Seven Myths of Military History

Seven Myths of Military History

Edited by John D. Hosler

Series Editors
Alfred J. Andrea and Andrew Holt

Hackett Publishing Company, Inc.
Indianapolis/Cambridge

For further information, please address
    Hackett Publishing Company, Inc.
    P.O. Box 44937
    Indianapolis, Indiana 46244-0937

    www.hackettpublishing.com

Cover design by Rick Todhunter and Brian Rak
Interior design by E. L. Wilson
Composition by Aptara, Inc.

Library of Congress Control Number: 2021944433

ISBN-13: 978-1-64792-043-2 (pbk.)
ISBN-13: 978-1-64792-044-9 (cloth)
ISBN-13: 978-1-64792-045-6 (PDF ebook)

CONTENTS

ABOUT THIS SERIES

The Myths of History series is dedicated to exposing and correcting some of the misconceptions, misjudgments, distortions, exaggerations, outdated interpretations, fallacies, seductive canards, and blatant lies that stick like super-glued Post-it notes to so many of history's most significant events and actors.

The series editors and the authors involved in this work do not believe that they are presenting pure *truth* or claim they are rendering the final word on the issues under examination. The craft of history does not allow its practitioners to speak with the voice of unquestionable authority, and the study of history does not produce immutable laws and timeless narratives that will never be revised in the light of further investigation. Rather, each historian involved in this series offers a counter-narrative that reflects the best, most up-to-date scholarship on some important element of the past that has become encrusted with misconceptions that wither when tested against the available evidence and the general consensus of the profession.

The reason for engaging such "myths" is simple. The past is neither dead nor forgotten. Carefully honed knowledge of our shared past informs our understanding of who we are and our place in the here and now, and it also allows us to place our current concerns into a broad perspective. This never-ending dialogue between the present and the past—a process we term "history"—is vital to our lives, our societies, our cultures, our world, and it is incumbent upon us to understand that past as correctly as the evidence and our fallible intellects allow.

Because of the value inherent in such an investigation and understanding of the past, each book in this series speaks to a general readership, namely students and the larger reading public. For that reason, no matter how complex a topic might be, the editors and authors are committed to presenting it clearly and without recourse to technical gymnastics and jargon. This is possible without sacrificing nuance and without any "dumbing down."

Many readers will note our debt to Matthew Restall's groundbreaking *Seven Myths of the Spanish Conquest*, which serves as a model for the series. Indeed, this series—to which Restall has granted his imprimatur—is an homage to his pioneering work.

Alfred J. Andrea
Andrew Holt

Series Editors' Foreword

It is with great pleasure that we present the fifth volume in Hackett Publishing Company's Myths of History series, *Seven Myths of Military History*. It is a worthy companion to earlier volumes that have dealt with myths surrounding the crusades, Africa in world history, the American Civil War, and Native American history. One thread binds all four predecessors together—conflict. The conflicts of holy and civil wars are obvious. Less obvious but just as real have been the conflicts of racist-driven colonialism and attempts at cultural genocide in Africa and North America. Clearly a book that deconstructs myths surrounding the interpretative study of military engagements is equally centered on the history of conflict.

Conflict is also at the heart of all historical myths and myth-busting—conflicts between evidence and misperception, between critical analysis and passionately held beliefs. In the case of military history, the potential for conflicts is vast and, perhaps, overwhelming. This is due in large part to the popularity of military history.

A survey of bookstores and websites reveals to even the most casual observer that no other area of history produces and sells as many books and journals. Added to that are numerous made-for-television documentaries and docudramas. What would television producers do without World War II or the American Civil War? And what about the legions of military reenactors and the popularity of their encampments and mock battles? The drive for "authenticity" in the dress, modes of maneuver and fighting, and general lifestyle of the soldiers and their associates whom the reenactors portray can reach the level of obsession. Such popularity inevitably engenders controversy among persons who find outlets for their fascination with military history in reading, viewing, and acting.

If so-called amateur historians are so passionate, imagine the heat generated by professionals. Military historians regularly debate and argue, quite energetically and sometimes sharply, the finer points of long-ago strategies and tactics, the consequences of various battles or wars, and the impact of social or cultural movements and new technologies on warfare and vice versa. They have much to ponder, yet through such internal debates they also often come to a general consensus about the evidentiary limits for certain issues and judgments. In those instances, their strength is not in declaring with absolute assurance what actually happened or the significance of something, but rather highlighting what the evidence will allow.

Yet such discussions are all too often held exclusively within the scholarly community of military historians. Although most military historians are exceedingly generous with their time and insights, giving public lectures in a wide variety of venues, all too often the latest advances in their scholarship fail to find an immediate audience and readership in popular media. This book is an attempt, and a successful one at that, to bridge the schism by communicating to a broader public how current scholarly interpretations are at odds with widespread perceptions of our military past.

Moreover, the men and women who train for and fight wars, especially they who hold high ranks, are avid students of military history. The military branches of many countries promote reading lists among their officers and enlisted personnel, and the scholarly works of the editor and contributors to this present volume prominently fill those lists. Former Marine Corps general James Mattis reportedly did not own a television set but kept a personal library of more than seven thousand books, from which he sometimes carried select titles with him into battle. The reasons for the interest of military leaders in military history are obvious. As strategists, tacticians, and persons intimately involved with intelligence, operations, and logistics, they want the most reliable and up-to-date scholarship to inspire their efforts. They cannot afford to base their battlefield decisions on myths. It is sometimes said that the debates in academia are so heated because the stakes are so small, but the stakes for military historians are conceivably much higher.

It is for these many reasons that we are pleased to welcome this addition to the Myths of History series.

Andrew Holt
Alfred J. Andrea

Editor's Preface

In 2017, I left my tenured professorship at Morgan State University, in Baltimore, Maryland, and began teaching mid-career officers at the US Army's Command and General Staff College. In a single stroke, I was no longer the only military historian on campus but rather just one of more than twenty-five military historians *in a single department!* The breadth, and depth, of my colleagues' knowledge here in the Department of Military History (DMH) immediately impressed me, as did their enthusiasm and collegiality. A remark often heard here is that "we have a great hallway"—that corridor of offices, daily abuzz with spirited discussions of warfare over the past millennium and more, provoked and nurtured the concept for this book.

I have been interested in myths since my undergraduate days at Iowa State University, where I recall a classmate referencing the premodern belief in the flat earth. The professor replied, "Did you know that's actually a myth?" and I was hooked. For those who might think otherwise, I am on no quest to eradicate myths from military history, or any history for that matter. Rather, I believe we historians should periodically ask ourselves *what* we know, what we *think* we know, *why* we think we know it, and finally, why it might *matter*. This book spans a long time period ("From Plato to NATO," to cite a popular phrase), which, I think, demonstrates the ubiquity of myths and mythologizing and a deeper human proclivity toward both. I can only hope that it merits a place alongside the other excellent volumes of the Hackett Myths of History series.

I would like to acknowledge the efforts of the series editors, Alfred Andrea and Andrew Holt, as well as Rick Todhunter and the three anonymous peer-reviewers. They, along with the superb roster of chapter authors, collectively helped bring out the best in this volume. Deserving of thanks, too, are certain of my colleagues in DMH who, while sometimes differing with me on the subjects contained herein, nonetheless broadened my perspective: Donald S. Stephenson, Mark Hull, William Nance, Joseph Babb, Jonathan Abel, and Gregory Hospodor. Once again, my wife Holly has patiently tolerated my late nights of editing and periodic anxious bursts. Finally, I thank my past and current students in Staff Group 18 here at Fort Leavenworth—this one's for you.

John D. Hosler

INTRODUCTION

Myths Too Convenient to Fade Away

> Myths are easier to learn and remember than most
> scholarly findings; they are more fun.
>
> —*Lillian E. Doherty*[1]

Like any other historical subfield, military history has its fair share of myths and legends. Scouring the internet, one can find a wild assortment of websites, essays, and journalistic pieces seeking to dispel this myth or that. Many are rather trivial, interesting to read about but not exactly earthshaking. Available books on military myths are more coherent but tend to center only on one particular war or period. Some persistent myths are based on popular misunderstandings (e.g., most American soldiers in Vietnam were drafted) that can prove difficult to dispel because of personal experiences and ingrained beliefs of those who participated in wars or lived through them.

In this book, however, the authors address a different aspect of myths: the mythologizing of historical constructs and historical arguments. Constructs, or models, are routinely used to explain individual or multiple events in the past. Sometimes they are discarded, typically once judged to obscure rather than reveal history. But what happens when a discarded construct is mythologized, that is, when it endures as a myth, a widely held misrepresentation of truth? Likewise, historical arguments—interpretations of the past—can be influential for long stretches of time before falling out of favor, but some interpretations have enormous staying power despite the evidence against them. This mythologizing keeps the constructs and interpretations alive and legitimizes them. On one level, the issue seems only academic—distortions of history obscure accurate readings of the past—but military history myths also have a discernible impact outside the bookstore and classroom because *military history* is regularly read by military professionals, heads of state, and even paramilitary/irregular leaders.

---

1. Lillian E. Doherty, *Gender and the Interpretation of Classical Myth* (London: Bloomsbury, 2003), 100.

Military History and Mythmaking

War has been a central concern of historians since Herodotus analyzed the Persian Wars 2,500 years ago. Yet military history itself took some time to bloom. Even by the late nineteenth century, it was taught in isolation from the contexts that conditioned and set in motion war in the first place, and then primarily by military officers: "The professors taught politics but excluded war, the soldiers taught war but excluded politics."[2] Today, however, military history is a complex, multifaceted area of study. Although it is frequently derided as nothing but "brass buttons," battles, and campaigns, in the decades since America's war in Vietnam the conversation has diversified tremendously. Historians have looked closely at issues of military organization and logistics/sustainment, the play between economic and social changes brought on by war and vice versa, war from the perspective of the soldiers themselves, as opposed to studies of generalship and strategy, and, more recently, critical approaches to war that have usefully employed questions of culture, religion, race, and gender in their analyses.[3] Military history may appear a niche subject, but in reality it exists in constant interplay with other subfields and its study finds purchase in most major aspects of history and life.

Such relevance is obvious in both popular and academic spheres. A glance through the weekend edition of any newspaper of record reveals reviews of military history books, which are also a common sight in airport bookstores and the like. These tend to sell quite well, especially when one includes biographies of famous generals.[4] Military history and war-studies courses are perennially popular at universities and colleges and typically well subscribed. Military historians themselves are increasingly diverse, and together practitioners have been incredibly productive, publishing a slew of interesting and influential books to a wide audience in the last three decades.

Military history *myths* are likewise influential in these diverse aspects. One could argue, in fact, that it is even more prone to mythmaking than other subfields of the historical discipline. Wars that have created nations or altered their conditions are essential for any coherent national narrative: one simply cannot understand, say, modern America sans the abolition of slavery and the Civil War, or modern China without the Long March or the second Sino-Japanese War. Commemorations of national historical events, accordingly, keep the wars front and center. In his seminal essay, "The Use and Abuse of Military History," Sir Michael Howard argued that because military history is frequently employed for patriotic purposes—so often do

---

2. *Delbrück's Modern Military History*, ed. and trans. A. Bucholz (Lincoln: University of Nebraska Press, 1997), 13.

3. Stephen Morillo and Michael F. Pavkovic, *What Is Military History?* 3rd ed. (Cambridge: Polity Press, 2018).

4. For example, Ron Chernow's *Grant* (New York: Penguin, 2017) became a *New York Times* best seller.

past wars contribute to national identities—a myth can be "so much a part of our world that it is anguish to be deprived of it."[5] Heritage rests on understandings of past conflict, whether accurate or not. Put another way, such myths "are designed to explain us as we wish to see ourselves. They establish the national character and set the standard for coming generations."[6]

Too Convenient by Far

Why does military history get mythologized? In a word: convenience. History professors routinely search for constructs to explain world events, and for good reason. A typical college term is too short to comprehensively cover complex subjects such as World War II. Thematic approaches can therefore be of great assistance to students and faculty alike, as can the encapsulation of large swaths of time within theoretical constructs and frameworks. Once enshrined in a popular textbook, such constructs—which occasionally get mythologized—are difficult to excise.

Three of the myths in this volume—military revolutions, feudalism, and the Western way of war—hold this sort of appeal. In its most prevalent form, the first sorts the progress of military art and science neatly into major developments that permanently transformed the ways in which wars were conducted, such as the French Revolution, industrialization, or the advent of nuclear power. In broad terms, students can rationalize such a breakdown because, clearly, something big happened when production was mechanized, and a train stuffed with soldiers clearly contrasts with a column marching slowly over endless terrain. This separation of military history into bite-sized chunks is eminently useful to instructors and students alike because it helps distill centuries of events, even if, as John France ably teases out here, the result is confusion between things that are truly revolutionary versus broad *continuity* featuring interesting moments of change in a more evolutionary sensibility.

Feudalism holds a similar appeal to teachers searching for a means of generalizing the dizzying array of political, legal, and economic customs of military obligation in the thousand-year medieval period. That the construct erroneously applies across hundreds of years of European and Near Eastern history a single problematic model, in which a knight was obligated to fight alongside his lord, to whom he had sworn an oath of fidelity, has been widely known since 1974, at least among medievalists. As Richard Abels's essay here notes, however, in the absence of a suitable alternative, a portion of medievalists have nonetheless resigned themselves to the convenience of retaining the mythical language. Pushing farther, Abels questions the practicality of

---

5. Reprinted as Michael Howard, "The Use and Abuse of Military History," *Parameters: Journal of the US Army War College* 11, no. 1 (1981): 11.

6. Gil Klein, "The Use of Myth in History," Colonial Williamsburg Foundation, accessed September 19, 2019, https://www.history.org/Foundation/journal/summer12/myths.cfm.

the "myth-busting" itself, arguing that enough "feudal" elements might be spied in the records to justify continued usage of the term. Here, then, is a fascinating chain of events: overreliance on the mythological "feudalism" resulted in a scholarly backlash that unwittingly obscured the kernels of reality formerly obscured by the myth itself!

Likewise, the Western way of war construct helps to frame interactions between Europe and the rest of the globe over the long duration. It promises an answer to what Niall Ferguson has called "the most interesting question a historian of the modern era can ask":

> Just why, beginning around 1500, did a few small polities on the western end of the Eurasian landmass come to dominate the rest of the world, including the more populous and in many ways more sophisticated societies of Eastern Eurasia?[7]

By arguing that something inherent in and specific to the culture of the West enabled a certain irresistible, and well-nigh invincible, "shock-combat" style of warfare, the construct's adherents offer a serious and comprehensive answer to Ferguson's question. When scholars point out, as Everett Wheeler does here, that this answer is based on a mythologizing of Greek warfare, adherents tend to shrug and fall back on the concept's usefulness as an interpretive tool.

Or is it, rather, obstinacy? Could it be that these propagators *know* the truth but persist in mythologizing because learning, and then teaching, more authentic historical interpretations would be a chore? Alternatively, perhaps they are simply true believers in the original construct and continue to "fight the good fight" out of integrity and expert judgment. Both are possibilities.

Other myths arise not so much through well-considered choices but rather because *not* doing so seems irrational. Andrew Holt's chapter on religion and war falls into this category. It seems irrational to deny that religion has been the cause of many, if not most, wars. In the eighteenth century, enlightened theorists conceived of ways to rationalize and control the military instrument: gone would be zealous religious wars, to be replaced by so-called good wars waged with humanitarian sensibilities. Yet as Holt points out, this widely held notion is, both quantitatively and qualitatively speaking, mythological in conception. There were not so many wars caused primarily by religion as we might imagine, and newly modern Europe fostered an increase in the number of nonreligious wars fought around the world. These, as well as wars waged in other parts of the globe, also intensified in scale and violence as industrialization created more lethal, more numerous, and longer-range killing instruments, culminating in two world wars.

---

7. Niall Ferguson, *Civilization: The West and the Rest* (London: Penguin, 2011), xv.

Military Myths in the "Real World"

It is not uncommon for historical interpretations to influence contemporary affairs. Military history often influences military practitioners, who seek to put history to work while solving strategic, operational, or tactical problems. Mythologizing, however, complicates the notion of "lessons learned." For example, the Wehrmacht's rapid dispatch of the Polish army in 1939 is true enough but has been mythologized by the story of the latter's cavalry—still on horseback!—charging heavily armed panzers: a juxtaposition of an advanced, modern, and technologically proficient Germany against a backward, inept, and hopelessly outclassed Poland. A skeptic might justifiably counter, "So what?"—horses or not, does not the tale illustrate the real, and staggering, discrepancies between the two nations' armies? Well, yes, but some historians argue that, had the Poles not tried to defend all of their borders at once, enough combat power existed to potentially repel assaults on Warsaw until help arrived from Great Britain and France. What lesson might military professionals take from this history? That the overmatched Poles simply had no chance? Or, rather, that conducting a large-scale "perimeter" defense in maneuver warfare carries risks that require careful planning?

This scenario illustrates an important second-order effect, which is the consequence of mythologizing both in and by professional militaries. In the United States, the chiefs of staff of the Army and Air Force, the Marine Corps commandant, and the chief of naval operations maintain annually updated professional reading lists, each of which includes military history titles. In addition, the study of military history is required at institutions of professional military education that prepare officers for higher ranks. On one hand, this must be celebrated because the study of history in this sense transcends the "life of the mind" and finds utility in the real world of modern conflict.

On the other hand, there are consequences when mythologizing replaces more accurate historical interpretation. In 2018, for example, the American general Stanley McChrystal helped author a book that argues excessive and ubiquitous mythologizing of commanders like Julius Caesar and George Washington has led, over time, to problematic conceptions of what leadership is, should be, or could be.[8] In another sense, as John Curatola argues in this volume, the mere promise of "Strategic Air Power"—a strategy "that employs aerial platforms to bypass the battlefield to achieve decisive political results in conflict"[9]—has prompted a chase for bloodless victories from the skies. Hesitant to commit "boots on the ground" and accept casualties that

---

8. Stanley McChrystal et al., *Leaders: Myth and Reality* (New York: Portfolio/Penguin, 2018), 1–7.

9. Robert Gerald Hughes, "Strategic Air Power," Oxford Bibliographies Online, accessed September 22, 2019, https://www.oxfordbibliographies.com/view/document/obo-9780199743292/obo-9780199 743292-0066.xml.

raise the ire of voting publics, risk-averse decision makers seek to win primarily from the aerial domain.

Airplanes are also rather expensive, and the belief that they, or any other particular pieces of new technology, hold the keys to victory has an economic consequence. "Force modernization" projects in modern state militaries are, after all, taxpayer funded. Are the new technologies worth the cost? It is undeniable that technological advances have changed the practice of warfare. The importance of scientific innovation, and the increased lethality that results from it, has been summarized by Martin van Creveld thusly: "War is completely permeated by technology and governed by

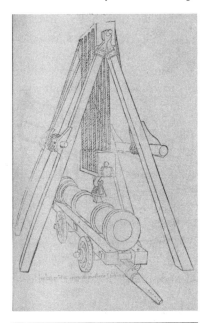

One of the many conceptual war machines illustrated in Roberto Valturio's 1455 book *De re militari.* Long have technologies of war captured the imaginations of artists, theorists, and military practitioners alike.

it."[10] There is, of course, the perennial debate over undue influence of defense contractors and the military-industrial complex.

Additionally, in a cultural sense modern minds tend toward a high valuation of material progress. Technological advancement is prized above all else. In the armed forces, the lure of the "latest and greatest" piece of new tech can be hard to resist because it represents *the* potential competitive edge a nation needs to win its next conflict. "Determinism," however, in which a single factor is the proximate cause for all significant historical change, is bound to be erroneous. As Rob Johnson relentlessly reminds us in his chapter, there are always human actors behind the technology, making choices about technological deployment: how, where, when, and why. To overly privilege material innovation risks forgetting what John Lynn has called "the unchanging reality of war as the domain of chance, violence, and politics," which primarily relate to this human, not technological, element.[11]

And lest we confine ourselves to national institutions, wars against non-state actors constitute part of the story. The library of Osama bin Laden is an interesting example. Captured during the raid on his compound in Pakistan in 2011, it included several titles relating to the history of military

10. Martin van Creveld, "Technology and War I: To 1945," in *The Oxford History of Modern War*, ed. C. Townshend (Oxford: Oxford University Press, 2005), 201.

11. John A. Lynn, "Forging the Western Army in Seventeenth-Century France," in *The Dynamics of Military Revolution, 1300–2050*, eds. M. Knox and W. Murray (Cambridge: Cambridge University Press, 2001), 56.

affairs, including Charles Townshend's *Oxford History of Modern War*, which, interestingly enough, contains essays on several of the subjects tackled in the present volume.[12] Bin Laden himself, the leader of the Islamic terrorist organization Al-Qaeda, waged what is often regarded as "asymmetrical war." In a 1962 commencement address to Army cadets at West Point, President John F. Kennedy characterized such war thusly:

> This is another type of war, new in its intensity, ancient in its origin—war by guerrillas, subversives, insurgents, assassins, war by ambush instead of by combat; by infiltration, instead of aggression, seeking victory by eroding and exhausting the enemy instead of engaging him. . . . It preys on economic unrest and ethnic conflicts.[13]

Of interest here is the phrase "new in its intensity." After Al-Qaeda's attack on the World Trade Center in New York City on 9/11, understanding this new sort of threat became an urgent matter and resulted in a flurry of studies. Later, American difficulties in locating and dispatching insurgent forces after Operation Iraqi Freedom eventually led to the creation of formal counterinsurgency doctrine and subsequent unit training to match it.[14]

Osama bin Laden. His library included Paul Kennedy's *The Rise and Fall of the Great Powers* (Vintage, 1989) and Willard C. Matthias's *America's Strategic Blunders* (Penn State University Press, 2001).

As William Kautt shows in his essay, however, this purported change in intensity leans on the mythologizing of certain historical developments. The "new" asymmetrical warfare is often credited to the works of Mao Zedong, but Mao's role has been mythologized and the sort of warfare he promoted had actually been on display since the late eighteenth century, and, more concretely, in the Irish conflict that preceded his rise to military influence. The general misconception of what asymmetry is, where

---

12. Office of the Director of National Intelligence, "Bin Laden's Bookshelf," accessed September 2, 2019, https://www.dni.gov/index.php/features/bin-laden-s-bookshelf?start=5. See *The Oxford History of Modern War*, ed. C. Townshend.

13. David L. Buffaloe, "Defining Asymmetric Warfare," Land Warfare Paper 58 (Arlington, VA: Institute of Land Warfare, Association of the United States Army, September 2006), 1.

14. Field Manual (FM) 3-24/Marines Corps Warfighting Publication (MCWP) 3-33.5: *Counterinsurgency* (Washington, DC: Department of the Army, 2006; updated in 2014).

it came from, and how it operates has played a role in delaying or impeding cohesive efforts to combat it. To repeat the point, then, military history myths hold the potential to influence the conduct of actual military affairs, in which lives are on the line.

Myth-Busting as a Virtue

We have arrived, then, at certain levels of gravity. At first thought, the mythologizing of the history, and historical constructs, in this volume seems rather benign: convenient historical constructs in the guise of teaching tools, which are not entirely accurate but nonetheless contain enough truth to help students grasp historical continuity and change. Yet mythologized constructs distort reality by conveying false or partial explanations for past wars and enable mischaracterizations of the past. At times, these mischaracterizations have transcended the academy altogether and moved into—and unduly influenced—national policy and strategy.

The mythological dimensions of military history, therefore, could use some proper scrutiny. They stand in the way of fuller understandings of the past and intellectually honest reckonings that could better serve historians, military professionals, and policy makers alike. Convenience be damned—it is time to confront them head-on in the pursuit of historical truth. For, as the poet Ovid once quipped:

> But gangren'd members must be lopt away,
> Before the nobler parts are tainted to decay.[15]

John D. Hosler

---

15. Ovid, *Metamorphoses*, trans. John Dryden (New York: Heritage, 1961), 1.10.

1. War and the Divine: Is Religion the Cause of Most Wars?

Andrew Holt

> It is somewhat trite, but nevertheless sadly true, to say that more wars have been waged, more people killed, and these days more evil perpetrated in the name of religion than by any other institutional force in human history.
> —*Richard Kimball*[1]

To uproarious laughter, the late comedian and social critic George Carlin once condemned God as the cause of the "bloodiest and most brutal wars" ever fought, which were "all based on religious hatred." He stated that millions have died simply because "God told" Hindus, Muslims, Jews, and Christians it would be a "good idea" for them to kill each other. Carlin's comedy routine, entitled "Kill for God!" has received rave reviews by its viewers for being "brilliant" and "spot on," with one anonymous fan confirming that religion is "by far the single biggest cause of human deaths."[2]

To be clear, it is not modern military historians who claim religion is the cause of most wars, but rather many prominent intellectuals, scientists, academics, and politicians, often with far greater influence over popular cultural assumptions than professional historians, who have popularized such claims. In a 2006 interview, the neuroscientist and cultural commentator Sam Harris stated, "If I could wave a magic wand and get rid of either rape or religion, I would not hesitate to get rid of religion. I think more people are dying as a result of our religious myths than as a result of any other ideology."[3] The Oxford University evolutionary biologist Richard Dawkins claimed in 2003 that religion is the "principal label, and the most dangerous one," by which human divisions occur, contributing to "wars, murders and terrorist attacks."[4]

---

1. Richard Kimball, *When Religion Becomes Evil: Five Warning Signs* (New York: Harper, 2002), 1.

2. George Carlin, "Kill for God," YouTube, accessed January 16, 2019, https://www.youtube.com/watch?v=WEi3Gaptaas.

3. Bethany Saltman, "The Temple of Reason: Sam Harris on How Religion Puts the World at Risk," *The Sun*, September 2006.

4. Richard Dawkins, *A Devil's Chaplain: Reflections on Hopes, Lies, Science, and Love* (Boston: Houghton Mifflin, 2003), 158.

Laurent Dabos's 1791 painting of the American revolutionary writer Thomas Paine.

Prominent American politicians have commented similarly. Richard Nixon argued in 1983 that the "bloodiest wars in history have been religious wars."[5] Perhaps unknowingly, Nixon was following his predecessor George Washington, who remarked in a 1792 letter that "religious controversies are always productive of more acrimony and irreconcilable hatreds than those which spring from any other cause."[6] That Washington held such views in the late eighteenth century is not surprising, given the rationalist spirit of his social class and times. Some of his contemporaries equally expressed their concern over the propensity for violence among traditional

5. Richard M. Nixon, *Real Peace: A Strategy for the West* (Boston: Little, Brown and Company, 1983), 14.

6. "George Washington to Edward Newenham, June 22, 1792," National Archives Founders Online, accessed January 16, 2019, https://founders.archives.gov/documents/Washington/05-10-02-0324.

religious believers. Thomas Paine is perhaps most notable in this regard. In *The Age of Reason* he argued that "the most detestable wickedness, the most horrid cruelties, and the greatest miseries, that have afflicted the human race have had their origin in this thing called revelation, or revealed religion. It has been . . . the most destructive to . . . the peace and happiness of man."[7]

Paine's views reflect a particular strain of thought that emerged in a slightly earlier period of the European eighteenth century, which many persons then and now have referred to as the "Enlightenment." While intellectuals of the period tended to emphasize religious toleration, many also wrote harshly about the negative social effects of traditional religion. Such concerns undoubtedly reflected the fact that they were writing in the wake of the so-called age of religious wars, during which Catholics and Protestants engaged in lengthy and destructive conflicts including, most notably, the French Wars of Religion (1562–98), the Thirty Years' War (1618–48), and the English Civil War (1642–51).[8]

None can challenge the claim that religion has often inspired or motivated violence, but has it truly been, as Harris claims, the "most prolific" source? Are, or were, religious wars, as Nixon wrote, the "bloodiest" sort of wars? Is it true that "more wars have been waged" and "more people killed" because of religion than any other institutional force, as Richard Kimball claims in the quotation that begins this essay?

Interestingly, these claims—often confidently asserted—that "more" wars have been waged and "more" people killed as a result of religion, can only be substantiated by both an accounting of all major wars of which we have historical knowledge and a means of separating the "religious" wars from other types of wars and counting the bodies. Such a list is destined to be incomplete and open to debate for many reasons, not least of which is the ambiguity surrounding many human conflicts. Was, for example, the English Civil War primarily a struggle over parliamentary rights vis-à-vis royal absolutism, or was it driven by a deep religious divide? Or was it both? Regardless of these pitfalls and uncertainties, such an accounting, no matter its imperfections, that seeks to understand the causes of particular wars and the degree of their lethality is possible. It is only with such an accounting that one can determine if religion is, indeed, the cause of most wars.

To most historians, this may seem an impossible task, with insurmountable methodological problems. Nevertheless, the critics cited here—neither specialists on warfare in any era nor trained historians—assume an ability to do this. Indeed, there is no other basis for making their claims without these assumptions.

---

7. Thomas Paine, *The Age of Reason, Part the Second: Being an Investigation of True and Fabulous Theology* (London: R. Carlisle, 1818), 82.

8. See Richard S. Dunn, *The Age of Religious Wars: 1559–1689* (London: Weidenfeld and Nicolson, 1970), ix; and Philippe Buc, *Holy War, Martyrdom, and Terror: Christianity, Violence, and the West* (Philadelphia: University of Pennsylvania Press, 2015), 29–36.

Rabbi Shlomo Goren blows the *shofar* (horn) by the Western Wall, Jerusalem, during the Six-Day War of 1967. That war can confound definitions: it has been called an Israeli defense against Pan-Arab, nationalist aggression but alternatively Zionist aggression in pursuit of territorial conquest.

The critics cited thus far do not provide such an accounting. Kimball and Harris imply that their claims are transparently obvious. For Kimball, religious ideologies and commitments are "indisputably central factors" in the "escalation of violence and evil around the world."[9] He states that this "evidence is readily available," after which he cites not data but the headlines of seven newspaper stories about contemporary religious violence.[10]

Yet this is anecdotal evidence. Moreover, alternative causality is dispensed with, as when Harris rejects out of hand the notion that the Hindu-Muslim conflict has political or economic roots.[11] Furthermore, neither author endeavors to sift through history's wars in order to make even a rough estimate of how many were primarily motivated by religious considerations, much less offering a method for how one distinguishes "religious" wars from all other types of wars. And neither acknowledges a basic proposition that all historians would accept: that most, if not all, wars are driven by multiple factors. At what point does a preponderance of religious factors, however they might be defined, outweigh secular motives or goals allowing for a war to be categorized as a "religious" war? The critics cited here appear to consider such questions and modes of inquiry irrelevant.

Of course, one could reasonably argue that firmly distinguishing between religious and nonreligious wars is so impossible that any effort to count and categorize all known wars in this manner is doomed to failure. Indeed, as I prepared this essay, I spoke with multiple historians who all inquired how one could possibly accomplish such a task, with some intonating it is not possible due to the complexity of warfare, which is almost always based on multiple causes and motivations. If this is true—that it is essentially impossible to distinguish "religious" wars from other types of war, much less provide accurate casualty figures for all wars ancient to modern—then the debate is over: there can be no basis to the argument that the former is the most frequent cause of war and/or the bloodiest type of human conflict. In sum, Harris, Kimball, and others would have zero basis for their claims. Likewise, those who seek to refute their charges would be unable to offer anything even approaching quantifiable evidence to support their objections. Game over.

But let us not fall prey to defeatism. Complexity and ambiguity pervade historical research and are elements in every conclusion reached by every historian. With that in mind, let us dare to hazard a definition of religious warfare.

Defining "Religious Warfare"

In attempting to define religious warfare, it first seems worthwhile to consider the origin of the term "religion." In its earliest Ciceronian sense, the Latin word *religio* meant

---

9. Kimball, *When Religion Becomes Evil*, 4.

10. Kimball, *When Religion Becomes Evil*, 4.

11. Sam Harris, *The End of Faith: Religion, Terror, and the Future of Reason* (New York: W. W. Norton, 2005), 27.

to have respect or regard for the gods, as demonstrated by the performance of obligatory rites in veneration of them.[12] Although a critic of Roman religion, Augustine of Hippo (d. 430) adapted the term in such a way that it could be uniquely applied to a Christian understanding of and relationship to the sacred. For Augustine, *religio* meant worship, the actions by which one renders praise to God, but he also sought to separate what he understood to be true worship from false worship.[13]

Yet while many in the West think of religion as worship centered around a god or gods, accompanied by adherence to theological doctrines and rituals, such a definition fails to embrace the totality of the worldwide religious experience, both past and present. Definitions evolve and change, and modern scholars of religion have come to accept a broader definition of religion, one that phenomenologists who specialize in comparative religion now generally embrace, which sees "religion" as any spiritual or pragmatic connection with a transcendental Other. This Other could include gods (or God), sacred forces, a supreme cosmic spirit, or even a universal law, like Buddhist Dharma.[14] Consequently, if "religion" represents belief in the Divine and reverence for the Other—and these beliefs influence the thoughts, morality, and deeds of believers—then it follows that "religious wars" are those conflicts in which religious belief or devotion plays a key role in the motivation of most of their originators and/ or participants.

The oft-cited Prussian military theorist Carl von Clausewitz famously argued that all wars are political.[15] Yet when religious motivations influence political goals, it becomes trickier to determine to what degree religion is the inspiration for a conflict. Must both sides in a conflict have religious motivations for it to be considered a "religious" war, or is one side sufficient? At what point do economic concerns, for example, outweigh religious concerns so that one would no longer consider a war "religious"? What if a war begins as religious but ends as an overtly political conflict, as was the case with the Thirty Years' War? Those who make the claim that religion is the most prominent cause of violence or warfare never seem to bother with such details, yet they, nevertheless, obviously define "religious wars" broadly enough to support them.

12. Cicero, *De Natura Deorum Academia*, trans. H. Rackham (Cambridge, MA: Harvard University Press, 1979), XLII.112–13. On *religio*, see Clifford Ando, *The Matter of the Gods: Religion and the Roman Empire* (Berkeley: University of California Press, 2008), 1–6; William T. Cavanaugh, *The Myth of Religious Violence: Secular Ideology and the Roots of Modern Conflict* (Oxford: Oxford University Press, 2009), 60–69.

13. Cavanaugh, *Myth of Religious Violence*, 63; Ando, *Matter of the Gods*, 4–5.

14. Alfred J. Andrea and Andrew Holt, *Sanctified Violence: Holy War in World History* (Indianapolis: Hackett, 2021), 1.

15. Carl von Clausewitz, *On War*, ed. and trans. M. Howard and P. Paret (Princeton, NJ: Princeton University Press, 1989), I.1.24–27: "War is merely the continuation of policy by other means"; "a true political instrument, a continuation of political intercourse, carried on with other means"; and, consequently, "all wars can be considered acts of policy."

To be clear, few would object to the proposition that religion or religious motivation often inspire violence. Many examples of religiously inspired warfare are to be found in the histories of the ancient Near East, Greco-Roman antiquity, Europe, the Far East, India, the Americas, and sub-Saharan Africa by members of various religions. Spanning the ancient to modern worlds, Mesopotamians, Chinese, Indians, Europeans, Arabs, Persians, Turks, Aztecs, and many others have embraced religious beliefs that at times led to, justified, or encouraged violence or warfare, sometimes resulting in a

A sixteenth-century depiction of Aztec human sacrifice: the removal of prisoners' still-beating hearts. The Aztecs and their neighbors engaged in ritualized "flower wars" to capture warriors worthy of sacrifice.

massive loss of human life. Yet the aforementioned critics of religious violence do not claim that religion *sometimes* inspires violence or warfare. If this were the case, then their claims would be noncontroversial. Instead, they claim that, more than any other factor, religious faith has led to *more* war throughout history and across all cultures.

If one is willing to hazard a definition of religious warfare, as I have just done, that allows for the distinct categorization of religious and nonreligious wars, then some data can be developed that might help us to evaluate these charges in a manner that is more systematic and logical than simply saying, "Your criticism of religion as the cause of most wars and bloodshed is without foundation." As demonstrated in the remainder of this chapter, some have been willing to provide such a twofold analysis, namely to categorize wars as "religious" or otherwise and to provide death estimates for various wars. Such data are not supportive of the claims of Kimball et al. To the contrary, the only data currently available on these topics suggest that the popular claim that religion is the cause of "more" wars than anything else . . . is a myth.

Religious War by the Numbers

Charles Phillips and Alan Axelrod's three-volume *Encyclopedia of Wars* includes an analysis of 1,763 wars covering the worldwide span of human history. It has become an influential reference in the popular sphere, often cited by persons seeking to define specific wars as religious or otherwise.[16] In their lengthy index entry on "religious wars," Phillips and Axelrod do not explain their classification methodology. They only provide clues in their limited commentary on the concept of religious wars in their introduction, where they seem to suggest that religion was often used as a sort of cover for premodern wars that resulted from more mundane causes, including territorial, ethnic, and economic concerns.[17] Yet each war they list in the index under the category "religious wars" contains clear references to its religious nature or features, providing an apparent justification for its classification as such.[18]

What, then, did Phillips and Axelrod find? Interestingly, of 1,763 wars they list only 121 entries fall under the heading "religious wars." In one case, two wars are considered in a single entry ("Sixth and Seventh Wars of Religion"), bringing their total to 122.[19] Thus, only 6.9 percent of the wars they considered are classified as religious wars.[20] One presumes they see the remaining 93.1 percent as primarily wars that took

---

16. *Encyclopedia of Wars*, ed. C. Phillips and A. Axelrod, 3 vols. (New York: Facts on File, 2005), III:1484–85. Commentators citing the *Encyclopedia of Wars* in this manner include the *Huffington Post*, Christian apologetics groups, such as the *Christian Apologetics and Research Ministry* (CARM), and the libertarian political/social commentator Theodore Beale, more commonly known as Vox Day. See Vox Day, *The Irrational Atheist: Dissecting the Unholy Trinity of Dawkins, Harris, and Hitchens* (Dallas: Benbella, 2008), 103–6; Robin Schumacher, "The Myth That Religion Is the #1 Cause of War," CARM: Christian Apologetics and Research Ministry, accessed March 13, 2019, https://carm.org/religion-cause-war; and Alan Lurie, "Is Religion the Cause of Most Wars?" *Huffington Post*, April 10, 2012.

17. *Encyclopedia of Wars*, I:xxii–xxiii.

18. In their entry titled "Charlemagne's War against the Saxons," e.g., Phillips and Axelrod refer to the effort to convert the Saxons to Christianity as one of Charlemagne's "major" objectives and describe his success. See *Encyclopedia of Wars*, I:307–8.

19. The common figure ascribed by various sources to the *Encyclopedia of Wars* is slightly different, usually listing 123 religious wars. See, e.g., Bruce Sheiman, *An Atheist Defends Religion: Why Humanity Is Better Off with Religion Than without It* (New York: Alpha, 2009), 117.

20. Phillips and Axelrod's list, reordered chronologically here, includes the following: First, Second, Third, and Fourth Sacred Wars (spanning 595 to 336 BCE); Roman-Persian Wars (421–22 and 441); Visigothic-Frankish War; Mecca-Medina War; Byzantine-Muslim Wars (633–42, 645–56, 668–79, 698–718, 739, 741–52, 778–83, 797–98, 803–9, 830–41, 851–63, 871–85, 960–76, and 995–99); Arab conquest of Carthage; revolt in Ravenna; First and Second Iconoclastic Wars, Charlemagne's invasion of Northern Spain; revolt of Muqanna; Charlemagne's War against the Saxons; Khurramites' revolt; Paulician War; Spanish Christian-Muslim Wars (912–28, 977–97, 1001–31, 1172–1212, 1230–48, and 1481–92); German Civil War (1077–1106); Castilian conquest of Toledo; Almohad conquest of Muslim Spain; Spanish conquests in North Africa (1090–91); First, Second, Third, Fourth, Fifth, Sixth, Seventh, Eighth, and Ninth Crusades (spanning 1095–1272); Crusader-Turkish Wars (spanning 1100–1146 and 1272–91); Aragonese-Castilian War; Wars of the Lombard League; Saladin's Holy War; Aragonese-French War (1209–13); Albigensian Crusade; Danish-Estonian War; Luccan-Florentine War; Crusade of Nicopolis; Portuguese-Moroccan Wars (1458–71 and 1578); War of the Monks; Bohemian Civil War (1465–71); Bohemian-Hungarian

shape due to other factors, such as geopolitics, economic rivalry, and ethnic divisions. One may certainly quibble over the omission of some wars from Phillips and Axelrod's list, but it would take a lot of quibbling to get to the point where religious wars represent the majority (882 out of 1,763) of the wars they count and consider. They also list other categories of warfare that have higher totals than religion. Under the heading of "colonial wars," they list 161 wars.[21] After cross-referencing both lists, one finds that Phillips and Axelrod only list two wars in both the "colonial" and "religious" categories, suggesting that they have made every effort to categorize these wars based on their primary causes, as they interpret them, rather than secondary ones.[22] Consequently, based on the total numbers presented by Phillips and Axelrod in each category, one could argue that imperialist ideologies, regardless of the latent religiosity that occasionally colors such endeavors, have historically and collectively been the primary inspiration of more wars than explicitly religious ideologies.

Again, historians could certainly look at Phillips and Axelrod's list of religious wars and criticize the omission of many and the inclusion of some. Indeed, in my rough accounting of the 1,763 wars they list in their encyclopedia, I would likely come up with a figure of religious wars that, perhaps, doubled theirs. Other historians may arrive at still different figures, both lesser and greater, based on how they choose to categorize "religious wars." Yet it seems highly unlikely that any historian would look at the 1,763 wars considered in the *Encyclopedia of Wars* and determine that a majority of them were primarily religious. If someone were to attempt to provide such a systematic accounting, their efforts would, indeed, be interesting to consider here, but nobody besides Phillips and Axelrod seems to have been bothered.

War (1468–78); Siege of Granada; Persian Civil War (1500–1503); Vijayanagar Wars; Anglo-Scottish War; Turko-Persian Wars (1514–17 and 1743–47); Counts' War; Schmalkaldic War; Scottish uprising against Mary of Guise; First, Second, Third, Fourth, Fifth, Sixth, Seventh, Eighth, and Ninth Wars of Religion (spanning 1562 to 1598); Javanese invasion of Malacca; Bohemian-Palatine War; Thirty Years' War; First, Second, and Third Bernese Revolts (spanning 1621 to 1629); Swedish War; Shimabara Revolt (1637–38); First and Second Bishops Wars; Maryland's Religious War; Transylvania-Hapsburg War; Portuguese-Omani Wars in East Africa; First Villmergen War; Covenanters' Rebellions (1666, 1679, and 1685); Rajput Rebellion against Aurangzeb; Camisard Rebellion; Second Villmergen War; Brabant Revolution; Vellore Mutiny; Great Java War; Padri War; Irish Tithe War; War of the Sonderbund; Crimean War; Tukulor-French Wars; Mountain Meadows Massacre; Serbo-Turkish War; Russo-Turkish War (1877–78); Ugandan Religious Wars; Ghost Dance War; Holy Wars of the "Mad Mullah"; raids of the Black Hundreds; Mexican insurrections; Indian Civil War; Bosnian War; and US War on Terrorism.

21. *Encyclopedia of Wars*, III.1447–48.

22. The two wars listed in both the "colonial wars" and "religious wars" categories by Phillips and Axelrod are the Tukulor-French Wars and the Vellore Mutiny, nineteenth-century conflicts involving a complex mix of potential religious and colonial/territorial causes that may have proven too difficult for the authors to categorize under one primary cause. See *Encyclopedia of Wars*, III.1158–59 and 1243.

In a similar way, Matthew White, a self-described "atrocitologist," is sometimes cited by those comparing religious wars to nonreligious wars. His 2012 book purports to list the one hundred greatest atrocities in human history, based on total deaths.[23] Although a popular-history writer, White's work was favorably reviewed in the *New York Times* and has won academic acclaim in some quarters, with Harvard psychologist Steven Pinker dubbing it, in a complimentary foreword, "the most comprehensive, disinterested and statistically nuanced estimates available."[24] Historians, as well, have praised White's efforts. Harvard University professor of history Charles S. Maier, in the same *New York Times* review, praised White for trying to arrive at "the best figures" and not being, like most historians when it comes to this type of research, "afraid to get his hands dirty."[25]

White is clear and upfront about both his methodology and the controversial nature of his statistics. He notes, for example, on the first page of his introduction, "Let's get something out of the way right now. Everything you are about to read is disputed. . . . There is no atrocity in history that every person in the world agrees on."[26] His methodology, as described in the *Times* review, is simple and transparent. He gathers all of the death estimates he can find for an event, with all data on his website available for public review, throws out the highest and lowest numbers, and then calculates the median, "arriving at what he acknowledges is often just an informed guess."[27] Yet, White's "informed guesses" appear to be the best ones currently available.

Like Phillips and Axelrod, White also categorizes and provides a list under the heading "Religious Conflict."[28] He notes that it is "impossible" to find a "common cause" in the various atrocities he considers, and that they can often fall under multiple headings. For example, White lists "Cromwell's Invasion of Ireland" under the categories of both "Religious Conflict" and "Ethnic Cleansing."[29] Yet even allowing for this, White lists only eleven atrocities that fall under the heading of "Religious Conflict." He provides insights into how he arrived at his list in a section of his work subtitled "Religious Killing," while pointing out that "no war is 100 percent religious (or 100 percent anything) in motivation, but we can't duck the fact that some conflicts involve more religion than others."[30]

---

23. Matthew White, *The Great Big Book of Horrible Things: The Definitive Chronicle of History's 100 Worst Atrocities* (New York: W. W. Norton, 2012).

24. Jennifer Schuessler, "Ranking History's Atrocities by Counting the Corpses," *New York Times*, November 8, 2011.

25. Schuessler, "Ranking History's Atrocities."

26. White, *Great Big Book of Horrible Things*, xiii.

27. Schuessler, "Ranking History's Atrocities." For White's figures, see "Death Tolls across History," Necrometrics, accessed March 15, 2019, https://necrometrics.com/.

28. White, *Great Big Book of Horrible Things*, 544.

29. White, *Great Big Book of Horrible Things*, 544–45.

30. White, *Great Big Book of Horrible Things*, 544 and 107–8.

In an attempt to solve a problem we have already noted here, White then asks how we can decide if "religion is the real cause of a conflict and not just a convenient cover story."[31] In response, he lists three primary principles that cumulatively address this question. The first is when "the only difference between the two sides is religion," for which he cites examples of people who look alike, speak the same languages, and live in the same communities yet engage in conflict over what can only be ascribed to religious differences. This would include Catholics and Protestants in Northern Ireland. The second is an ability to describe a conflict without reference to religion or religious trappings. For this, he gives the example of the US Civil War, which he notes certainly had religious elements, but can also be described in a detailed history without ever referencing those elements. White argues this would be impossible, for example, in writing a history of the crusades. Finally, the third is when the parties themselves declare religious motives. Here White notes that "we should at least consider the possibility that they are telling the truth," especially if there are not other significant potential reasons.[32]

With these rules in mind, White lists eleven atrocities from the one hundred that he classifies as "Religious Conflicts": Taiping Rebellion, Thirty Years' War, Mahdi's Revolt, crusades,[33] French Wars of Religion, War in the Sudan, Albigensian Crusade, Panthay Rebellion, Hui Rebellion, Partition of India, and Cromwell's Invasion of Ireland.[34] Thus, according to White's study, only 11 percent of the one hundred worst atrocities in history can be attributed, in some major part, to religion, with 89 percent primarily attributable to some other cause. Yet there are other atrocities in White's book that seem to deserve to be grouped under a more general heading of religiously inspired atrocities, even if they do not meet his definition of "conflict." These include the Roman gladiatorial games and Aztec human sacrifice, both of which White categorized separately under "Human Sacrifice."[35] If we add these two atrocities to the eleven listed under religious conflict, this would bring the total of the one hundred greatest atrocities, based on White's death estimates, attributed primarily to religious motivations (a broader category than just "conflicts") up to thirteen, or only 13 percent.

A final breakdown, depending on how one evaluates White's work, is therefore as follows: 11/100 (or 11 percent) of the worst atrocities in history can be ascribed to

---

31. White, *Great Big Book of Horrible Things*, 107.

32. White, *Great Big Book of Horrible Things*, 107–8.

33. Presumably, only the crusades that took place in the East.

34. White, *Great Big Book of Horrible Things*, 544.

35. White, *Great Big Book of Horrible Things*, 548. One could argue that Mesoamerican human sacrifice is more correct, as even societies like the Maya appear to have performed it, even if apparently on a lesser scale. The scale of Aztec human sacrifice—from only 150 sacrificial victims to 250,000 per year—is a debate; see Matthew Restall's book *When Montezuma Met Cortés: The True Story of the Meeting that Changed History* (New York: Ecco, 2018), 85–95.

"Religious Conflict," and 13/100 (or 13 percent) of the worst atrocities in history can be ascribed to "Religious Conflict" or "Human Sacrifice." Although these percentages are higher than Phillips and Axelrod's more comprehensive findings (6.9 percent), none supports the claim that religion has been and remains the cause of most wars. Indeed, "Hegemonial War," a category that White defines as similar countries fighting "over who's number 1," and "Failed State" conflicts, involving the collapse of a central government and the division of lands among warlords that results from the civil war that follows, individually account for more of the "worst atrocities" on his list than "Religious Conflict."[36]

Again, one may quibble about White's categories, arguing that he omitted some significant wars and instances of mass violence or incorrectly included others, but it seems highly unlikely that any historian reviewing White's list of the one hundred greatest atrocities in history would see a majority of them as primarily religious. An alternative accounting would be welcome for consideration here, but nobody else has offered one, certainly none of the prominent voices proclaiming religion as the cause of the "bloodiest" wars.

Steven Pinker has provided his own rankings, based largely on White's research, of the twenty-one worst wars or atrocities based on death tolls in his widely reviewed 2011 book, *Better Angels*.[37] His list includes the following: Second World War, reign of Mao Zedong, Mongol conquests, An Lushan Revolt, fall of the Ming dynasty, Taiping Rebellion, annihilation of the American Indians, rule of Joseph Stalin, Mideast slave trade, Atlantic slave trade, rule of Tamerlane, British rule of India, World War I, Russian Civil War, fall of Rome, Congo Free State, Thirty Years' War, Russia's Time of Troubles, Napoleonic Wars, Chinese Civil War, and the French Wars of Religion. Pinker then provides a unique perspective by factoring in population differences at the times such events occurred. While Pinker lists 55,000,000 deaths resulting from World War II in the mid-twentieth century and only 36,000,000 for the An Lushan Revolt in mid-eighth-century China, he then uses population estimates to adjust the rankings per capita between the different periods.[38] Using this "mid-twentieth-century equivalent," he finds that the An Lushan Revolt would move

---

36. White, *Great Big Book of Horrible Things*, 543–44.

37. Steven Pinker, *The Better Angels of Our Nature: Why Violence Has Declined* (New York: Penguin, 2011), 195. His categorizations are often problematic, as reflected in his consideration of the "Fall of Rome" as an "atrocity."

38. Pinker draws his figure of 36,000,000 for the An Lushan Rebellion from White, *Great Big Book of Horrible Things*, 93. White notes, "The census taken in China in the year 754 recorded a population of 52,880,488. After ten years of civil war, the census of 764 found only 16,900,000 people in China. What happened to 36 million people? Is a loss of two-thirds in one decade even possible? Perhaps. Peasants often lived at the very edge of starvation, so the slightest disruption could cause a massive die off, particularly if they depended on large irrigation systems. . . . [Moreover] many authorities quote these numbers with a minimum of doubt."

from fourth place to first place on his list with a mid-twentieth-century equivalent of 429,000,000 deaths, far surpassing World War II.[39]

While Pinker singles out religious conflicts/events in neither his ranking based on total deaths nor his population-adjusted rankings, it is interesting to note that religious conflicts appear to play a minor role in both. Only three of the conflicts would clearly seem to qualify as primarily religious conflicts or religiously inspired events: the Taiping Rebellion, the Thirty-Years' War, and the French Wars of Religion, resulting in only 14.2 percent of the twenty-one worst atrocities in history as referenced by Pinker. It is worth pointing out that at least four of the twenty-one atrocities listed by Pinker could be attributed not to religion but rather *Marxist* efforts to establish or develop communist states, including the reign of Mao Zedong, the reign of Stalin, the Russian Civil War, and the Chinese Civil War, equaling 19 percent of the total. Consequently, one could argue that Marxism is a greater cause of violence and atrocities in Pinker's study than religion!

The numbers, therefore, as provided by our three major studies to enumerate history's most violent wars and conflicts, break down as follows: 6.9 percent of Phillips and Axelrod's 1,763 historical wars were religious conflicts; 13 percent of White's 100 worst atrocities in history can be ascribed to "Religious Conflict" or "Human Sacrifice"; and 14.2 percent of Pinker's 21 worst atrocities in history were religiously inspired. Thus, our only existing quantitative analyses suggest that religious motivations inspire only a relatively small percentage of all conflicts. Moreover, there seem to be other causes or motivations that have inspired more wars or atrocities than religion.

Distinguishing Religious Wars from Secular Wars

One can disagree with such an approach in considering to what degree religion was the cause of a particular conflict. Such disagreements among historians are not surprising. War is messy, after all, and conflicts usually emerge from a complex mix of factors that might incorporate economic, political, ethnic, and religious concerns on one or both sides.

William T. Cavanaugh, a theologian and professor of Catholic studies at DePaul University, has considered the issue of defining and distinguishing religious warfare from other types of conflict in a highly influential 2009 book. Cavanaugh argues that various scholars have made "indefensible assumptions about what does and does not count as religion."[40] He considers the claims of nine scholars who have suggested that "religion is particularly prone to violence" based on arguments that religion is,

---

39. Pinker, *Better Angels*, 195.
40. Cavanaugh, *The Myth of Religious Violence*, 4.

among other things, absolutist, divisive, and/or irrational.[41] He rejects their respective arguments, noting that "they all suffer from the same defect: the inability to find a convincing way to separate religious violence from secular violence."[42] Indeed, as Cavanaugh argues, secular violence is often motivated by similar degrees of absolutism, division, and irrationality, but in nonreligious forms.

Among the scholars that Cavanaugh considers is Charles Kimball. He argues that Kimball's book (which, incidentally, was chosen by *Publishers Weekly* as the top book on religion in 2002) "suffers" from its inability to "distinguish the religious from the secular."[43] Kimball postulates that there are various "warning signs" that religion could turn evil. Among such warning signs, for example, are calls for blind obedience and the belief that the end justifies the means. Cavanaugh argues in rebuttal that all of the warning signs offered by Kimball could equally apply to nationalism or nationalist ideologies. Concerning Kimball's claim about blind obedience as a marker of religious conflict, for example, Cavanaugh points out that "obedience is institutionalized" in the US military, as there is no allowance for "selective conscientious objection."[44] Yet Cavanaugh appears most dismissive of the claim that the end justifies the means is uniquely associated with religious conflict, noting that the history of modern conflict is "full of evidence" that demonstrates how secular states have embraced such a view. Among such evidence, he references "the vaporization of innocent civilians in Hiroshima" and "the practice of torture by over a third of the world's nation states, including many democracies."[45]

To be clear, Cavanaugh is not rejecting the notion that religion can sometimes inspire violence. Instead, he is arguing that Kimball's efforts to clearly distinguish religious violence as somehow worse than secular violence, and more prone to fanaticism, are unconvincing.

Similarly, Cavanaugh also challenges the claims of sociologist Mark Juergensmeyer, who argues that "religion seems to be connected with violence virtually everywhere," perpetually and across all religious traditions.[46] Juergensmeyer, like Kimball, makes sharp distinctions between religious and secular violence, highlighting what he claims are significant differences. These include, for example, the notion that religious violence is "accompanied by strong claims of moral justification and enduring

41. Cavanaugh, *The Myth of Religious Violence*, 15–56. In addition to Kimball, he considers the academic arguments of John Hick, Richard Wentz, Martin Marty, Mark Juergensmeyer, David C. Rapoport, Bhikhu Parekh, R. Scott Appleby, and Charles Selengut.

42. Cavanaugh, *The Myth of Religious Violence*, 8.

43. Cavanaugh, *The Myth of Religious Violence*, 21–24.

44. Cavanaugh, *The Myth of Religious Violence*, 23.

45. Cavanaugh, *The Myth of Religious Violence*, 24.

46. Mark Juergensmeyer, *Terror in the Mind of God: The Global Rise of Religious Violence*, 3rd ed. (Berkeley: University of California Press, 2003), xi.

absolutism" as a result of the intense religious conviction of those carrying it out.[47] In response, Cavanaugh points out how secular warfare is often "couched in the strongest rhetoric of moral justification and historical duty," citing, for example, Operation Infinite Justice, the US military's initial name for the post-9/11 war in Afghanistan.[48] In another example, Juergensmeyer argues that secular conflicts are briefer, concluding within the lifetimes of the combatants, whereas religious conflicts can last for hundreds of years.[49] Cavanaugh objects by noting that, "Juergensmeyer himself says that US leaders have given every indication that the 'war against terror' will stretch indefinitely into the future" and that this war "seems so absolute and unyielding on both sides."[50] To this one might also cite the examples of the so-called Hundred Years' War, lasting from 1337 to 1453, as well as the Second Hundred Years' War, lasting from 1689 to 1815, both of which have traditionally been interpreted, and rightly so, as secular conflicts rather than religious ones.

Cavanaugh does not confine himself to refuting only Kimball's and Juergensmeyer's arguments. He critiques the positions of several other scholars who have made similar claims about religion, emphasizing their presumed inability to define religious wars or violence in a way that cannot also be applied to secular institutions or ideologies. He further argues that modern distinctions between religious violence and other types of violence "are part of a broader Enlightenment narrative that has invented a dichotomy between the religious and the secular . . ." that frames religious violence as "irrational and dangerous" in comparison to various forms of secular violence.[51] He then rejects the notion, convincingly, I think, that religious ideologies are inherently "more inclined toward violence" than secular ideologies or institutions, arguing that distinctions between the two have not been properly established by the scholars who make such claims.[52]

Secular Ideologies as a Type of Religion?

Another problem is that people often define religion and its essential qualities quite differently. Some scholars even debate whether or not nationalism, Marxism, liberalism, or intersectionality are essentially religious in nature as a result of varying demands for philosophical and political "orthodoxy" from adherents to the worldviews promoted by these ideologies. Yet the definition of religion provided earlier in this essay, based on the earliest meanings of the term, centered on belief in, respect

---

47. Juergensmeyer, *Terror in the Mind of God*, 220.

48. Cavanaugh, *Myth of Religious Violence*, 32.

49. Juergensmeyer, *Terror in the Mind of God*, 158.

50. Cavanaugh, *Myth of Religious Violence*, 32.

51. Cavanaugh, *Myth of Religious Violence*, 4.

52. Cavanaugh, *Myth of Religious Violence*, 5.

for, and devotion to a transcendental Other, obviously excludes secular ideologies from qualifying as "religions." Moreover, modern adherents of the major faiths, which include Islam, Christianity, Hinduism, among others, who embrace the Divine as a mover of historical events and the afterlife, in some form, as a reality, would see such secular ideologies, devoid of any emphasis on the sacred or the Divine, as something very different from how they define religion.

Similarly, Marxist governments, as well, have generally embraced atheism and typically rejected any associations of their beliefs with religion. Karl Marx himself disparaged "religion" as the "opium of the people," serving only as a palliative that those in power offered to mask the suffering of the proletariat and, thereby, harmfully preventing the oppressed from perceiving the oppression that was the cause of their pain.[53] Marx did not see his conclusions, which he based on his study of history, economics, and government, as a faith or "religion." To his mind, his insight was scientific truth, not empty belief, and he understood it to be a rational and true alternative to the irrational illusion of religion.

Consequently, while some may classify certain secular ideologies as essentially religious, when claiming that religion is the cause of more wars than anything else critics like Harris or Dawkins certainly do not. They are not, after all, referring to secular atheists or agnostics (like themselves), progressives, or Marxists, as the cause of most wars or violence, but rather those who are inspired to acts of war because of their belief in the Divine.

Secular Ideologies and Violence

As noted at the beginning of this essay, Kimball argues that "more people" have been killed in the name of religion "than by any other institutional force in human history."[54] Yet other ideologies appear to have proven far deadlier (and in a shorter amount of time) than religiously inspired conflict. Consider the comments of Sam Harris, who devotes a portion of his introductory chapter in *The End of Faith* to the collective horrors and atrocities that have resulted from historic Hindu-Muslim animosity and highlights political efforts to accommodate Hindu-Muslim religious divisions through the establishment of the modern nations of Pakistan and India. Harris then asks, "When will we realize that the concessions we have made to faith in our political discourse have prevented us from even speaking about, much less uprooting, the most prolific source of violence in our history?"[55]

---

53. Karl Marx, *A Contribution to the Critique of Hegel's "Philosophy of Right,"* trans. A. Jolin and J. O'Malley (Cambridge: Cambridge University Press, 1972), 131.

54. Kimball, *When Religion Becomes Evil*, 1.

55. Harris, *The End of Faith*, 26–27.

Concerning Harris's suggestion that "concessions" in our "political discourse" to religious faith have been the main obstacle to reducing violence from its "most prolific" source (religious faith), it is worth noting that there has, indeed, been a political discourse that not only refused to make concessions to religious faith, particularly Christianity, but also outright attacked it—communism.[56] Indeed, the communist government of the Soviet Union initially attacked Christianity as a source of all evils, destroying churches and persecuting clergy during the 1920s, as it sought to *uproot*, to borrow Harris's term, Christianity from Soviet society. Yet this did not stop violence in the Soviet Union or hinder the extensive Soviet promotion of revolutionary

Vladimir Lenin and Joseph Stalin.

conflicts around the world. To the contrary, the twentieth century is grimly notable for the deaths of, so it has been estimated, nearly one hundred million people by communist governments.[57] Some estimates run even higher. R. J. Rummel, for example, studied governments responsible for mass killings of their own citizens, a phenomenon he called "democide."[58] He attributed far higher numbers of deaths to the reigns of Mao or Stalin than did Pinker or White: seventy-three million to Mao (vs. forty), and thirty-eight million to Stalin (vs. twenty).[59] Similarly, in White's statistical breakdown, by cause, of the deaths attributed to the one hundred greatest historic atrocities, multiple categories rank higher than religion. Of White's estimated 455 million collective victims of these atrocities, he calculates that about 47 million were due to

56. Special thanks to Professor Florin Curta of the University of Florida for drawing my attention to this point in a private conversation.

57. Stéphane Courtois et al., *The Black Book of Communism: Crimes, Terror, Repression*, trans. J. Murphy and M. Kramer (Cambridge: Harvard University Press, 1999), 4.

58. R. J. Rummel, *Death by Government* (New Brunswick, NJ: Transaction, 1994), 36–38.

59. Rummel revised his figures in 2005; see Andrew Holt, "The 20th Century's Bloodiest 'Megamurderers' According to Prof. R. J. Rummel," apholt.com, accessed January 16, 2019, https://apholt.com/2018/11/15/the-20th-centurys-bloodiest-megamurderers-according-to-prof-r-j-rummel/.

religion, or only around 10 percent of the total.[60] In contrast, White estimates that communist ideology is responsible for 67 million deaths, or nearly 15 percent of the total.[61]

Conclusion

As I have tried to make clear throughout this essay, none of what I have written here is meant to imply that religions are always, or even typically, peaceful, or that members of various religious faiths cannot exhibit the same degree of violence as those otherwise motivated. Religious peoples are often willing to engage in warfare. To the contrary, my argument is that claims that religious wars are *more violent* and *greater in number* than other types have no empirical evidence to support them. Such arguments are wholly anecdotal, which almost certainly explains why professional historians have not embraced them. Available quantitative analyses of history's wars in this regard, as flawed as they are, point in a different direction: that religious conflicts are but a relatively modest percentage of the total and that other causes or ideological motivations have inspired as much or more conflict than religion. Thus, until new data are collected that demonstrate otherwise, the claim that religion is the greatest cause of war is an unsubstantiated myth.

---

60. White, *Great Big Book of Horrible Things*, 554; in a footnote, he offers, "A friend once wondered aloud how much suffering in history has been caused by religious fanaticism, and I was able to confidently tell her 10 percent, based on this number."
61. White, *Great Big Book of Horrible Things*, 554.

2. The Western Way of War:
Battle, Imperialism, and Ethnocentrism[1]

Everett L. Wheeler

Man does not take the field for the fight, but for victory. He does everything in his power
to suppress the former and to assure the latter. Often in our time war among savage
peoples, even the Arabs, is a war of ambushes by small groups of men of which each, at
the moment of surprise, chooses, not his opponent, but his victim, and assassinates him.
                    —*Colonel Charles Ardant du Picq (c. 1870)*[2]

Now, I want you to remember that no bastard ever won a war by dying for his
country. He won it by making the other poor dumb bastard die for his country. . . .
Americans, traditionally, love to fight. . . . That's why Americans have never lost and
will never lose a war. Because the very thought of losing is hateful to Americans.
                    —*General George S. Patton (1944)*[3]

These quotations, roughly seventy years apart, reflect aspects of a supposed "Western way of war" (WWW). For Ardant du Picq, non-*Westerners* pursue underhanded means, here surprise and ambush, violations of an assumed honorable norm of open battle and face-to-face confrontation, although he also emphasizes that battle's purpose is not the fight itself but winning with the least expense—an immediate contradiction, since surprise and ambush can bring victory at less cost to the attackers. Patton adds American, that is, Western, triumphalism: the West always wins.

Ethnocentrism, the tendency to evaluate other cultures by the standards and customs of one's own, generally with the assessor's belief in his own culture's superiority, underlies the notion of a WWW and fosters a mentality of an in-group versus an out-group (us vs. them). This phenomenon occurs in most pre-state societies, each of which conceived its own state as the center of the universe. For Europeans, the broader idea of Western versus non-Western differences and eventually hostility

---

1. In memoriam Roger J. Spiller (1944–2017), historian and friend.

2. *Études sur le combat: Combat antique et combat moderne* (repr., Paris: Éditions Champ Libre, 1978), 7. My translation.

3. *Patton* (20th Century Fox, 1970), opening monologue, adapted from Patton's "pep talks" to the US Third Army, June 1944.

began only c. 500 BCE, when Greeks first conceived non-Greek speakers, now collectively called "barbarians," as distinct from themselves in more than just use of a different language. Simultaneously, a Greek sense of sharing a common language, religion, and culture intensified despite their political division into individual city-states. The Persians' attempt to expand their Asian empire into Europe, which the Greeks repulsed in two wars (490, 480–479 BCE), exacerbated this new Greek-barbarian dichotomy. Herodotus, the Greek historian of these wars, traced the dichotomy's origins to the mythical period of the Trojan War, whereby he reflected a trend, new in the fifth century, to see the Trojan War as a Greek-barbarian conflict, a perspective absent in the Homeric poems centuries before.[4] Earlier, however, in *The Persians* (472 BCE), a historical tragedy focused on the Greek naval victory at Salamis in 480 BCE, the Athenian Aeschylus, a veteran of the Persian Wars, disdained the Persians as morally and culturally inferior barbarians. Thus originated a concept of "Orientalism," a Western view of Asian peoples as exotic, but backward and uncivilized.[5]

By the fourth century BCE, Greeks began to dehumanize barbarians, by their inferior character only a step above wild beasts and fit to be slaves or worthy of extermination.[6] Traits common in pre-state peoples' relations with "outsiders," such as trickery, faithlessness in agreements, and refusal to fight in open battle, were generalized to all barbarians regardless of their level of political, social, and economic development. The Persians, rulers of a rich, sophisticated, multiethnic empire stretching from the Aegean Sea to the Indus River of India, fell into the same category as primitive tribal societies.[7] Indeed the Chinese, no less ethnocentric than Greeks, could also identify "barbarians" (non-Chinese) as beasts.[8]

Barbarians occurred at all points of the compass, not exclusively in Asia. Romans, although adapting the Greek-barbarian dichotomy, legalistically distinguished a *iustus hostis*, a public enemy with whom they could engage in a proper war, from brigands outside the rules of civilized behavior, to whom no restraints in military conduct were owed. Barbarians were brigands. Further, wars fought with civilized foes in competition for honor and empire differed in practices and ferocity from wars for survival

---

4. Herodotus, 1.4.3–4; 8.144.2 (Greek nationalism). English translations are conveniently available in the Loeb Classical Library series.

5. Patrick Porter, *Military Orientalism: Eastern War Through Western Eyes* (New York: Columbia University Press, 2009), 27–29.

6. Aristotle, *Nicomachean Ethics*, 7.1.3, 5.6; *Politics*, 2.8.12; Isocrates 12.163; Ps.-Plato, *Menexenus*, 242d.

7. Cf. Polyaenus, *Strategica*, 7 preface, in Polyaenus, *Stratagems of War*, ed. and trans. P. Krentz and E. L. Wheeler (Chicago: Ares Publishers, 1994), 623.

8. Andreas Alföldi, "Die ethische Grenzscheide am römischen Limes," *Schweizer Beiträge zur allgemeinen Geschichte* 8 (1950): 48–49.

against barbarians. Limits (in theory) circumscribed the former, but not the latter.[9] Thus from its origins the *idea* of a WWW stressed that non-Westerners (the uncivilized) pursued a different military style from civilized Westerners and in fighting non-Westerners a different set of "rules" for military behavior applied.

In the Middle Ages the Greek/Roman-barbarian dichotomy morphed into Christians versus infidels. European overseas expansion from c. 1500 permitted transfer of the Graeco-Roman concept of barbarians to pre-state and non-Christian populations, outsiders to the legal and religious European community. By the late nineteenth century and into the twentieth, the term "savages" replaced "uncivilized" with the political and moral imperative ("the white man's burden") to "civilize" and Christianize non-European peoples according to European standards, despite murky definitions of "civilized" and "uncivilized." In 1945, the United Nations Charter, declaring the legal equality of all peoples and states regardless of different levels of political and economic development, created a universal international community and—in theory—finally eliminated this dichotomy.[10]

Since 1945, large-scale conventional wars between major powers, prominent in the view of a WWW, have largely disappeared. Instead, guerilla insurgencies, terrorism, and "small wars" provoke outrage at enemies who shun the WWW's open, direct confrontation of a "fair fight." For some, a "clash of civilizations," perpetuation of a traditional West-East dichotomy, underlies multiple conflicts.[11] Hence in the popular imagination the concept of a WWW flourishes as the polar opposite of unconventional or asymmetric warfare, an overused term in the early twenty-first century for almost any conflict in which the opponent refuses open combat.[12] Indeed the medieval rhetoric of the crusades (Christians vs. infidels) resurfaced in public discourse of the 1990s, just when academic historians were turning to "culture" as an analytical approach to war. Yet for others, the cultural clash may be more "rhetoric than reality" and "culture" can be problematic in assessing Western and non-Western military behavior.[13]

---

9. *Justinian's Digest* 49.15.24; Cicero, *On Duties* 1.38; Alföldi, "Ethische Grenzscheide," 37–50.

10. A brief overview at Liliana Obregón Tarazona, "The Civilized and the Uncivilized," in *The Oxford Handbook of the History of International Law*, ed. B. Fassbender and A. Peters (Oxford: Oxford University Press, 2012), 917–40.

11. Samuel Huntington, *The Clash of Civilizations and the Remaking of World Order* (New York: Simon and Schuster, 1996); Anthony Pagden, *Worlds at War: The 2,500-Year Struggle between East and West* (New York: Random House, 2008).

12. Hew Strachan, "A General Typology of Transcultural Wars–the Modern Ages," in *Transcultural Wars from the Middle Ages to the 21st Century*, ed. H-H. Kortüm (Berlin: De Gruyter, 2006), 103.

13. Jeremy Black, *Rethinking Military History* (New York: Routledge, 2004), 76 and 83; Porter, *Military Orientalism*, 7–13.

The concept of a WWW raises complaints about oversimplification of world history and military history in particular.[14] Can world military history really be reduced to monolithic blocks of consistent behavior, especially when the concept of a WWW homogenized all non-Western practices as primitive from its origins?[15] Is it true that the West, with an unbroken continuity of practice over 2,500 years and prone to imperialism, fights decisive battles, relies on infantry forces, delights in killing, and wages wars of annihilation, whereas the non-West prefers cavalry, avoidance of battle and casualties, touts trickery and indirect means, and favors victory by attrition? Does Western military thought differ from the non-Western?

A neat dichotomy of Western and non-Western military behavior cannot escape reality's quagmire of messy contradictions. Both the West and the non-West display different styles and varieties of conduct in various epochs and even within the same epoch. A hypothesized "non-Western way of war" would be just as dubious as a "Western" way.[16]

Rather, a WWW is an ideology, subject to reinvention over time—evident in the transformation of barbarians into first, infidels, then the uncivilized. Likewise the concept of Orientalism is fluid.[17] Popular perceptions of a WWW clash with the historical realities of how Westerners and non-Westerns have conducted wars.[18] The very term "WWW," in fact, imitates earlier attempts to formulate national ways of war for the United Kingdom and the United States.[19] The former is now generally rejected and the later contested.[20] Yet the current reinvention of the WWW anachronistically projects nineteenth-century ideas about decisive battle and successful Western imperialism into the distant past. Through various questionable interpretations WWW advocates claim that only the West fights real battles, engages in true war, seeks total victory and unconditional surrender, and emphasizes killing. Instead of a concern for obtaining objectives and winning a war by other means, the WWW advocates fixate

14. Strachan, "General Typology," 102n49.

15. Black, *Rethinking*, 68.

16. See, e.g., Gérard Chaliand, *The Art of War in World History* (Berkeley: University of California Press, 1994).

17. Harry Sidebottom, *Ancient Warfare: A Very Brief Introduction* (Oxford: Oxford University Press, 2004), x, xiv, and 115–24; Porter, *Military Orientalism*, 23–32.

18. John A. Lynn, "Discourse, Reality, and the Culture of Combat," *International History Review* 27 (2005): 475–77 and 480.

19. B. H. Liddell Hart, *The British Way in Warfare* (New York: Macmillan, 1933); Russell Weigley, *The American Way of War: A History of United States Military Strategy and Policy* (Bloomington: Indiana University Press, 1973).

20. Michael Howard, *The Causes of Wars*, 2nd ed. (Cambridge: Harvard University Press, 1984), 169–87; A. J. Echevarria, *Reconsidering the American Way of War: US Military Practice from the Revolution to Afghanistan* (Washington, DC: Georgetown University Press, 2014); cf. on the "Arab way of war": Porter, *Military Orientalism*, 179.

on battles and blood, as if it were the sole means of military effectiveness.[21] Since antiquity, however, trickery as an alternative to open battle was advocated, even in the West. The political philosopher Thomas Hobbes (d. 1679) assigned fraud equal status with force as war's two cardinal virtues.[22]

The WWW's current manifestation dates to 1989, when Victor Davis Hanson coined the phrase in his application to classical Greek warfare of John Keegan's much-imitated "face-of-battle" approach to studying combat. For Hanson, the WWW's origin lay in the Greek invention of decisive battle, the direct clash of hoplite, or heavy infantry forces, of Greeks versus Greeks in the fifth century BCE and earlier, whereby a relatively brief but intense act of violence decided the war and spared lives from a prolonged conflict.[23] An elaboration of the Greek-WWW connection followed.[24] Hanson's WWW, already contested in 1990,[25] would probably have fueled only scholarly debate, had not the initial publication of his *Carnage and Culture*, expanding coverage to world history, roughly coincided with the tragic events of September 11, 2001.[26] With debate about a clash of civilizations in progress and the American response to 9/11 (Operation Enduring Freedom) underway in Afghanistan, a new assertion of a WWW and Western (American) dominance harmonized with patriotic fervor and outrage. *C&C* became a best seller in an atmosphere of "the Primordial East driven by visceral or pre-modern urges, against the West, rational and modern."[27]

But even before 9/11, Keegan endorsed Hanson's WWW and an East-West dichotomy in an anthropologically inspired treatment of world military history.[28] A WWW then found favor in analysis of Western war and its ethics from the Greeks to the Middle Ages.[29] The variety of favorable views of the WWW can be seen in a massive attempt at an "evolutionary" global history of warfare from the Stone Age to the present, stressing geographic, environmental, and economic factors,[30] besides a series of

---

21. Cf. Black, *Rethinking*, 20; Jason Sharman, *Empires of the Weak: the Story of European Expansion and the Creation of the New World Order* (Princeton, NJ: Princeton University Press, 2019), 22.

22. Thomas Hobbes, *The Leviathan* (repr., Baltimore: Penguin, 1968), 188 (pt. 1, chap. 13).

23. Victor Davis Hanson, *The Western Way of War: Infantry Battle in Classical Greece* (New York: Alfred A. Knopf, 1989); hereafter the italicized *WWW*.

24. Victor Davis Hanson, *The Wars of the Ancient Greeks and Their Invention of Western Military Culture* (London: Cassell, 1999).

25. Everett L. Wheeler, *Journal of Interdisciplinary History* 21, no. 1 (1990): 122–25.

26. Victor Davis Hanson, *Carnage and Culture: Landmark Battles in the Rise of Western Power* (New York: Doubleday, 2001); hereafter *C&C*.

27. Porter, *Military Orientalism*, 192.

28. John Keegan, *A History of Warfare* (New York: Alfred A. Knopf, 1993).

29. Doyne Dawson, *The Origins of Western Warfare: Militarism and Morality in the Ancient World* (Boulder, CO: Westview, 1996).

30. Azar Gat, *War in Human Civilization* (New York: Oxford University Press, 2006), 396.

works from Geoffrey Parker, who wedded the WWW to his thesis of an early modern "military revolution" underlying Western expansion.[31]

Since 1989, the current version of a WWW has provoked innumerable criticisms among scholars, attacking the supposed uniqueness of Western practices and thought besides the alleged unbroken continuity of a WWW between the Greeks and the present.[32] Nor has the WWW escaped the current "culture wars" with assertions of the topic's politicization.[33] Here only further nuance and context on some key themes will be added to others' detailed rebuttals.

Definitions of the WWW and Pre-State Warfare

Recent efforts to explain the WWW disfigure the notion even more. Major WWW advocates have disagreed on key elements of its composition and differed in the thrust of their arguments. Keegan, aware of Hanson's faulty case for continuity, ignored the problem.[34] Further, if Greeks invented "decisive battle," they declined to pursue the unconditional surrender and total victory, which WWW advocates assert.[35] Nor was decisive battle exclusively Western: Keegan concedes one at Ain Jalut, where the Egyptian Mamelukes defeated the Mongols in 1260. Other examples could be cited, such as Hormizdagan in 224 CE, where Ardashir I's victory ended after over four hundred years of the Parthian Arsacid dynasty's rule of an Iranian empire and placed his own family, the Sasanids, in power.[36]

Greek invention of the WWW rests on WWW advocates' misunderstanding of pre-state warfare in general and initially ignoring non-Western warfare before c. 500

---

31. *The Cambridge Illustrated History of Warfare: The Triumph of the West*, ed. G. Parker (Cambridge: Cambridge University Press, 1995; rev. ed. 2008); *The Cambridge History of Warfare*, ed. G. Parker (Cambridge: Cambridge University Press, 2005; rev. ed. 2020); hereafter *CHW* 2005/*CHW* 2020; summary in Geoffrey Parker, "What Is the Western Way of War?" *Military History Quarterly* 8, no. 2 (1996): 86–95; hereafter *MHQ*.

32. E.g., John A. Lynn, *Battle: A History of Combat and Culture* (Boulder, CO: Westview, 2003); Beatrice Heuser, *The Evolution of Strategy: Thinking War from Antiquity to the Present* (Cambridge: Cambridge University Press, 2010); Steven J. Willett, "History from the Clouds," *Arion* 10, no. 1 (2002): 157–78; Black, *Rethinking*, 1–2, 57–58, and 83.

33. Black, *Rethinking*, 57; Porter, *Military Orientalism*, 17n102; cf. F. J. González Gracía and P. López Barja de Quiroga, "Neocon Greece: V. D. Hanson's War on History," *International Journal of the Classical Tradition* 19, no. 3 (2012): 129–51.

34. Keegan, *History of Warfare*, 232 and 244; cf. Lynn, *Battle*, 5, 7–9, and 46–47.

35. Keegan, *History of Warfare*, 364; contra, Hanson, *C&C*, 21 and 430; Parker, *MHQ*, 94; *CHW* 2020, 5.

36. Keegan, *History of Warfare*, 35, 210–11; Everett L. Wheeler, "Present but Absent: Marathon in the Tradition of Western Military Thought," in *Marathon, the Day After*, ed. K. Buraselis and E. Koulakiotis (Athens: European Cultural Centre of Delphi, 2013), 267; cf. Morgan Dean, *Decisive Battles in Chinese History* (Yardley, PA: Westholme, 2018).

Hoplites depicted on the famous *Chigi Olpe* (pitcher), a mid-seventh-century BCE vessel from Corinth discovered in an Etruscan tomb north of Rome.

BCE, particularly in the Bronze and Iron Ages Near East, as if Egyptians, Assyrians, Persians, and others did not fight real wars. Neither strategic design nor a fear of fighting produced the relative rarity of pitched battles in the Iron Age Near East. Hanson would even impute to Philip II of Macedon (382–336 BCE, Alexander the Great's father) the introduction of "decisive war."[37]

Hanson's original concept stressed decisive battle, a confrontation of rival infantry forces in a "fair fight," face-to-face, open combat, whereby Greeks, with their infantry in the closely ordered rectangle of a phalanx, disdained missile weapons, cavalry, strategy (battle plans), and trickery.[38] The Greek phalanx as a *tactical model* for the Romans and early modern military theorists, inspired by Greek and Roman texts, is not in dispute, but the meaning and context of battle is. Hanson derived his WWW from societal factors, generalized as "culture" (a term not defined), as if culture is independent of the physical and material factors of its geographical setting.[39]

---

37. Sarah C. Melville, "Win, Lose, or Draw? Claiming Victory in Battle," in *Krieg und Frieden im Alten Vorderasien*, ed. H. Neumann et al. (Münster: Ugarit-Verlag, 2014), 527; Hanson, *C&C*, 77.

38. Hanson, *WWW*, 9–17 and 223–27.

39. *C&C*, 8–9, 15–19, and 359; on culture, see David A. Graff, *The Eurasian Way of War: Military Practice in Seventh-Century China and Byzantium* (London: Routledge, 2016), 9–11; Porter, *Military Orientalism*, 7–11.

Discipline (for Hanson *innately* Western), civic militarism, and lethality feature prominently in the analysis.[40] Civic militarism, a supposed Western trait for over 2,500 years, is equated with free, landholding citizens equipped as heavy infantry, fighting for freedom, which denotes not only political independence but also capitalism's free markets. Motifs of freedom and the moral value of heroism reflect the seminal 1851 book of Sir Edward Creasy on decisive battle. Emphasis on Western freedom echoes the German philosopher G. W. F. Hegel's uncritical acceptance of Herodotus on the Persian Wars as a struggle of Greek freedom versus Oriental despotism. Ignored in Hanson's exaggerated discussion is a blatant contradiction of "freedom": Herodotus largely rehearses fifth-century-BCE Athenian propaganda to justify the Athenian Empire, an unwanted tyranny over numerous subject cities, as Thucydides later asserts.[41] Stronger states easily manipulate abstract terms like "freedom" and "liberation" for their own political purposes.

In *C&C* "military necessity" justifies for Hanson the West's admittedly amoral emphasis on lethality. Killing is good, if done openly, and *all* war should be total with a complete defeat of the enemy.[42] Like culture, military necessity, a much-debated concept and a common defense in trials for war crimes, is left undefined.

For Hanson and Keegan the WWW is a cultural tradition. In contrast, Parker emphasizes Western innovation and adaptability to changing circumstances, spawning resilience and lethality—a challenge/response model in the mode of Arnold Toynbee.[43] The WWW's supposed tradition of aggression supports Parker's early modern military revolution underlying the West's global dominance by 1800. Hence the WWW becomes a template for superpower status, a survival of the fittest à la Social Darwinism, in which not even all Western states could compete, but Japan in certain eras could.[44] The thrust of Parker's version is technology and the means to finance it, not Hanson's culture.[45] His cultural appeals to antiquity reveal idealized (even erroneous) notions, such as highly disciplined Greek hoplite armies (true perhaps for Sparta, but not other states), Western freedom of thought and systematization of knowledge dating from Plato's Academy (ignoring Plato's advocacy of censorship), and misinterpretation of an ancient source influential in the Dutch military reforms of Maurice of Nassau (1590s).[46]

---

40. *C&C*, 168 and 257.

41. Hanson, *C&C*, 39 and 46–55; Wheeler, "Present but Absent," 242n5; Thucydides 1.122.2–3, 124.3; and 2.63.

42. Hanson, *C&C*, 21, 430; cf. on the firebombing of Tokyo, 348.

43. Parker, *MHQ*, 86 and 94; *CHW*, 2005, 1, 5, 414, and 416; Arnold Toynbee, *A Study of History*, 12 vols. (London: Oxford University Press, 1934–61).

44. Parker, *CHW* 2020, 10.

45. Lynn, "Discourse," 479–80.

46. Parker, *MHQ*, 89; *CHW* 2005, 5, 431; *CHW* 2020, 2–5; cf. more accurately Parker, "The Limits to Revolutions in Military Affairs: Maurice of Nassau, the Battle of Nieuwpoort (1600), and the

Foibles in the WWW advocates' definition of war surface in Keegan's anthropological assessment, in which culture becomes the chief factor in styles of warfare. He aimed to replace an emphasis on politics/policy, associated with the Prussian military theorist Carl von Clausewitz in *On War* (1832), with culture: "war is culture by other means."[47] An East-West dichotomy figures prominently with sharp contrasts between states with infantry forces and "horse peoples."

For Keegan true war must include organization or occupation of conquered territory.[48] Certainly ecology and geography explain why some cultures developed infantry and others cavalry, but one type of force is not always superior to the other. Too many variables (e.g., political, temporal and topographical dispositions, generalship, etc.) preclude that generalization. Manchu cavalry, after all, conquered Ming China in the seventeenth century.[49] A strict dichotomy between European infantry and "horse peoples" of Central Asia is less applicable to China, originally an agrarian, not herding, culture.[50] Pre-state warriors could also profit from war and expand their territory.[51]

Not all wars are fought for territorial expansion. An argument similar to Keegan's discounts any Parthian or Sasanid Persian threat on Rome's eastern frontier because the Iranian powers did not attempt to annex Roman territory west of the Euphrates River. When an opportunity occurred, however, the Sasanid Chosroes II seized Roman Anatolia, the Levant, and Egypt (603–29 CE). No one would dispute that Rome and Iranian powers fought real wars.[52] Likewise a contention that Alexander the Great, Chinggis Khan, and Tamerlane only raided without consolidating their gains is just as dubious as Hanson's view that Alexander sought annihilation of all enemy combatants and destruction of cultures that opposed his rule.[53] Rather, Alexander tried to keep the Achaemenid Persian Empire intact and attempted to assimilate himself with Persian, Babylonian, and Egyptian cultures.[54]

Legacy," *Journal of Military History* 71 (2007): 338–58 and 361–66; Plato, *Republic*, 3.398a–b and 10; Aelianus Tacticus, *Tactica Theoria*, 28: not a discussion of *Roman* volley fire with javelin throwers and slingers, as Parker alleges.

47. Porter, *Military Orientalism*, 11.

48. Keegan, *History of Warfare*, 92 and 122.

49. Black, *Rethinking*, 169.

50. Gat, *War in Human Civilization*, 391–99.

51. Lawrence H. Keeley, *War before Civilization* (New York: Oxford University Press, 1996), 99–112 and 116.

52. Everett L. Wheeler, "Methodological Limits and the Mirage of Roman Strategy," *Journal of Military History* 57 (1993): 33–35, correcting Benjamin Isaac, *The Limits of Empire: The Roman Army in the East* (Oxford: Clarendon Press, 1990), 22, 28, and 52–53.

53. Keegan, *History of Warfare*, 74, although at 204–7 he attributes the conduct of "true war" (not pre-state war) to Chinggis Khan; Hanson, *C&C*, 83.

54. See F. S. Naiden, *Soldier, Priest, and God: A Life of Alexander the Great* (Oxford: Oxford University Press, 2019).

The objective in war, not always battle and conquest (unless imperialism is the motivation), is imposing one belligerent's will in a dispute. The threat of violence can be just as effective. Hunnic peoples of Central Asia learned this lesson early in imposing their will on ancient Chinese rulers. Attila successfully extorted Roman concessions with the same technique, whereby he exploited a Roman practice to pay border peoples to behave.[55] Subsidies were cheaper. Some new acquisitions would not repay the cost of conquest.[56] Thucydides and later the Romans recognized the difference between power, a psychological but often fragile perception, and force, a limited, expendable physical and material entity. Actual employment of force could expose the illusion of power and its limits.[57]

Further, WWW advocates confound their East-West dichotomy with the difference between pre-state (primitive) warfare involving tribes or kin groups and the real war of states. Thucydides's brief analysis of barbarian (pre-state) warfare, stressing reluctance of numerically superior but unarmored and unordered Illyrian tribesmen to close with densely deployed Greek heavy infantry, is generalized into a barbarian fear of hand-to-hand combat.[58] From another perspective, the barbarians on this occasion did not fear fighting, but declined combat on Greek terms.

Non-Westerners allegedly, on the supposition that pre-state warfare was ritualistic and relatively bloodless, refuse close combat or battles altogether and prefer stratagems (trickery, deceit, surprise, and indirect means) to frustrate and exhaust the enemy rather than to compel a confession of defeat in direct confrontation.[59] Of course some horse peoples, Attila's Huns, Chinggis Khan's Mongols, and Tamerlane's Turco-Mongols, all seekers of battle, offer embarrassing exceptions.[60]

The myth of pre-state warfare as relatively bloodless and highly ritualized conflicts with strict, almost gamelike, rules derives from anthropologists of the 1920s–1960s positing theories of societal development based on "progress" as a guiding principle, and often seeking the eighteenth-century philosopher Jean-Jacques Rousseau's peace-loving "noble savage." WWW advocates err in accepting this view. They portray Greek hoplite battles as a break from primitive playing at war to real war with profuse bloodletting. Major battles of the ancient Near East in the Bronze and Iron Ages, not to mention the large armies and horrendous casualties in Chinese warfare, especially

55. Thomas Barfield, *The Perilous Frontier: Nomadic Empires and China* (Cambridge: Blackwell, 1989), 4–9; Edward N. Luttwak, *The Grand Strategy of the Byzantine Empire* (Cambridge, MA: Belknap, 2009), 12–13, 38–39, and 54–55.

56. Wheeler, "Methodological Limits," 216n137.

57. Thucydides, 6.11.4; Edward N. Luttwak, *The Grand Strategy of the Roman Empire* (Baltimore: Johns Hopkins University Press, 1976), 3 and 195–200; Black, *Rethinking*, 20.

58. Thucydides, 4.126, with Hanson, *WWW*, 13; cf. 17.

59. Dawson, *Origins*, 13–14; Keith F. Otterbein, *How War Began* (College Station: Texas A&M University Press, 2004), 188; and even Chaliand, *Art of War*, 7.

60. Keegan, *History of Warfare*, 189 and 387–88; Heuser, *Evolution*, 42–44.

in the Warring States period (475–221 BCE), escape notice.[61] Yet work since the 1990s has exploded the myth of relatively bloodless pre-state warfare.[62] Nor does modern warfare lack rituals, canonized in laws of wars, Geneva Conventions, and procedures for surrender.[63]

In 1949, Harry Holbert Turney-High synthesized anthropological views of primitive warfare. Accordingly, state warfare emerged when a society's development crossed a "military horizon." Five elements were discerned: (1) a political state capable of assembling forces and providing a *group* (not individual or kinship based) motive; (2) adequate supply; (3) tactical operations, including column and line formations in combat; (4) command, control, and training of combatants; and (5) the ability to conduct a protracted campaign beyond a single battle.[64] Modern (Western) practices became the criteria for evaluation. Keegan based his *History of Warfare* on Turney-High's views.[65] Likewise, Turney-High's military horizon (e.g., group motive, organization, supply, discipline, command) inspired Hanson's lists of the WWW's components.[66]

Inconveniently, however, other anthropologists had rejected Turney-High's military horizon since the 1980s and even earlier. An emphasis on an evolutionary continuum from pre-state to state warfare has replaced the developmental approach of attaining a threshold or horizon.[67] Command, planning, and training of combatants can occur in pre-state warfare, which sometimes, protracted beyond a single battle, even extends for generations. The degree of lethality often varies by the character of the opponent, whether part of a common linguistic and cultural in-group, thus often encouraging limits, or an external out-group, not owed restraints.[68] An in-group/out-group distinction characterized Chinese warfare of the Spring and Autumn period (771–476 BCE) and the phenomenon is now extended to analysis of medieval

---

61. Keegan, *History of Warfare*, 73–74. On Chinese warfare, see Lynn, *Battle*, 35–46; Ralph D. Sawyer, *The Seven Military Classics of Ancient China* (Boulder, CO: Westview, 1993), 11–16; Willett, "History from the Clouds," 176–77; cf. Dean, *Decisive Battles in Chinese History*.

62. Keeley, *War before Civilization*; Otterbein, *How War Began*; Steven A. LeBlanc, with Katherine E. Register, *Constant Battles: Why We Fight* (New York: St. Martin's, 2003).

63. Keeley, *War before Civilization*, 61–65; Robin Wagner-Pacifici, *The Art of Surrender: Decomposing Sovereignty at Conflict's End* (Chicago: University of Chicago Press, 2005).

64. Harry Holbert Turney-High, *Primitive Warfare: Its Practice and Concepts*, 2nd ed. (Columbia: University of South Carolina Press, 1971), 21–38, and *The Military: The Theory of Land Warfare as Behavioral Science* (Hanover, MA: Christopher Publishing House, 1981), 33–36.

65. Keeley, *War before Civilization*, 12, 205n40; Keegan, *History of Warfare*, 92.

66. *C&C*, 21, 308–9, and 332–33 (quotation); see Turney-High's influence regarding Isandlwana (1879) at 96.

67. Keeley, *War before Civilization*, 42; Keith F. Otterbein, "The Anthropology of War," in *Handbook of Social and Cultural Anthropology*, ed. J. J. Honigmann (Chicago: Rand McNally, 1973), 945.

68. Maurice R. Davies, *The Evolution of War* (repr., Port Washington, NY: Kennikat Press, 1968), 16–21; Keeley, *War before Civilization*, 65.

and modern state-level warfare.[69] Indeed Turney-High's military horizon represents not a tactical, but a political and economic threshold.[70]

Hanson's decisive battle belongs to a type of limited warfare called agonistic, reflecting the view of war as competition (*agōn*) and fitting Stephen Morillo's view of intracultural warfare. Possession of the battlefield determined the victor. Subsequent capture/demolition of the opponent's city was not an objective of either side.[71] Greek agonistic warfare, like the pre-state warfare of cultural in-groups, both limited casualties and sometimes included the idea of "battles by appointment" (designation in advance of the time and place of battle).[72] Hoplite battle's conventions apparently *evolved* from armed settlement of local border disputes, in which battle (as in pre-state warfare) could sometimes assume the ritualistic character of duels (not bloodless) between individual "champions" or small groups.[73] Details, so far as known for the seventh and sixth centuries BCE, do not permit discerning a sharp break from pre-state warfare or crossing Turney-High's military horizon. Further, the mechanics of Hanson's hoplite battle in his *WWW* represent a mosaic of evidence from various periods with the whole explicitly attested in none.[74]

The Persian Wars initiated major changes in the Greek conception and conduct of war, as larger strategic aims, especially acquiring and retaining an empire, eliminated the restraints of an in-group system of rival city-states. Athenian imperialism and the generation-long Peloponnesian War (431–404 BCE) expanded these changes, generalizing the unlimited warfare of the Greek periphery to the Greek world as a whole, but without producing a "military revolution."[75] In comparison, China's Warring States period offers a striking parallel: transition from a ritualistic, aristocratic conduct of war to a more ruthless, no-holds-barred style. In both areas the transition fostered the origins of written military theory stressing trickery.[76]

---

69. Chinese: James A. Aho, *Religious Mythology and the Art of War* (Westport, CT: Greenwood, 1981), 110–11; medieval-modern: Stephen Morillo, "A General Typology of Transcultural Wars– The Early Middle Ages and Beyond," in *Transcultural Wars*, 29–42.

70. Keeley, *War before Civilization*, 12–14, 42–48, and 65.

71. Morillo, "General Typology," 31–33 and 40.

72. Keeley, *War before Civilization*, 59–60; Whitman, *Verdict of Battle*, 34 (medieval examples); cf. Polybius, 13.3.5; Livy, 42.47.5; Cassius Dio, 47.42.1.

73. E.g., Homer, *Iliad* 3.74–461; Herodotus, 9.48.3–49.1.

74. An alternative is Everett L. Wheeler, "Land Battles," in *The Cambridge History of Greek and Roman Warfare*, ed. P. Sabin et al. (Cambridge: Cambridge University Press, 2007), I:186–223.

75. Arther Ferrill, *The Origins of War from the Stone Age to Alexander the Great* (London: Thames and Hudson, 1985), 107–86.

76. Everett L. Wheeler, "The Origins of Military Theory in Ancient Greece and China," *International Commission of Military History, Acta 5, Bucharest 1980* (Bucharest: Romanian Commission of Military History, 1981), 74–79; Lynn, *Battle*, 35–37; cf. Christopher C. Rand, *Military Thought in Early China* (Albany: State University of New York Press, 2017).

Hanson omits that Greeks also practiced "war without herald," a conflict without the normal "rules" of formally declared wars. Thucydides implies that the Peloponnesian War became a war without herald.[77] Yet the conventions of Greek limited (agonistic) warfare applied only in a formally declared war. The war without herald suspended the normal rules, thus permitting surprise attacks, ambushes, raids, and trickery—traits of Morillo's subcultural combat.[78]

Decisive Battle

If, as WWW advocates assert, the Greeks invented decisive battle, curiously neither Greeks nor Romans had a term distinguishing decisive battle from other engagements. Likewise no such term is found in languages of the ancient Near East, such as Akkadian, the lingua franca of Mesopotamia in the Bronze and Iron Ages. Although many ancient wars (including those of the Near East) were one-battle affairs and *some* battles could be discerned as more important than others, battles served as a chronological reference or a memory of success or defeat.[79] Marathon, for example, where the Athenians defeated the Persians (490 BCE), became at Athens a patriotic symbol shrouded in myths and legends, a classic example of a historical event succumbing to memory.[80] Rhetorical exaggeration might posit a battle to determine a "ruler of the world," as in Polybius's account of the prelude to Zama (202 BCE), Scipio Africanus's defeat of Hannibal, but the idea of a decisive battle in the sense of a total victory that changed the course of history developed only in the eighteenth and nineteenth centuries.[81] Certainly a view that Herodotus's account of Marathon originated the concept of decisive battle should be rejected.[82]

Battles, never war's most common form, rank in frequency behind raids and sieges. Plundering raids, from the pre-state era on, yielded immediate gains and could become a form of economic warfare and attrition, avoiding the risks and losses of battle.[83] Nevertheless, armies had to be prepared for battle, even if battle was not the

---

77. Thucydides, 1.146; 2.1; "war without herald": *Armies of Classical Greece*, ed. E. L. Wheeler (Aldershot, UK: Ashgate, 2007), xliv–xlv.

78. Everett L. Wheeler, "Greece: Mad Hatters and March Hares," in *Recent Directions in the Military History of the Ancient World*, ed. L. L. Brice and J. T. Roberts (Claremont, CA: Regina Books, 2011), 78–92; and review of R. Konijnendijk, *Classical Greek Tactics: A Cultural History*, in *Ancient History Bulletin Online Reviews* 9 (2019) 35–45; Morillo, "General Typology," 36–40.

79. Melville, "Win, Lose, or Draw?" 528; Wheeler, "Present but Absent," 247–48.

80. Wheeler, "Present but Absent," 241–59.

81. Polybius, 15.9.1–5; cf. Livy, 30.32.1–3.

82. Cathal J. Nolan, *The Allure of Battle: A History of How Wars Have Been Won and Lost* (Oxford: Oxford University Press, 2017), 19–20.

83. Stephen Morillo, introduction to *The Battle of Hastings: Sources and Interpretations*, ed. S. Morillo (New York: Boydell, 1996), xvii; Gat, *War in Human Civilization*, 117; James Q. Whitman,

Lady Butler's 1881 painting of the charge of the Royal Scots Greys at the Battle of Waterloo.

primary strategic objective.[84] From the seventeenth century on, some European commanders began to seek a speedier resolution than a conflict prolonged from clever maneuvering and/or sieges. Results did not always match desires.[85] If a battle ended a specific war, the duration of that peace depended on multiple variables, some unseen or yet undeveloped.

Already the French political philosopher Montesquieu (d. 1755) doubted that a war-ending battle had larger social repercussions. Edward Gibbon, whose monumental *Decline and Fall of the Roman Empire* (1776–88) drew inspiration from Montesquieu, had similar views.[86] Indeed three contemporary military theorists saw nothing exceptional about the Battle of Waterloo (June 18, 1815), which later merited little attention in Clausewitz's *On War*.[87]

The Verdict of Battle: The Law of Victory and the Making of Modern Warfare (Cambridge: Harvard University Press, 2012), 25–26 and 28; Parker, *CHW* 2005, 414.

84. Cf. John France, "Close Order and Close Quarter: the Culture of Combat in the West," *International History Review* 27, no. 3 (2005): 504.

85. The elusive nature of early modern decisive battles: Russell F. Weigley, *The Age of Battles: The Question for Decisive Warfare from Breitenfeld to Waterloo* (Bloomington: Indiana University Press, 1991); Whitman, *Verdict of Battle*; Nolan, *Allure*; Yuval N. Harari, "The Concept of 'Decisive' Battles in World History," *Journal of World History* 18, no. 3 (2007): 251–66.

86. C.-L. Montesquieu, *Considerations on the Causes of the Greatness of the Romans and Their Decline*, trans. D. Lowenthal (repr., Indianapolis: Hackett, 1999), 50–51 (chap. 4), 120 (chap. 13), 169 (chap. 18); Wheeler, "Present but Absent," 246; Whitman, *Verdict of Battle*, 38–39, and (on Gibbon) 92n132 and 242–43.

87. Beatrice Heuser, "Who Won at Waterloo? Rühe von Lilienstern, Jomini, Clausewitz and the Decisive Battle," *British Journal of Military History* 1, no. 3 (2015): 134–48.

A union of the two senses of decisive battle, the war-ending clash (the military aspect) and the conflict opening a new historical period (the cultural), began with the French Revolution and the Napoleonic era. Napoleon's ghost, haunting military thinkers and practice from 1815 to 1914, encouraged quick pursuit of a major battle. Interpreters of Napoleonic operations rethought the history of warfare accordingly. Eventually, the most influential of these thinkers, Clausewitz, advocated in his *On War* the indispensable role of battle and achievement of a "battle of annihilation," although he also cautioned about its rarity.[88] Nevertheless, Clausewitz, scarcely read in military circles outside Germany before the 1870s and little appreciated among the general public before the twentieth century, did not invent the idea of decisive battle.[89]

A different view emerged with the French Revolution and the blending of nationalism with Romanticism. The unexpected victory of a French revolutionary army at Valmy on September 20, 1792, over German and Austrian regular forces caused the early Romantic Johann Wolfgang von Goethe (d. 1832), a participant in the battle, to hail the dawn of a new era.[90] Later, Hegel's 1822 lectures on the philosophy of history elevated the Battle of Marathon into a "turning point" in history. The idea that victory in a major battle inaugurated a new millennium appealed to Romantics and Hegelians from the 1830s on, besides nationalistic historians. Further, Waterloo, concluding a generation of war with France, also seemed to mark a new epoch. A battle between thousands with its drama, sense of theater, and the epic clash of history's cosmic forces stimulated the imagination of poets and painters. Its battlefield soon attracted tourists.[91] Minutiae of who did what at Waterloo spawned the painstaking research of Captain William Siborne (d. 1849), beginning in the 1830s, for construction of a gigantic model of the battle's climax with hundreds of miniature lead figurines—at that point the most detailed investigation of any battle ever attempted and a forerunner of the current "face of battle" phenomenon.[92]

By the 1850s, battle books, battlefield monuments, and tour guides began to proliferate.[93] Battles were "popular" and Clausewitz had nothing to do with it. A new impetus came in 1851. Creasy coined the phrase "decisive battle" in his *Fifteen*

---

88. Clausewitz, *On War*, IV.11.

89. See Wheeler, "Present but Absent," 247n24; Christopher Bassford, *Clausewitz in English: The Reception of Clausewitz in Britain and America 1815–1945* (New York: Oxford University Press, 1994).

90. Wheeler, "Present but Absent," 244n15.

91. Wheeler, "Present but Absent," 242n5; Whitman, *Verdict of Battle*, 16, 46, 216–26, and 243; John Keegan, *The Face of Battle* (London: Penguin, 1976), 117–19.

92. Supplemented by *History of the War in France and Belgium* (London: T. and W. Boone, 1844); on Siborne, see Keegan, *Face of Battle*, 119–20; Philip Abbott, "William Siborne's New Waterloo Model," *British Journal for Military History* 2, no. 3 (2016): 78–100.

93. Whitman, *Verdict of Battle*, 243.

THE

FIFTEEN DECISIVE

BATTLES OF THE WORLD;

FROM MARATHON TO WATERLOO.

By E. S. CREASY, M.A.,

PROFESSOR OF ANCIENT AND MODERN HISTORY IN UNIVERSITY COLLEGE, LONDON;
LATE FELLOW OF KING'S COLLEGE, CAMBRIDGE.

Those few battles, of which a contrary event would have essentially varied
the drama of the world in all its subsequent scenes.—HALLAM.

IN TWO VOLUMES.

Sir Edward Creasy's 1851 book coined the term "decisive battle" and proved to be enormously influential.

Decisive Battles of the World, a Victorian classic.[94] Not size or number of casualties made a battle "decisive," but rather its long-term repercussions on social and political conditions. Decisive battles preserved important aspects of Western civilization. Their violence, though distasteful, contributed to the "progress" of mankind, besides offering moral instruction through examples of heroism and self-sacrifice, each an exemplar of the then current racial notions that placed contemporary northern Europeans at the apex of human development. Marathon headed Creasy's list, which included Tours/Poitiers (732 CE, Charles Martel's defeat of Arab raiders); Waterloo ended it. Hegel and Creasy turned Marathon, hitherto a political symbol, into a decisive battle.

Creasy's views of decisive battle popularized the concept and initiated a still persistent deluge of battle books, especially among nonscholarly Anglophone readers. History thus became (from a political and military perspective) a series of battles as pivotal turning points. Decisive battles soon intertwined with the nineteenth century's fascination with the "great men" who fought them. More recently, the 2,500th anniversary of Marathon and the Persian Wars elicited several Creasyesque "battle that changed the world" tomes.[95]

Although Creasy had no knowledge of Clausewitz, the Clausewitzian battle of annihilation, intertwined (accurately or not) with notions of decisive battle, has contributed to current perceptions of a WWW, whose advocates can tout over 150 years of battle books often asserting Western glory. Yet even Creasy realized that distinguishing "decisive" battles from others was preferential, not objective. Some believe,

---

94. *Fifteen Decisive Battles of the World: From Marathon to Waterloo* (repr., New York: Dorset Press, 1987), vii–x, 404; Keegan, *Face of Battle,* 55–61; Dennis E. Showalter, "Of Decisive Battles and Intellectual Fashions: Sir Edward Creasy Revisited," *Military Affairs* 52, no. 4 (1988): 206–8; Hanson, *C&C,* 8–11.

95. E.g., Tom Holland, *Persian Fire: The First World Empire and the Battle for the West* (London: Little, Brown, 2005); Richard Billows, *Marathon: How One Battle Changed Western Civilization* (New York: Overlook, Duckworth, 2010).

for example, the Arabs' failed siege of Constantinople (717–18) was more significant than Tours/Poitiers in halting Muslim expansion in Europe.[96]

Political considerations can also render battles prominent, if not decisive. Many historians perpetuate the myth of a Roman obsession with the Parthian victory at Carrhae (53 BCE), thereby ignoring that propaganda of the emperor Augustus, a generation later, magnified this Roman defeat to glorify his own Parthian agreement (20 BCE). Similarly, the heroic stand of about 150 British regulars against 3,000–4,000 Zulus at Rorke's Drift (January 22–23, 1879), a prime example of the WWW in Hanson's *C&C*, initially attracted attention in contemporary media and from the British government to obscure the overwhelming British defeat at Isandlwana (January 22, 1879).[97] Carrhae and Rorke's Drift fit a pattern: disciplined Western forces defend themselves in an isolated position, often on a frontier, against an alien culture's overwhelming hordes. Although Western incompetence or intelligence failures may have produced the situation, the Western heroism/martyrdom on display, representing the self-sacrifice required to sustain the "good" civilization against barbarians, becomes a popular inspirational adventure story.[98] Creasy's specter still lurks behind the WWW.

Accuracy also comes into play. WWW advocates often perpetuate antiquated or uncritical interpretations. Hanson's Creasyesque view of Tours/Poitiers prompted rebuttals.[99] Nor does Marathon fare better. Keegan erroneously claimed Marathon the first Greek-Persian battle, ignoring that the Persians suppressed a revolt of Ionian Greeks in Anatolia in the years before Marathon.[100] A WWW did not make Greek victory inevitable. Persians could defeat Greeks. For Hanson, Marathon set a pattern of East-West confrontation virtually unchanged for three centuries, but he accepts at face value Herodotus's account, which may not even be accurate. Later Greeks imagined Marathon and the relatively small-scale island-hopping operation of 490 BCE through the lenses of the major Persian effort of 480–479 BCE.[101]

---

96. Creasy, *Decisive Battles*, vii–x; Chaliand, *Art of War*, 25.

97. See Everett L. Wheeler, "Roman Treaties with Parthia: *Völkerrecht* or Power Politics?" in *Limes XVIII. Proceedings of the XVIIIth International Congress of Roman Frontiers Studies*, ed. P. Freeman et al. (Oxford: Archaeopress, 2002), 287–92; Rorke's Drift: Hanson, *C&C*, 280–333; Porter, *Military Orientalism*, 46.

98. Porter, *Military Orientalism*, 43–45.

99. Hanson, *C&C*, 135–69, rejected by France (a medievalist), "Close Order," 501, and Nolan, *Allure*, 30n44.

100. Keegan, *History of Warfare*, 253.

101. Hanson, *CHW* 2020, 17 and 23, perpetuating a Greek myth that Near Eastern armies relied on numbers; Wheeler, "Present but Absent," 245–58; Christopher Tuplin, "All the King's Horse: In Search of Achaemenid Persian Cavalry," in *New Perspectives on Ancient Warfare*, ed. G. G. Fagan and M. Trundle (Leiden: Brill, 2010), 101–82; Michael Charles, "Herodotus, Body Armour, and Achaemenid Infantry," *Historia* 61, no. 3 (2012): 257–69.

In the tradition of Creasy, Hanson does not dispute the pivotal role of battles in history.[102] Not all, however, espouse the validity or even the existence of decisive battles. The German sociologist, Max Weber (d. 1920), rejected Marathon and other supposed decisive battles as fantasies—the product of unclear historical thinking. By 1944 Liddell Hart opined that the mystical sense of decisive victory in military language rarely matched its actual effects and Nolan now rejects the idea that battles win wars.[103]

Achilles versus Odysseus

From war's very beginnings debate has raged on whether success is better obtained by strength and direct confrontation or surprise, deception, and trickery—the contrast of brawn versus brains. After all, the Trojan Horse was a stratagem. Legal scholars, who subdivide military necessity into violence and ruse, have a valid point. Contrary to the WWW's perspective, winning, war's real objective, depends not exclusively on violence and battle.

The Roman historian Sallust (86–c. 35 BCE) summarized the brawn versus brains debate, attested already in Homer and the Homeric tradition, where Achilles came to represent the "fair fight," emphasizing open, direct combat, strength, and numbers, and Odysseus the use of trickery, deception, surprise, and indirect means, although not necessarily avoidance of battle under advantageous conditions.[104] Hanson equates the WWW with this Achilles ethos: ambush, stratagems, and battle plans are bad; open battle is good.[105] But major powers frequently assume the righteous cloak of the Achilles ethos. Roman Republican propaganda preached Rome as the people of good faith and manly courage, who never resorted to trickery on or off the battlefield. But the prominence of stratagems in pre-state warfare, Roman legalistic chicanery in domestic and foreign affairs, and demonstrable ruses before 218 BCE undermine Roman pretensions to uprightness.[106]

Yet WWW advocates inaccurately portray the Western tradition of written military theory. Stratagems became the chief motif of Graeco-Roman military thought and subsequently that of the Byzantines, whose survival for centuries depended on

---

102. *C&C*, 8–9, 15–19, and 359.

103. Weber: Whitman, *Verdict of Battle*, 259; B. H. Liddell Hart, *Thoughts on War* (London: Faber and Faber, 1944), 50; Nolan, *Allure*.

104. Sallust, *Catiline*, 1.5–6.2; Homer, *Odyssey*, 8.75; later ancient commentators: Everett L. Wheeler, "Polyaenus: *Scriptor Militaris*," in *Polyainos. Neue Studien/Polyaenus. New Studies*, ed. K. Brodersen (Berlin: Verlag Antike, 2010), 27n87.

105. Hanson, *WWW*, 13–14 and 224; *C&C*, 22, 97, and 348.

106. Polybius, 13.3.3; Livy, 42.47.4–8; Hanson, *C&C*, 119 (Romans do not use stratagems); Dawson, *Origins*, 144; contra, Everett L. Wheeler, "Anti-Deceit Clauses in Greek Treaties: An Apologia," *Electrum* 14 (2008): 58–59 and n. 9.

The *Mykonos Pithos* (storage jar of 657 BCE), which shows the earliest depiction of the Trojan Horse.

astute diplomacy, stratagems, and indirect means.[107] Vegetius's *Epitome of Military Science* (c. 390) and Pseudo-Maurice's *Strategikon* (c. 600) represented compendia of a *doctrine* stressing stratagems running from Herodotus and Thucydides in the fifth century BCE to writers of the Roman era. Accordingly, war must be waged with intelligence, not simply numbers and brute force; generals should devise ingenious means to win at both the strategic and tactical levels. Collections of stratagems like Frontinus's *Stratagems* (84–88 CE) and Polyaenus's *Strategica* (c. 162 CE), the sole survivors of an extensive genre, had a didactic purpose to instruct on past successes and to provide models for inspiration. Attrition and avoidance of battle could also be Western.[108]

Stratagems permitted winning with less expense of blood and treasure and avoiding the risk of battle, where luck, not skill, courage, or numbers, could determine victory. In fact stratagems could counter numerical superiority and permit the weak to

107. Walter E. Kaegi, *Some Thoughts on Byzantine Strategy* (Brookline, MA: Hellenic College Press, 1983); Luttwak, *Grand Strategy of the Byzantine Empire*, 235–321 and 338–92.

108. Lynn, *Battle*, 25; Porter, *Military Orientalism*, 80.

beat the strong—the real meaning of Marathon in Western military thought.[109] Stratagems, not (for the most part) in any way illegal, merely circumvented an opponent's expectations engendered in the warrior code of the Achilles ethos. The most common ancient reproach of stratagems is that they were shameful, not illegal. Indeed the Western juristic tradition from antiquity to the present has recognized their legitimacy, if perfidy (violation of an oath or pledged agreement) is avoided.[110] Contrary to WWW advocates' preference to fit military conduct into mutually exclusive boxes or downplay contrary evidence, practitioners of the Odysseus ethos cannot be limited to a single epoch, war, ethnicity, or individual commander. Preference for Achilles or Odysseus can be fluid and situational. In contrast to Alexander's assumption of the Achilles ethos at Gaugamela, Polyaenus includes thirty-two stratagems of the Macedonian.[111]

The Odysseus ethos and the doctrine of stratagems did not prohibit battle, only avoiding or postponing engagements for favorable situations. Hannibal, the most infamous perpetrator of stratagems in the Roman tradition, certainly fought battles. At Cannae (216 BCE), the classic example of tactical double envelopment, Hannibal devised a variant of the common use of feigned retreat to lure the enemy into ambush. Maurice de Saxe (d. 1750), a devout student of Vegetius and Onasander's *Strategikos* (c. 49 CE), advocated avoiding battle, although he fought bloody engagements like Fontenoy (May 11, 1745).[112] Despite notable battles, Frederick the Great (in Delbrück's view) pursued a strategy of attrition, thus disputing the German General Staff's view of Frederick's Clausewitzian strategy of annihilation.[113] Similarly, non-Western warfare was not exclusively based on attrition and an indirect approach: in the fourth century BCE, Sun Tzu did not oppose battle and offensive initiative when opportune.[114]

For WWW proponents study of Greco-Roman military treatises in the Middle Ages (though ignoring the Byzantines) and the early modern era prove the WWW's continuity, as if such works emphasized battle and civic militarism.[115] In reality, these works advocated stratagems. Even Machiavelli's *Art of War* (1521), although preaching

---

109. Wheeler, "Polyaenus," 26–30, and "Present but Absent."

110. For a survey, Everett L. Wheeler, "Ruses and Stratagems," *International Military and Defense Encyclopedia*, ed. T. N. Dupuy (Washington, DC: Macmillan-Brassey's, 1993), V:2334; cf. Whitman, *Verdict of Battle*, 191.

111. Polyaenus, 4.3, in *Stratagems of War*, 331–67.

112. Maurice de Saxe, *Reveries on the Art of War*, trans. T. R. Phillips (repr., Mineola, NY: Dover, 2007), 121.

113. Hans Delbrück, *History of the Art of War within the Framework of Political History*, trans. W. J. Renfroe Jr. (Westport, CT: Greenwood, 1985), IV:369–82.

114. Chaliand, *Art of War*, xxv, 42; Sun Tzu: Lynn, "Discourse," 479; Heuser, *Evolution*, 89–90 and 390.

115. Hanson, *C&C*, 129; Parker, *MHQ*, 89–90; *CHW* 2005, 3–4.

the virtue of a civilian militia over mercenaries, copied extensively from Vegetius and Frontinus.[116] In the late Middle Ages, stratagems could also be reconciled with concepts of chivalry and just war.[117]

Stratagem collections, often combining ancient with modern examples, continued in the Renaissance and early modern eras. At least one new book on the importance of deception and surprise in war still appears nearly every year, as if a new idea. Liddell Hart's "strategy of indirect approach," exploiting the line of the enemy's least expectation, descends from the classical doctrine of stratagems.[118] Extensive Allied deception prepared the way for D-Day (June 6, 1944) in World War II and Norman Schwarzkopf won the Gulf War (February 23–27, 1991) through the deception and feints of stratagem. The Achilles-Odysseus debate remains palpable in contemporary strategic culture.[119]

Indeed the West's rediscovery of Sun Tzu in the second half of the twentieth century and his subsequent popularization reflected the West's ignorance of its own tradition of stratagems, which the Napoleonic mystique of decisive battle and Clausewitzian theory had obscured. Conceptually, Sun Tzu and the Chinese tradition of military theorists, in origin contemporary with (not anterior to) Western developments, offer little not in Greco-Roman sources, although more succinctly expressed.[120]

In sum, WWW-proponents propagate a myth of Western theory and practice, in which direct confrontation in battle and annihilation of the enemy, the traits of brawn, are contrasted with a supposed non-Western preference for use of dishonorable means to exhaust an opponent through attrition, erroneously equated with the Odysseus ethos and avoidance of battle.

WWW and Imperialism

WWW advocates closely associate the WWW with imperialism and European expansion, which (in their view) a Western tradition of aggression honed from intense competition between European states fostered. For Hanson, classical precedents rendered Western imperialism permissible and natural. Greek equation of non-Greeks (barbarians) with wild beasts, turned war into a form of acquisition similar to hunting. Plato, an advocate of limited war between Greeks, is converted into an imperialist.

---

116. Porter, *Military Orientalism*, 72, noting Machiavelli's ambivalence between Achilles and Odysseus.

117. David Whetham, *Just Wars and Moral Victories: Surprise, Deception and the Normative Framework of European War in the Later Middle Ages* (Leiden: Brill, 2009).

118. Chaliand, *Art of War*, 42, imprecisely equates "indirect approach" with attrition.

119. Porter, *Military Orientalism*, 72–77; Wheeler, "Ruses and Stratagems," in *Military and Defense Encyclopedia*, 2333–34.

120. Wheeler, "Ruses and Stratagems," 2330–32; Black, *Rethinking*, 88–90; Lynn, *Battle*, 50 and 66–70; Heuser, *Evolution*, 390.

For Parker, the WWW underlies the West's rise to world domination and "Roman war," the lust to exterminate, was the key to Western expansion.[121] Space precludes discussion of Parker's imprecise notion of Roman war and lethality as uniquely Western. Horrendous losses of population from Mongol, Mughal, and Manchu conquests are ignored.[122] A strict Western/non-Western dichotomy would suggest intercultural wars as more brutal. In reality, civil and internal religious conflicts, descending into subcultural warfare, incited the most brutality.[123] Lethality as a cardinal WWW trait privileges events of c. 1500–1945. Arrogance or belief in one side's cultural superiority, often with a dehumanizing or demonizing of the opponent, removes restraints on conduct, as does the conflict's dynamics, in which the degree of ferocity follows the general rule of reciprocity: the fiercer the enemy, the fiercer the opponent's response.[124] In contrast to Hanson, Parker does not have the WWW justify imperialism, but rather his early modern military revolution facilitated Western expansion.

Parker's general conception of the WWW invites other criticisms. Parker appropriates from the non-Western sphere surprise and attrition.[125] Surprise, an Odyssean trait, hardly fits with Hanson's identification of the WWW with the Achilles ethos. Parker's three examples of Western attrition, generally taken as a non-Western method of shunning battle, are portrayed as exceptions. Attrition, however, neither always produced the hypothesized goal of total victory for the West, nor avoided battle. The Duke of Alba, commanding Hapsburg forces against Dutch rebels 1567–73, declined battles (but not sieges) and attempted to exhaust the rebels' financial means. But he failed and was replaced. U. S. Grant's "hammering" of Robert E. Lee's Army of Northern Virginia in 1864 employed superior Union manpower and resources: battle became the means of attrition, not its opposite. Much the same can be said for the German Erich von Falkenhayn (a replacement for Grant in Parker's 2020 version of the WWW), in his attempt to "bleed the French white" at Verdun (February 21–December 18, 1916) in World War I.

Of course the most famous example, Fabius Maximus, later called the "Delayer," bequeathed a Western notion of "Fabian strategy." He frustrated Hannibal (217 BCE) in the Second Punic War not only by refusing pitched battle but also by skillful maneuver and harassment. For WWW advocates, obsessed with battle-eager Romans hungry for slaughter, a contradiction emerges. Augustus, in creating a hall of fame in the Roman forum (2 BCE) for Roman "greats," commemorated Fabius Maximus with the highest distinction afforded any general. He alone was called "most skilled

121. Parker, *MHQ*, 90–91; *CHW* 2005, 5 and 413.

122. Hanson, *C&C*, 21, 362–63, and 430; Parker, *MHQ*, 90–91 and 94; *CHW* 2005, 5; on Mongols, etc., see Willett, "History from the Clouds," 177.

123. Morillo, "General Typology," 35–38.

124. Peter Karsten, *Law, Soldiers, and Combat* (Westport, CT: Greenwood, 1978), 55; on the Pacific theater of World War II: Black, *Rethinking*, 52.

125. Parker, *MHQ*, 88 and 98; *CHW* 2020, 5.

in warfare." Indeed Fabius played a key role in establishing at Rome a new cult, *Mens* (literally, "Mind," but to be understood as "practical wisdom"), adding a religious element to his policy of delay as an example of Roman ingenuity against Hannibal's craftiness.[126]

Other examples (not trivial) of Western attrition escaped Parker. As noted, in Delbrück's view Frederick the Great pursued a strategy of attrition. George Washington in the American Revolution generally avoided open battle after 1776. The victories at Trenton (December 26, 1776) and Princeton (January 3, 1777) were both un-WWW-like surprise attacks. Yet the most obvious omission, the so-called Periclean strategy of the Peloponnesian War featured, if Thucydides can be believed, Athenian avoidance of the traditional hoplite battle, while harassing Sparta through amphibious raids to compel, not a Clausewitzian total victory, but frustration.[127] Parker blurs the border between other WWW advocates' clear distinction between Western and non-Western styles of war. Attrition, maneuver, surprise, and Fabius Maximus belong to the Odysseus ethos and the Western tradition of stratagems.[128]

Decisive Battle and the End of the WWW

Napoleonic warfare and its interpreters like Clausewitz occasioned rethinking the history of warfare to stress battles, but only the nineteenth century's emphasis on battle fits the WWW hypothesis. So, too, Western empires, c. 1500–1945, generated a supposed WWW prevailing since c. 500 BCE.[129] But times have changed.

A different era of warfare after World War II continues in the twenty-first century. A novel prominence of non-state actors (guerillas, terrorists) with the increase of regional, ethnic, and religious conflicts even suggests a return to pre-state warfare.[130] Enemies motivated through religious revelation and eschatological beliefs are disinclined to confess defeat, as the WWW desires. The WWW's wish for a "fair fight" in open battle goes begging, nor do superior technology, institutional organization, and logistics produce success, as seen in the United States' Vietnam experience, when attrition, will, and patience drove a so-called asymmetrical war. Non-Western, non-state

---

126. *Inscriptiones Latinae Selectae*, ed. H. Dessau (repr., Chicago: Ares, 1979), I:16–17 and n. 56; Joseph Geiger, *The First Hall of Fame: A Study of the Statues in the Forum Augustum* (Leiden: Brill, 2008), 145–46.

127. C. Schubert and D. Laspe, "Perikles' defensiver Kriegsplan: Eine thukydideische Erfindung?" *Historia* 58 (2009): 373–94.

128. Everett L. Wheeler, *Stratagem and the Vocabulary of Military Trickery* (Leiden: Brill, 1988), 46, 55–56, 68, and 74.

129. Sharman, *Empires of the Weak*, 123; Heuser, *Evolution*, 502.

130. Turney-High, *The Military*, 24; Everett L. Wheeler, "Terrorism and Military Theory: An Historical Perspective," *Journal of Terrorism and Political Violence* 3 (1991): 6–33; Keeley, *War before Civilization*, 79–80.

actors continue their disdain of Western norms. Simultaneously, the West's aversion to casualties, its humanitarian concerns for the effects of military violence, and even its previous technological and economic superiority in an age of globalization undermine tenets of the WWW.

The post-1945 changes elicit differing responses from WWW advocates. Hanson sees no end to Western domination and the WWW.[131] Parker's hybrid form of the WWW, appropriating attrition and surprise from the non-Western sphere, emphasizes superior technology as in the pre-1945 period. Azar Gat, recognizing the post-1945 changes and an aversion to war in Western liberal democracies, posits a "new WWW," abandoning aggressive direct confrontation.[132] Thus for Gat and, to a certain extent, Parker, the WWW is whatever the West does, not a continuation of a supposed Western tradition of 2,500 years, sharply distinguished from non-Western practices. A unique WWW evaporates, as these WWW advocates refute themselves and confirm the WWW as a frequently re-invented ideology. Keegan, more radically, declared that the WWW exterminated itself in World Wars I and II through the massive destruction wrought on military and civilian populations via mechanization and weaponry's increased lethality. Good riddance (in his view), as the WWW's demise ended the Clausewitzian connection of war and politics.[133] Thus only Hanson, of four major WWW advocates, asserts that the "old" WWW is alive and well. The demise of decisive battle, total victory, and unconditional surrender, supposed WWW hallmarks, remain to complete the WWW's obituary.

Battles simplify narratives. Resolved in a day or two with a definite beginning and end, their ceremonial and theatrical aspects served a dramatic function in comparison to long, ugly sieges, even if sieges better tested the two belligerents' technology and resources. For some, Clausewitzian pretensions about decisiveness underlie retention of the term "battle" for extended engagements like the Somme (July 1–November 18, 1916) in World War I or Fallujah (April–May, November–December 2004) in the Iraq War.[134]

Further, battles were not always decisive strategically in ending either a campaign or a war, much less in changing the course of history, nor even tactically decisive. If a battle ended without a clear winner, such as one side routing the other, both parties could claim victory. Possession of the battlefield often indicated victory, but not always. One side's orderly retreat overnight or the next day to fight again elsewhere permitted the opponent to claim victory, although in drawn battles the side with fewer losses and/or greater loot could do likewise, even after abandoning the battlefield. Both the French and the British claimed victory at Malplaquet on September

---

131. Hanson, *C&C*, 14 and 448.

132. Gat, *War in Human Civilization*, 610–11.

133. Keegan, *History of Warfare*, 390–92.

134. Harari, "Concept of 'Decisive' Battle," 262–65.

11, 1709. Indeed the debate over definition of victory, whether possession of the battlefield or the fewest casualties, dates to at least the eighth century BCE in the Near East with some later Greek instances.[135]

Like battles, wars can also be indecisive or end in stalemate. A WWW hardly prevailed in the Korean War with repercussions still evident—a conflict WWW advocates choose to ignore in asserting as a WWW principle total victory with a complete, Clausewitzian demolition of enemy capabilities and unconditional surrender.[136] Sometimes the political situation (both international and at home) precludes pursuit of a total victory, nor are all wars intended to be "total." Fear of Chinese and/or Russian intervention and the prospect of a larger conflict restrained American efforts in Vietnam. Likewise the coalition backing American efforts in the Gulf War did not support Saddam Hussein's overthrow, accomplished in the Iraq War but with deleterious results.

For WWW advocates, Japanese and Muslim ways of war forego total victory and seek only the defeated's concessions. In the WWW tradition an enemy must confess defeat and surrender unconditionally.[137] The concept of a state's "unconditional surrender," erroneously identified as an American idea from either the Civil War or World War II, actually dates to the Roman practice of *deditio*, although from 1945 on unconditional surrender morphed from a strategic to a legal doctrine, bestowing the victor's right to remake the defeated's society.[138] From a European perspective, the emphasis on unconditional surrender belongs not to the WWW, but to an American cultural trait reducing war to a "crusade" of good versus evil, defending democracy against tyrants, and dehumanizing the enemy.[139] Even Japan's unconditional surrender in 1945, the last instance in a major war, emerged as policy only after heated debates.[140]

Victory as compelling the enemy to confess defeat, an ancient idea, belongs to the Achilles ethos. The Odysseans had their own response: defeat by stratagem not only brought victory at less expense, but also exposed the loser's negligence or gullibility and subjected him to ridicule.[141] A single decisive battle has not terminated a war between major powers since Königgrätz on July 3, 1866, in the Austro-Prussian War.[142] An enemy's confession of defeat involves a psychological turning point, which,

135. Whitman, *Verdict of Battle*, 173–80 and 234; Melville, "Win, Lose, or Draw?" 527–37.

136. Geoffrey Parker and Williamson A. Murray, "The Post-War World 1945–2004," in *CHW* 2005, 366–70.

137. Hanson, *C&C*, 362–64; Wagner-Pacifici, *Art of Surrender*; *How Fighting Ends: A History of Surrender*, ed. H. Afferbach and H. Strachan (Oxford: Oxford University Press, 2012).

138. Heuser, *Evolution*, 141–42; Whitman, *Verdict of Battle*, 260: *deditio*: Livy, 1.38.

139. Chaliand, *Art of War*, xxv, 42; Heuser, *Evolution*, 456–57; cf. Whitman, *Verdict of Battle*, 252.

140. Marc Gallicchio, *Unconditional: The Japanese Surrender in World War II* (New York: Oxford University Press, 2020).

141. Vegetius 3.22.12–13; John Chrysostom, *On the Priesthood*, 1.8, in *Patrologicae Cursus, series Graeca*, ed. J-P. Migne (Paris: Imprimerie Catholique, 1862), XLVIII: 629–30.

142. Whitman, *Verdict of Battle*, 212; cf. 7.

since the mid-nineteenth century, battle has not delivered. Not casualties, not capture of a capital, not destruction of an army necessarily breaks an enemy's will. Even occupation of an opponent's territory can be problematic.[143] A people's will to resist need not coincide with a government's surrender, as the Prussians learned after Sedan (September 1–2, 1870) in the Franco-Prussian War. A final outcome in a stalemate of symmetrical forces may come not from a victory, but a collapse of will from war weariness and loss of morale.[144]

For the post-1945 world, definitions of "victory" and "defeat" lack their former supposed clarity. In fact "victory" in its traditional sense is no longer espoused by the United Nations, nor in NATO doctrine.[145] Superior Western resources and technology can still win battles, but not wars, as Parker admits.[146] President George W. Bush's proclamation of "mission accomplished" (May 1, 2003) ended by WWW standards an Iraq War, which failed to resolve basic issues and hostilities within Iraq, still evident after withdrawal of American combat troops in 2011—scarcely a triumphal act. Similarly, Hanson's 2002 postscript for a paperback edition of *C&C* considered the WWW successful in Afghanistan—hardly the case nineteen years later.[147] Superior technology and force alone cannot break an opponent's will nor secure a lasting peace, however short-lived in the ever-changing circumstances of human history.

As simplified world history, the WWW appeals to popular readers, whose enthusiasm for the theme persists—an irony, as military history's popularity in the publishing world corresponds to the decline of actual military service among the populations of major Western powers and the reluctance of universities to support study of military history.[148] As this chapter has attempted to show, demythologizing the WWW can demonstrate commonalities between the West and the non-West in the conduct of war and reassert military history's value as a legitimate pursuit in understanding the plague of armed conflict. But the WWW's Romantic roots run deep. Even some WWW advocates concede its ethnocentrism, thoroughly outdated in an age of globalization and the WWW's ineffectiveness after 1945. The aim of war is not battles and blood, but imposing one belligerent's will on an opponent with hopefully a subsequent long peace or at least a *modus vivendi*. In both the West and non-West, the style of warfare, varying over time and within epochs, contradicts postulating a stark dichotomy. As Vergil queried, "Trick or courage, who among the enemy would ask?"[149]

---

143. Liddell Hart, *Thoughts on War*, 20; Black, *Rethinking*, 10–11.

144. Liddell Hart, *Thoughts on War*, 22.

145. Heuser, *Evolution*, 444–47 and 476–77.

146. Parker, *CHW* 2005, 412; likewise Black, *Rethinking*, 20, 68–69, and 234; Nolan, *Allure*, 580–82; Sharman, *Empires of the Weak*, 7 and 133.

147. Hanson, *C&C*, 457–71.

148. Black, *Rethinking*, 234–35.

149. *Aeneid*, 2.390. My translation.

3. THE MYTHS OF FEUDALISM AND THE FEUDAL KNIGHT

Richard P. Abels

Once the precarious Pax Romana had disintegrated and waves of invaders swept over it . . . it is not surprising that an entire social pattern should have come into being to enable the peoples of Europe to survive in such an environment: the pattern to be known to later generations of historians as "feudalism."

—*Michael Howard*[1]

This crisis in the military history of Europe [caused by Viking and Magyar raids] coincided with the breaking up of all central power in the shipwreck of the dynasty of Charles the Great. In the absence of any organized national resistance, the defence of the empire fell into the hands of the local counts, who now became semi-independent sovereigns. To these petty rulers the landholders of each district were now commending themselves, in order to obtain protection in an age of war and anarchy. At the same time, and the same reason, the poorer freemen were "commending" themselves to the landholders. Thus the feudal hierarchy was established and a new military system appears, when the "count" or "duke" leads out to battle his vassals and their mounted retainers.

—*Charles W. C. Oman*[2]

"Feudalism" was once accepted by academic and popular historians alike as a defining, if not *the* defining, feature of medieval society. For military historians, the High Middle Ages, the period from around 1000 to 1300, was once the age of the feudal knight. This is no longer the case. Today scholars who study the Middle Ages avoid the term like the plague. (One can almost imagine the cry "Bring out your dead constructs!") If they use it at all in their writings or classrooms, it is usually to dismiss it. Feudalism has joined the "Dark Ages," "the right of the first night," and Viking horned helmets in the myriad ranks of myths of the Middle Ages. In historiographical terms, this happened fairly recently. The transformation only began in 1974 with the

---

1. Michael Howard, *War in European History*, rev. ed. (repr., Oxford: Oxford University Press, 2009), 1.

2. Charles W. C. Oman, *The Art of War in the Middle Ages* (repr., Ithaca, NY: Cornell University Press, 1953), table of contents and 19.

appearance of American historian Elizabeth A. R. Brown's article, "The Tyranny of a Construct: Feudalism and Historians of Medieval Europe," in the *American Historical Review*. It was substantially completed twenty years later with the publication of Susan Reynolds's *Fiefs and Vassals*.[3] These two works shifted the paradigm of medieval history by crystallizing doubts about the construct harbored by many historians of the Middle Ages. But, like many myths, feudalism and the feudal knight have kernels of truth to them.[4]

While feudalism has become the "F-word" for academic medievalists, nonspecialists have been slow to follow their lead. The relegation of the term to the historiography rather than the history of the Middle Ages has been the cause of consternation, especially for non-medievalists assigned to teach Western and World Civilization surveys. When one is covering millennia over the course of one semester, generalizations are not only useful but necessary. As someone who spent four decades teaching civilization surveys to undergraduates, I can attest to that. Over the last decade, civilization surveys have begun to reflect the new professional consensus. Medieval historians responsible for chapters on the Middle Ages in these textbooks shy away from the term "feudalism," although many continue to use its adjectival form, "feudal."[5] This reticence is less evident in civilization textbooks lacking a medievalist among the collaborators. In several of these we still encounter the "feudal Middle Ages" presented without apology, as well as comparisons drawn between Japanese, Chinese, and medieval Western feudalisms.[6] This is even truer for general surveys of military history. One continues to find feudalism and feudal warfare in the "updated" 2009 edition of Sir Michael Howard's influential *War in European History*. Howard, perhaps the most prominent military historian of his generation, begins the chapter entitled "The Wars of the Knights" with an account of the historical origins of feudalism.

Whether or not the assigned textbook mentions feudalism, most instructors of broad surveys probably continue to use the term because it is familiar to them and to their students. As one of my colleagues, an American historian, commented, "I'm going to keep on teaching feudalism until you guys come up with some other generalization I can use." Given this shift in the treatment of one of the key

---

3. Elizabeth A. R. Brown, "The Tyranny of a Construct: Feudalism and Historians of Medieval Europe," *American Historical Review* 79 (1974): 1063–88; Susan Reynolds, *Fiefs and Vassals: The Medieval Evidence Reinterpreted* (Oxford: Oxford University, 1994).

4. The historiography section of this chapter is adapted from my article on the subject in *History Compass*. See Richard Abels, "The Historiography of a Construct: 'Feudalism' and the Medieval Historian," *History Compass* 7, no. 3 (2009): 1008–31.

5. See, e.g., Barbara Rosenwein's explanation in L. Hunt et al., *The Making of the West: Peoples and Cultures*, 2nd ed. (Boston: Bedford/St. Martin's, 2005), 343.

6. Peter N. Stearns et al., *World Civilizations: The Global Experience*, 5th ed. (New York: Pearson/Longman, 2007), 59, 327–28, and 395–97; the seminal work is *Feudalism in History*, ed. R. Coulborn (Hamden, CT: Archon Books, 1965). This approach underlies Peter Duus, *Feudalism in Japan*, 3rd ed. (New York: McGraw-Hill, 1993).

concepts for the study of the Middle Ages, a brief overview of how we got to this point is in order.

Feudalism to the 1970s

In the 1960s and 1970s, academic historians were as comfortable using the term "feudalism" to characterize medieval society as they were with labeling the thousand years between the "Fall of Rome" and the Italian Renaissance the "Middle Ages." This is to say, they used both with the understanding that they are historical constructs rather than historical facts: that is, useful generalizations and shorthand expressions for shared social, political, economic, and military institutions that identified this period as a particular historical era. There was a problem with feudalism as a construct that was tacitly recognized by all medievalists: there was no agreement about what that term actually meant. This was, in fact, the genesis of Brown's skepticism about the validity and utility of using that word at all. The multiplicity of meanings assigned to feudalism helps explain its appearance in almost every book published on the Middle Ages.

The meaning of feudalism as used by scholars differs according to nationality and historical subdiscipline. The oldest, early modern definition of feudalism, the pedigree of which can be traced to the Italian Renaissance jurists who coined the term "feudal," is the legal framework for the possession and descent of a type of property known in English as a "fief" or "fee" (*feudum* in Latin, hence feudalism). Fiefs were lands and estates held as dependent tenures by retainers, known as vassals, from their lords, social superiors to whom they had sworn loyalty, in return for a combination of military and social duties (e.g., attendance at the lord's court, hospitality to the lord and his men) and miscellaneous payments (feudal incidents) that reflected the lord's continued rights over the property. The most important of the services required from a fief-holder in the Middle Ages was knight service.[7]

Eighteenth-century Enlightenment *philosophes* used the adjective "feudal" to characterize the unequal and unjust economic, social, and political institutions of the *ancien régime*. Montesquieu, in his *The Spirit of the Laws* (1748), used the expression "feudal law" to describe a system of exploitation of peasants viewed against the backdrop of the parceling out of national sovereignty to private individuals. For them *féodalité* denoted the aggregate of seigneurial privileges and prerogatives that could be justified neither by reason nor justice. When the National Constituent Assembly

---

7. "Knight" as used in this essay refers to members of the medieval aristocratic elite who defined themselves as those who fought on horseback. In Latin, these men were *milites* and *caballarii*; in French, *chevaliers*, and German, *Ritter*. The social status and political and military functions of knights evolved between the eleventh and fourteenth centuries. In the eleventh, they were the armed and mounted retainers of nobles; by the end of the thirteenth century, "knight" was a term of nobility and designated membership in an order of society.

abolished the "feudal regime" in August 1789 this is what it meant. Across the English Channel, Adam Smith in the *Wealth of Nations* (1776) coined the phrase "feudal system" to describe a form of production governed not by market forces but by coercion and force. For Smith, the feudal system was the economic exploitation of peasants by their lords, which led to an economy and society marked by poverty, brutality, exploitation, and wide gaps between rich and poor. In the writings of Karl Marx, Smith's feudal system became a stage of economic development in his theory of historical materialism, the mode of production situated between the slave economy of the ancient world and modern capitalism.

Non-Marxist modern French historians also tend to use feudalism to mean a socioeconomic system in which landed lords, bound to one another by personal ties, dominated peasants economically and judicially, requiring from them rents, labor, and dues while enjoying seignory over those who lived on and worked their lands, although following the canon of modern historical methodology, they did so in "objective" terms, without moral judgment. German historians, more so than French, understand feudalism as a stage of political development characterized by personal ties of allegiance, and a hierarchy of fiefs and powers, stretching from the king down to minor lords.[8]

Discomfort with the ambiguity and multiple meanings assigned to feudalism led the influential twentieth-century French historian Marc Bloch to avoid defining the term at all in his two-volume *Feudal Society*. Instead, Bloch described what he called "feudal society," the key elements of which were a subject peasantry; widespread use of the fief instead of money to compensate service; supremacy of a warrior elite; ties of obedience and protection that bound man to man, and which among the warrior elite took the specialized form of vassalage; and the fragmentation of central authority, leading to endemic social and political disorder.[9]

British and American historians of the twentieth and twenty-first centuries, especially military historians, chose a narrower and more technical definition, one that locates feudalism in the union between vassalage and the fief. In its Anglo-American incarnation, feudalism is shorthand for a political, military, and social system that bound together the warrior aristocracy of Western Europe between c. 1000 and c. 1300. This system, it is asserted, only gradually took shape and differed in detail from region to region. Its key institutions were lordship, vassalage, and the fief. Lordship and vassalage represent two sides of a personal bond of mutual loyalty and military service

---

8. Frederic Cheyette, "Feudalism: A Brief History of the Idea," accessed September 18, 2019, http://dl.icdst.org/pdfs/files/c41a55a954061f27d1bed427310b61c7.pdf. See also Karl Kroeschell, "Lehnrecht und Verfassung im deutschen Hochmittelalter," *Forum historiae iuris: Erste europäische Internetzeitschrift für Rechtsgeschichte*, April 27, 1998, accessed September 18, 2019, https://forhistiur.de/1998-04-kroeschell/?I=de.

9. Marc Bloch, *Feudal Society*, trans. L. A. Manyon, 2 vols. (Chicago: University of Chicago Press, 1964), 2:446.

between nobles of different rank that found its roots in the Germanic warrior band. The superior in this relationship was termed a lord, and the subordinate, who swore loyalty on holy relics, became his "vassal." The pledge of fealty was confirmed by the performance of homage, a symbolic ritual of subordination in which the vassal knelt before his lord and placed his hand between his lord's. The lord promised on his part to

A thirteenth-century miniature painting that resembles the paying of homage, from the Archives Départementales de Pyrénées-Orientales 1B31.

maintain and protect his vassal. Not all vassals were invested with fiefs, only those who inherited lands from kinsmen or had so distinguished themselves as household knights as to merit the reward of a fief or the hand of an heiress whose right of marriage belonged to the lord. Many younger sons of lesser nobility spent their entire careers as members of a noble's household. Some were maintained through money-fiefs, a fixed annual payment of money instead of land, while others became mercenary knights.[10]

British and American historians have traditionally regarded knight service as feudalism's raison d'être. For them, feudalism was essentially a military recruitment system. Most have illustrated the military workings of feudalism through the example of Norman England, a conquest kingdom in which, they claim, feudalism was newly introduced by William the Conqueror. As a consequence of his policy of confiscating lands of rebels and his need to reward those who had won him his kingdom, within a decade of the Conquest, King William had redistributed most of the land in England not belonging to the Church to his Norman and French followers. These lands were granted in the form of fiefs held from the king. Each was allocated a specified quota of knights owed to the king, its *servitia debita*, when the holder was summoned to join the royal host. Castle-guard, the duty of providing troops to garrison the king's primary castles, was equally important. The tenants-in-chief fulfilled their *servitium*

---

10. See the entries for feudalism (John Bell Henneman Jr.), feudal incidents, and fief (both Theodore Evergates) in *Medieval France: An Encyclopedia*, ed. W. W. Kibler et al. (New York: Garland, 1995). Brian Tierney and Sidney Painter, *Western Europe in the Middle Ages: 300–1475*, 6th ed. (Boston: McGraw-Hill College, 1999), 157–65. The sixth edition acknowledges that "some modern scholars" have grown skeptical about using a single general term to characterize the complexities of medieval society.

debitum by calling upon their own enfeoffed vassals. This military service was unpaid and a lord was responsible for ensuring that all his knights were equipped with proper armor and horses. The length of service was limited by custom. In Norman England it was sixty days a year, a reflection of the continuing influence of Anglo-Saxon military institutions. A century later, this had been reduced to forty days, to bring it into accordance with the customary term of service in northern France. In frontier polities, such as the crusader states of the Levant and the expanding Christian kingdoms of Spain, where the threat of war was omnipresent, the length of service was more open-ended.[11]

Exposing the Construct?

So why is "feudalism" a myth? Elizabeth Brown advanced two arguments. First, its multiple definitions make it impossible to know precisely what any particular historian means by it.[12] Using the word "feudalism" in place of analyzing social, economic, and political relations as they actually appear in the sources is sloppy and lazy historical writing. That brings up her second, and more critical, objection. Feudalism, in whatever incarnation it takes, is just a historical construct, a generalization used to characterize an era or economic, political, or intellectual regimes and movements. In the words of Joseph Strayer and Rushton Coulborn:

> The idea of feudalism is an abstraction derived from some of the facts of early European history, but it is not itself one of those facts. . . . [Eighteenth-century] scholars, looking at certain peculiar institutions which had survived to their day, looking back to the period when these institutions had originated and flourished, coined the word feudalism to sum up a long series of loosely related facts.[13]

They, and other medieval historians, accepted this caveat as a given, so obvious perhaps to them that they felt no need to state that explicitly. Feudalism was a generalization, but a useful one, as it helped students to understand medieval European society. Coulborn went even further, arguing that feudalism reveals to the social scientist uniformity in history, as this abstraction can be found, in one form or another, in all parts of the globe as a response to the collapse of empire.[14] It is a construct with universal application.

---

11. Philippe Contamine, *War in the Middle Ages*, trans. M. Jones (Oxford: Blackwell, 1984), 51–54, 59, 64, and 77–79.

12. A point previously made by Frederic Cheyette. "Some Notations on Mr. Hollister's 'Irony,'" *Journal of British Studies* 5 (1965): 1–14.

13. Joseph Strayer and Rushton Coulborn, "The Idea of Feudalism," in Coulborn, *Feudalism in History*, 3. See also Bloch, *Feudal Society*, 2.446–47 (on Japan).

14. Coulborn, *Feudalism in History*, 384–95.

Brown rejected this reasoning. The term "feudalism," she asserted, even if narrowly defined, is so divorced from the reality on the ground that it has neither practical nor pedagogical value.[15] Brown's challenge went far beyond the use of the term. All historical constructs—feudalism, capitalism, socialism, and the like—that claim to capture in a word the essential characteristics of an era, its modes of organization, movements, and doctrines are specious, and historians know that they are lies. They are simplifications that distort historical reality by claiming for it a nonexistent coherence. They are self-validating, as they lead historians to impose preconceived interpretations on historical research rather than examine evidence with an open mind. Feudalism is a lens that distorts, lulling researchers and students alike into accepting a phantom of coherence and uniformity rather than engaging the complexity and uniqueness of historical reality.[16]

Susan Reynolds developed Brown's criticisms in *Fiefs and Vassals*. Brown had asserted that the construct of feudalism did not accurately describe social and political relations at any time in the Middle Ages. Reynolds set out to prove that Brown was right about the feudo-vassalic model of feudalism. She identified and analyzed the textual evidence for dependent military tenures and vassalage in England, France, Germany, and Italy in what was supposed to be feudalism's heyday, the tenth through twelfth centuries. Her method was to interpret "feudal" vocabulary found in these texts in historical context, deriving their meanings rather than assuming them. She concluded that "fief" (*feudum*), "benefice" (*beneficium*, recompense or favor), and "vassal" (*vassus*/*vasselus*) had multiple meanings until the late twelfth century, when they were given legal definition by the Italian lawyers who produced the *Libri Feudorum* (Book of Fiefs), a mid-twelfth-century collection of texts relating to the tenure and descent of fiefs. In essence, Reynolds argued that in the early Middle Ages custom rather than law ruled, and that this custom was both highly localized and mutable. There is no evidence, to her mind, for precise feudal institutions or obligations in the tenth or eleventh centuries.

Historians have wrongly assumed, according to Reynolds, that if the words *feudum* or *beneficium* appear in a tenth- or eleventh-century document they must mean a knight's fee. Their mistake was to assume that such words belonged to a technical vocabulary of land law that did not exist before the middle of the twelfth century. Rather, historians need to read a text without preconceptions and derive from it what the drafter meant by these words. By doing so, Reynolds discovered that *feudum* and *beneficium* in tenth- and eleventh-century charters were as likely to refer to property that was freely owned as to land held in return for service. If anything, in the eleventh century dependent tenures were less important than inheritable family lands, and horizontal bonds of association were more important than the vertical bonds of lord and vassal that historians have traditionally emphasized. Reynolds argues for the

15. Brown, "Tyranny of a Construct," 1078.
16. Brown, "Tyranny of a Construct," 1080.

persistence of public power in the form of kingship and the centrality of community in the eleventh century.[17] The feudalism of history textbooks, Reynolds concludes, owes far more to the *Libri Feudorum* of the late twelfth-century professional northern Italian lawyers and to systematizing seventeenth-century English antiquarians like Sir Henry Spelman than to the institutions and practices of earlier centuries. In these Lombard legal texts *feudum* acquired the technical definition of a dependent tenure held by a vassal from a lord in return for service. The *Libri Feudorum* thus prepared the ground for King Henry II of England's insistence that all the land in his realm was held as fiefs either directly or intermediately from the Crown. Unlike his contemporaries, King Louis VII (r. 1137–80) of France and Holy Roman Emperor Frederick Barbarossa (r. 1159–90), Henry (r. 1154–89) had the advantage of ruling a kingdom that his forebears had conquered. England was more "feudal" because William the Conqueror had redistributed much of its land to his Norman followers. Just as importantly, Henry and his successors had the power to turn theory into political reality. The feudal pyramid familiar in medieval history textbooks came to have a semblance of reality in England (and later France and Germany), not from organic growth in the tenth and eleventh centuries but by royal imposition in the late twelfth. Feudalism, rather than being the consequence of the collapse of central authority, was actually an instrument for advancing it.

Susan Reynolds's critique of feudalism largely swept the field, and other historians were inspired by it to challenge received wisdom about feudalism. Even those who profoundly disagreed with Reynolds notably were reluctant to publicly challenge her. Within a few years it had become the new orthodoxy, at least in Britain and the United States. Medieval history in these countries now experienced what the historian of science Thomas Kuhn termed a "paradigm shift." The reasons for this would entail a discussion of changing norms in academia that would take us far afield from the central focus of this chapter. What is clear, however, is that feudalism went from being a staple of textbooks and classrooms to being a "myth" of the Middle Ages. Global "feudalism," in particular that which supposedly characterized the *bakufu* government of Kamakura Japan (1185–1333), has begun to follow suit.[18]

In at least one respect, Reynold's critique of feudalism did not go far enough. Europe in the Middle Ages is generally described as feudal in older textbooks but, even if one discounts the arguments against feudalism as a system, this characterization is wrong, as a great portion of what today constitutes Europe knew neither fiefs

---

17. Reynolds, *Fiefs and Vassals*, 34–46; and chap. 8 in Susan Reynolds, *Kingdoms and Communities in Western Europe, 900–1300*, 2nd ed. (Oxford: Oxford University Press, 1997).

18. See Conrad Totman, "English Language Studies of Medieval Japan," *The Journal of Asian Studies* 38, no. 3 (1979): 541–49; Jeffrey Mass, "The Early Bakufu and Feudalism," in *Court and Bakufu in Japan*, ed. J. Mass (Stanford, CA: Stanford University Press, 1982), 123–42; and, most fully, Karl Friday, "The Futile Paradigm: In Quest of Feudalism in Early Medieval Japan," *History Compass* 8, no. 2 (2010): 179–96.

nor vassalage in the Middle Ages. Brown and Reynolds, like virtually every other historian of medieval feudalism, myself included, focused their attention on France, England (after 1066), Germany, Italy, and the territories conquered and settled by their military elites in what the historian Robert Bartlett termed the "aristocratic diaspora."[19] If one looks farther east, one discovers completely different sociopolitical and military systems. In the medieval kingdom of Hungary and in the Slavic states of central and eastern Europe military organization was based on hereditary classes of freemen.[20]

Hungarian society under the Árpád dynasty (1000–1301) was structured as a four-tiered hierarchy: noblemen; two classes of freemen, hereditary warriors and the much more numerous commoners; and serfs. Military organization in the twelfth and thirteenth centuries was based on a network of about 150 castle districts that answered to the authority of royally appointed counts and barons from noble families, who commanded the military contingents raised from their territories. For most of this period, the arms-bearing class was known as "castle warriors" and constituted a privileged landowning elite. In return for their tax-exempt status, they governed the local villagers, garrisoned royal castles, and went on royal expeditions. The military service of castle folk was restricted to local defense and supplying provisions for royal armies. Castle warriors were bound by ties of lordship to the counts and barons under whose banners they marched. Their military service was limited neither geographically nor temporally; they served at the pleasure of the king.[21] By contrast, the military service of the great nobility after 1222 was largely voluntary. King Andrew II (1205–35) fundamentally altered the relationship between the Crown and the magnates by making extensive grants of royal lands, castles, and villages to his noble supporters. Unlike fiefs, these lands were given as hereditary possessions without any services, military or otherwise, attached to them. When Andrew levied heavy taxes to pay debts he had incurred on the Fifth Crusade, the great nobles rebelled and forced him to issue the Golden Bull of 1222, a charter of liberties that exempted them from all royal taxes, the jurisdiction of royally appointed courts, and military service on royal expeditions outside of Hungary, and limited their military obligation within Hungary to a mere fifteen days. Andrew and his successors compensated for the loss of the military service of the magnates by ennobling castle knights and granting them property, creating a class known as "royal servants," and hiring German mercenary knights.[22] They

---

19. Robert Bartlett, *The Making of Europe: Conquest, Colonization and Cultural Change 950–1350* (Princeton, NJ: Princeton University Press, 1993), 24–59.

20. See Jean W. Sedlar, *East Central Europe in the Middle Ages, 1000–1500* (Seattle: University of Washington Press, 1994), 58–64 and 197–256.

21. Pál Engel, *The Realm of St Stephen: A History of Medieval Hungary 895–1526* (London: I. B. Tauris, 2001), 17–18, 41–42, 66–74, and 183–86.

22. Sedlar, *East Central Europe*, 20–29.

Arthur Orlenov's Battle of Grunwald, July 15, 1410, in which allied forces of the Grand Duchy of Lithuania and the Kingdom of Poland crushed the Teutonic Knights.

also held their lands freely. It was only in the fourteenth century, with the advent of a French royal dynasty, that ideas of feudal tenure were introduced to Hungary.

Although primary-source evidence is scarce, what there is suggests that military service in the Slavic polities of the Baltic, Czech lands, Poland, and Belarus was broadly similar to that in Hungary. In the eleventh- and twelfth-century Duchy of Bohemia, all adult Czech males had an obligation to answer the duke's summons to war. The duke himself had an obligation to personally lead the mustered troops. German settlers were exempt from all military service except *pro patria*, that is, in defense of the town or locale. By the end of the twelfth century, military service, while still obligatory, had become more selective and a separation grew between those who were better trained and armed for war and the mass of peasants. There is also some evidence that at least a few wealthy magnates maintained warrior retainers through grants of land tenure to aid them in disputes with neighbors.[23] In all of these, military service was a combination of the war bands of nobles and musters of free men.[24] In the Kingdom of Poland military obligation became tied to landowning in the thirteenth century with the emergence of a wealthy landed nobility. Every Polish noble who held land by "military" law was required to serve personally in the royal army, if physically capable, accompanied by a suitable retinue of warriors, all of

23. Lisa Wolverton, *Hastening Toward Prague: Power and Society in the Medieval Czech Lands* (Philadelphia: University of Pennsylvania Press, 2001), 37–41 and 71–73.

24. Jahor Novikaŭ, *A Military History of Belarusian Lands Up to the End of 12th Century A.D.*, vol. 1 (Minsk: Łohvinaŭ, 2007).

whom he was responsible for arming and maintaining.[25] Unlike fourteenth-century Hungary, the association of military service with land tenure was an internal development rather than due to the introduction of Western practices.

Historians have discarded the once popular origin story for feudalism that traced its beginning to the early eighth-century Frankish ruler Charles Martel's distribution of Church lands as fiefs to his vassals, but it is interesting that feudal institutions seem to have developed only in areas that had once belonged to the Carolingian Empire.

The Kernel of Truth in the Myth of Feudalism

As observed at the beginning of this chapter, myths tend to have kernels of truth, and this is truer of the "myth of feudalism" than most. Reynolds and Brown may have effectively banished feudal*ism* from historical conferences and academic publications. What they did not accomplish is to persuade many medieval institutional and military historians, myself included, that medieval lordship and dependent military tenures are historical fictions. Feudalism as a historical construct or ideal type might never have existed. Lords, retainers, and dependent tenures, however, did, and were critical elements in the governance of early medieval polities. By the early thirteenth century, the institutions of lordship and the fief had become ubiquitous throughout Western Europe, and this development probably had less to do with professional Italian lawyers systematizing feudal law than with the realization by rulers that they could enhance their authority by defining themselves as royal liege lords of all free men and as the fount of all landholding in their realms. It is telling that the most "feudalized" societies of the twelfth and thirteenth centuries were Anglo-Norman England and Ireland; the Norman Kingdom of Sicily, comprising the island of Sicily and southern Italy; the Latin states of Syria-Palestine; and the Latin Empire of Constantinople's feudal states and baronies into which Greece, Macedonia, Thessaly, and some Aegean islands were divided after the Fourth Crusade. What all had in common is that they were polities established through crusade and conquest between the eleventh and the early thirteenth centuries.

Even if one agrees with Reynolds that the Norman Conquest of 1066 did not introduce full-blown feudalism into England, it is difficult to avoid seeing in William the Conqueror's great land register known as *Domesday Book* and late eleventh- and early twelfth-century royal writs and legal compilations the outlines of a sociopolitical system based on the institution of vassalage—even if the word "vassal" itself was largely restricted to literary works—and grants of land tenure. William the Conqueror's distribution of lands to his followers was on the basis of fiefs. *Domesday Book* describes the lands of England's tenants-in-chief in 1087 as held *de rege* (from the king). It is true that *Domesday Book* does not provide information about or even

---

25. Sedlar, *East Central Europe*, 206.

mentions in passing knight service owed from these estates, but another royal administrative document compiled eighty years later records that the barons of England owed William's son Henry I (r. 1100–1135) the service of some 5,000 knights, presumably on the basis of knights' fees created by the Conqueror. This document, known as the *Cartae baronum* (Charters of the barons), was the product of a royal inquest ordered by King Henry II to ascertain the military obligation attached to lands held from the Crown.[26] Henry had ascended the throne after a generation of chaotic civil war fought between his uncle King Stephen and his mother Empress Matilda, and he devoted much of his reign to restoring order and enhancing the Crown's authority over landholders and land. In 1166, Henry ordered every tenant-in-chief in England to report the number of knights that he or his predecessor had owed to Henry I, and the number of additional knights' fees that they had created since the death of his grandfather. Two hundred and eighty-three tenants-in-chief reported a total of 6,278 7/8 knights' fees, considerably higher than the 5,000 knights they owed the Crown. Six years later Henry undertook a similar inquest in his duchy of Normandy and found that as duke he was owed the service of 581 knights from about 1,500 enfeoffments.[27] Whether or not Normandy (or Anglo-Saxon England) was "feudal" in 1066, it is indisputable that William structured the Norman settlement of his newly acquired kingdom on the principle of dependent military tenures, and that a century later, a king of England could raise an army of up to 5,000 knights on the basis of *servitia debita*—the service owed by the kingdom's tenants-in-chief.

A similar case can be made for "Outremer" (the land across the sea), the Kingdom of Jerusalem, the Principality of Antioch, the County of Tripoli, and the County of Edessa, which even more than Norman England was the product of conquest. The argument for systematic feudal military service in the Latin East is based on three thirteenth-century lawbooks. The *Livre au roi* (*King's Book*), the earliest and briefest, was composed between 1198 and 1205. Around 1260, Philip of Novara, a knight and writer born in Italy who spent most of his adult life in Cyprus, described the High Court of Cyprus and its feudal law in the *Livre de forme de plait* (*Book of Legal Procedure*). In 1264–65, John of Ibelin, count of Jaffa, drew on Novara's work for his own treatise on the legal procedures and laws of the Kingdom of Jerusalem, *Le livre des assizes* (an assize was a legal inquest). All three describe feudal systems in which knights and more lightly armed mounted sergeants held fiefs in return for military service. Unlike in Western Europe, this service could last up to a year and had to be fulfilled in person along with the quota of knights owed from the fief. The extended duration of service, which is also found in medieval Castile, was a necessity if feudal service was to be at all useful given the perpetual threat of war faced by these states. Kings of Jerusalem had to justify service beyond the borders of the realm as defending

---

26. Thomas K. Keefe, *Feudal Assessments and the Political Community under Henry II and His Sons* (Berkeley: University of California Press, 1983), 1–19.

27. Contamine, *War in the Middle Ages*, 79.

the royal honor or in promotion of the common good. The *Assizes of Romania* (composed between 1333 and 1346) shows that feudal law in the Principality of the Morea (the Peloponnese), one of the states of Frankish Greece subject to the Latin Empire of Constantinople, drew heavily on the *Assizes of Jerusalem*, unsurprising given the similarities between these polities established by crusade and surrounded by enemies.[28]

Peter Edbury, the editor of John of Ibelin's treatise, provides the clearest exposition of the operations of feudalism and feudal military services in both Cyprus and the Kingdom of Jerusalem.[29] An admirer of Susan Reynolds's book, he attempted to apply her model to the evidence from the Latin East in the twelfth century. The result was not, I think, what he anticipated. He found no explicit evidence that the great lords of the "First Kingdom" had a formal obligation to produce a stipulated number of knights to the king when he went on campaign, or that their lordships were termed *feoda*. On the other hand, he uncovered a great deal of evidence for lesser landowners holding their lands as fiefs (in the sense as dependent tenures) in return for fixed quotas of military service, and by the 1180s the great nobles of the kingdom were conceived of as "vassals" of the king. Archbishop William of Tyre's account of an oath of fidelity in 1183 sworn by the higher nobility to the new regent, Guy of Lusignan, explicitly represents the higher nobility of the Kingdom of Jerusalem as such. Edbury also found that knights holding fiefs (in the traditional sense of the word) from magnates in return for heavy military service was the norm in the twelfth century. He admits that the most cogent and logical explanation for the military quotas and the absence of fiscal dues is that these knights' fees "dated from early in the kingdom's history and had come into being at a time of acute manpower shortage." The main argument against that conclusion is that it contradicts Reynolds's model.[30]

Brown's and Reynolds's arguments to the contrary, it is difficult to deny that the Normans who conquered England and southern Italy in the second half of the eleventh century and the French who settled in the Latin East and Byzantine Greece from the late eleventh to early thirteenth centuries brought with them a concept of dependent tenures held from lords in return for military service. The nexus of dependent tenures with military service in the earliest of these polities may at first have been ill defined. The obligations attached to fiefs (whether in the form of land or money or direct maintenance) probably depended more on practical circumstances than law or

---

28. Peter Edbury, "Feudal Obligations in the Latin East," *Byzantion* 47 (1977): 328–56; John of Ibelin, *Le livre des assizes*, ed. P. Edbury (Leiden: Brill, 2003).

29. Edbury, "Feudal Obligations"; Edbury, "Philip of Novara and the *Livre de forme de plait*, in *Praktika tou tritou diethnous kyprologikou sunedriou*, ed. A. Papageorgiou (Nicosia, 1966), 2:555–69; Edbury, *The Kingdom of Cyprus and the Crusades, 1191–1374* (Cambridge: Cambridge University Press, 1991).

30. Peter W. Edbury, "Fiefs and Vassals in the Kingdom of Jerusalem: From the Twelfth Century to the Thirteenth," and Susan Reynolds, "Fiefs and Vassals in Twelfth-Century Jerusalem: A View from the West," *Crusades* 1 (2002): 49–52, 59–60, and 29–48 for Reynolds's tortured attempt to explain away fiefs and vassals in the early Latin Kingdom.

even custom in Norman England, southern Italy, and Outremer, as the institutions of governance and society evolved in response to dynamic conditions.[31] Nonetheless, it seems to me that Anglo-Norman and Angevin England, the Norman kingdom of Sicily, and the Frankish principalities of the Levant and Greece established in the wake of crusades might be termed "feudal societies" without apology.

Feudalism and Medieval Knights

For historians of medieval England, going back to the late nineteenth century, the question has not been whether dependent military tenures existed but when they first appeared in England, a key issue in the ongoing debate over the impact of the Norman Conquest. Two related questions about English feudalism have also received a great deal of scholarly attention. The first, to what degree did medieval English kings rely on feudal obligations to raise armies? The second, when did English kings and barons begin to retain their men with the payment of monetary fees rather than grants of land? The argument that William the Conqueror introduced feudalism into England can be traced back to Spelman in the early seventeenth century, as he was the first to recognize the applicability of the feudal terminology formulated by early modern French legal writers to describe the laws governing the descent of fiefs to the situation of medieval England.[32] The modern debate, however, began in 1891 with the publication of an essay by J. H. Round on the introduction of knight service into England. Taking exception to Edward A. Freeman's argument for continuity in English tenurial and political history, Round represented the Conquest as a dividing line between a prefeudal and feudal England. According to Round, William the Conqueror revolutionized the military organization of England by imposing on the fiefs he distributed to his followers precisely defined quotas of knight service. Round, who had previously argued that 1066 marked a tenurial revolution, posited that the Norman Conquest marked a dramatic and absolute break with English traditions of military service, which he saw as arising from a public duty incumbent upon all free men. The most prominent advocate of Round's thesis was the doyen of Anglo-Saxon history Sir Frank Stenton (1880–1967), who rejected Round's animus against the

31. Alan V. Murray has argued for the importance of money-fiefs for military recruitment during the early decades of the Latin Kingdom of Jerusalem. The money came from the tolls levied on ports and were especially well suited to endowing newly arrived knights lacking the family or prestige to warrant a lordship; see "The Origin of Money-Fiefs in the Latin Kingdom of Jerusalem," in *Mercenaries and Paid Men: The Mercenary Identity in the Middle Ages*, ed. J. France (Leiden: Brill, 2008), 275–86.

32. J. G. A. Pocock, *The Ancient Constitution and the Feudal Law: A Study of English Historical Thought in the Seventeenth Century* (Cambridge: Cambridge University Press, 1987), 102–11.

Anglo-Saxons but nonetheless embraced his view that 1066 marked the beginnings of English feudalism.[33]

Some historians of Anglo-Saxon England disagreed, as they detected a similar system of vassalage and military service in pre-Conquest England. John Gillingham critically reexamined the meager evidence for William the Conqueror's imposition of knight service on landholdings and found that it better supported continuity than revolutionary change.[34] C. Warren Hollister found elements of continuity between the military organizations of Anglo-Saxon and Anglo-Norman England, and, more radically, demonstrated that "feudal" military service never constituted the main source of warriors for the Norman kings.[35] My *Lordship and Military Obligation*, touched indirectly on this debate, as I demonstrated that Anglo-Saxon armies at the time of the Conquest were organized according to the principle of lordship, and consisted of landowners and their dependents, who owed sixty days of unpaid service for every five "hides" of land (notionally, six hundred acres) they held directly from the Crown, with rights of jurisdiction.[36] The implication, therefore, is that pre-Conquest England had elements of "feudalism." David Bates has come at the question from a different perspective, demonstrating that Normandy before 1066 was not as "feudal" as Round had supposed.[37] The consensus at present is that both England and Normandy possessed rudimentary elements of a "feudal system"—dependent tenures, lordship, and dependent military tenures—before 1066 but they coexisted with other forms of tenure and military obligation. English feudalism, as exemplified by the twelfth-century legal treatise known as "Glanvill" and its early thirteenth-century successor "Bracton," was the result of an evolutionary process that had much to do with the unsettled conditions that followed the Norman Conquest.[38]

This brings us to a second, related myth of the Middle Ages, and one that is even more central to the military history of the period, the myth of the feudal knight. This myth, first fully articulated by C. W. C. Oman, places the mounted feudal knight and the castle at the center of warfare in the High Middle Ages.[39] Between the Battle of Hastings in 1066 and the "infantry revolution" of the fourteenth century, according

---

33. Eric John, *Orbis Britanniae* (Leicester, UK: Leicester University Press, 1966), 135–36.

34. John Gillingham, "The Introduction of Knight Service into England," *Anglo-Norman Studies* 4 (1982): 53–64.

35. C. Warren Hollister, *The Military Organization of Norman England* (Oxford: Oxford University Press, 1965); Hollister, "The Irony of English Feudalism," *Journal of British Studies* 2 (1962): 1–26.

36. Richard P. Abels, *Lordship and Military Obligation in Anglo-Saxon England* (Berkeley: University of California Press, 1988).

37. David Bates, *Normandy Before 1066* (London: Longman, 1982).

38. See David Bates, "England and the 'Feudal Revolution,'" in *Il feudalesimo nell'alto medioevo*, Settimane di Studi del Centro Italiano di Studi sull'Alto Medioevo 47 (Spoleto, 2000), 646.

39. Oman, *Art of War*; idem, *A History of the Art of War in the Middle Ages*, 2 vols. (repr., London: Greenhill, 1999).

to Oman, the art of warfare had stagnated. True generalship had all but disappeared in the West with the Fall of Rome, and with it, strategy and logistics. The only part of military science that showed any advancement was in fortifications and siege warfare, which did not impress him overly, as he saw battles as central to warfare through the ages. With neither standing armies nor professional soldiers in the modern sense, warfare had degenerated into a series of disorderly battles and skirmishes between small armies of ill-disciplined, heavily armored knights on horseback with few or no strategic goals. This was an age of the warrior rather than the soldier, as chivalry, courage, and honor replaced discipline and training.

The scarcity of large-scale battles in the High Middle Ages was for Oman further evidence for the degeneration of the art of war in this era. On the surface, it presented a paradox. A military aristocracy eager to prove themselves in combat should have sought out battle as much as possible. To break the monotony of long drawn-out sieges, knights representing the besieging army and the defending garrison might agree to engage in melees that had no military purpose and which resembled tournaments more than warfare. That battles were rare could not have been due to strategic intent, given the amateurishness of medieval commanders. Rather, battles were rare because armies, wandering about without any definite strategic aims and lacking reconnaissance scouts, had trouble finding each other. The only way of guaranteeing that a battle would take place is if one military commander issued a formal challenge to another, naming the time and place it should occur. When a battle did occur, it would quickly descend into a confused mess of men striking at one another.

The hierarchy of command, the little that existed, was based on social rank rather than martial experience or skill. A baron's or knight banneret's (a knight leading a squadron under his own banner) place in it was determined solely by his title of nobility and the size of his contingent of knights. Military commanders, even kings, proudly bore the title of knight, which was fitting, as they were expected to demonstrate the same degree, if not more, of courage and prowess on the battlefield as the barons and knights they led. The perceived performance of a commander in battle was critical for the morale of his troops, as was the battlefield oration he delivered before hostilities commenced. The absence of a true chain of command combined with the lack of training and discipline in the ranks allowed for only the most rudimentary battle tactics. Any tactical planning had to be done prior to battle, as once the fighting had begun, a military commander, engaged in hand-to-hand combat, had no way of controlling his troops. The same pattern of battle occurred over and over again: two armies would draw up face-to-face on the chosen battlefield, about four hundred yards apart. Each force would consist of two or three "battles," ad hoc cavalry formations three or four ranks deep, which could either be arrayed sequentially in parallel lines or linearly. These battles were made up of disparate companies of feudal knights serving under the banners of their individual lords, the only military commanders whose authority they recognized. This was virtually the only order and cohesion that an army of this period possessed. Although the armies had troops of foot soldiers raised from the peasantry and towns, they were lightly armed and even more poorly trained than the knights. They had little military value in battle, but were useful for sieges and wreaking casual destruction on the enemy's countryside.

In this, Oman's model, the centerpiece of battle was a cavalry charge of knights, their feet firmly planted in stirrups and their lances couched. After the initial collision, the battle would degenerate into a chaotic melee, featuring individual duels between knights intent more on demonstrating personal prowess than on any military objective, which would continue until one side fled the battlefield. Most knights served out of feudal obligation to their immediate lords, compelled by duty and inspired by the desire to win chivalric glory and spoils. They rode into battle under the banner of their lord, to whom they owed their primary loyalty and obedience. Rulers who could afford it, especially those threatened by rebellious barons, either supplemented or replaced feudal knights entirely with mercenaries, who, though inferior in morale, greedy, and ferocious, were more amenable to discipline and would serve as long as they were paid. The feudal knight, on the other hand, prized honor above all else, and honor demanded demonstrations of courage. But honor also led to rivalry and jealousy within the ranks, and unrestrained courage, to rashness in combat. A battle could turn on the actions of even a minor baron or knight banneret, who might precipitate a charge prematurely or break formation prompted by his desire for glory. A battle's outcome depended as much on chance as on numbers or skill. The death of the king or count in command, always a possibility given that he fought in the mix, could turn likely victory into sudden defeat. Oman, who silently judged the competency of medieval commanders against those of the Napoleonic era, found all of this distasteful. His assessment of the military quality of armies in the age of the feudal knight was blunt and brutal: "Assembled with difficulty, insubordinate, unable to maneuver, ready to melt away from its standard the moment that its short period of service was over, a feudal force presented an assemblage of unsoldierlike qualities such as have seldom been known to coexist."[40]

Oman may not have invented this myth, but his *A History of the Art of War in the Middle Ages* established it firmly. For English-language historians, at least, Oman's authority as a military historian was unimpeachable. His contributions to the discipline at a time when military history still commanded respect in academia were recognized by his peers, who elected him Chichele Professor of Modern History at Oxford University and president of the Royal Historical Society, culminating in 1920 with his being invested as a Knight Commander of the Most Excellent Order of the British Empire (KBE), appropriately a British order of chivalry. Oman's influence is evident in the work of one of the other giants of early twentieth-century military history, the German historian Hans Delbrück. Delbrück, in his masterwork, *The History of Warfare in the Framework of Political History*, presented warfare as a cultural feature

---

40. Oman, *Art of War*, 57–58.

of societies, subject to evolution and influenced by the economy and the political system. His volume on the Middle Ages explains the political and cultural foundations that supposedly undergirded the type of medieval warfare that Oman described.[41] Like Oman, Delbrück distinguished between knights, who were merely mounted *warriors*, and true cavalry, organized and disciplined companies of mounted soldiers. The former were independent fighters, unable to join with others and form units with tactical significance. For Delbrück, a medieval host was the military manifestation of the political incoherence of the age.

Oman's portrait of medieval warfare remained unchallenged until the 1950s. Two seminal works, by J. F. Verbruggen and R. C. Smail, which appeared only two years apart, profoundly reshaped historians' understanding of medieval warfare.[42] Verbruggen shared Oman's opinions that military history should be most concerned with battles, and that the feudal knight was the most important actor on the battlefields of the High Middle Ages. Where he disagreed with Oman was in his assessment of the military capability of medieval commanders and knights. Medieval knights, he argued, received both individual and collective training. The former occurred when he was a child and fostered in the court of a relation or associate of his father. There he learned the skills of the courtier and the profession of arms, including horsemanship and the proper use of the weapons appropriate to his status, lance and sword. He demonstrated skill with horse and lance in the game of quintain, in which he charged on horseback with couched lance attempting to solidly strike a target, usually a shield fixed to a stake. Hunting was not only a sport but training in horsemanship. It helped the youth to become comfortable with blood and gore. Collective training took place in tournaments, which in the twelfth and early thirteenth centuries resembled mock battles. Although the goal was to demonstrate individual prowess, knights participated as members of teams, representing the retinues of great lords. The same men who fought under the banner of a lord in tournaments also fought under his banner in battle. This last point was one of Verbruggen's most important discoveries. Armies of knights did not lack discipline and cohesion, as Oman had posited. Reevaluating the sources, Verbruggen concluded that, if viewed without preconception, armies of knights were organized, disciplined, and demonstrated close cohesion at the squadron level. These squadrons were the *conrois*, or banners, of a lord, bonded together by a shared loyalty to their lord and by common training in his court and in tournaments.

As a Belgian, Verbruggen was understandably interested in the urban militias of Flemish towns. By the early fourteenth century, these infantry forces, he found, exhibited equal, if not greater, organization, training, and discipline than feudal hosts, traits

41. Hans Delbrück, *The History of Warfare in the Framework of Political History*, vol. 3, *The Middle Ages*, trans. W. J. Renfroe (Lincoln: University of Nebraska Press, 1990).

42. J. F. Verbruggen, *The Art of Warfare in Western Europe during the Middle Ages: From the Eighth Century to 1340*, trans. S. Willard and Mrs. R. W. Southern, 2nd ed. (Woodbridge, UK: Boydell, 1997); R. C. Smail, *Crusading Warfare 1097–1193* (Cambridge: Cambridge University Press, 1956).

that allowed them to stand their ground when facing down a cavalry charge of heavily armored knights. This was dramatically illustrated by the victory at Courtrai in 1302 of an infantry army made up of urban militias from Bruges and other towns of Flanders over a "superior" force of French knights.[43] Of the 10,500 men in the Flemish army, only about 500–600 were knights, and all fought on foot armed with pikes and particularly nasty clubs sarcastically known as *goedendags* (Flemish for "good days"). The urban militias were raised by the town authorities and organized into contingents representing various guilds. The French army they destroyed consisted of about 3,000 knights under the command of Robert II, Count of Artois, and an unknown number of foot soldiers, who played virtually no role in the battle. The Battle of the Golden Spurs, so called because the victorious Flemings presented five hundred pairs of golden spurs to the Church of Our Lady in Courtrai, did not mean that infantry had suddenly become superior to cavalry—the French avenged the defeat at Cassel in 1328—but it did demonstrate what a disciplined and well-armed force of foot soldiers could do if fighting in a dense defensive formation on favorable terrain. Courtrai, the role played by English longbowmen in the battles of the Hundred Years' War, and victories by Scots and Swiss foot soldiers against mounted knights gave rise to the idea of an "infantry revolution" in the fourteenth century.[44] This is an exaggeration. Infantry had been an important element in battles throughout the High Middle Ages. The Battle of Hastings in 1066, which Oman used to mark the beginning of the age of the feudal knight, was actually a close-run affair. The cavalry forces of William the Bastard, Duke of Normandy (afterward King William I, "the Conqueror" of England) needed the ploy of a feigned retreat to lure the English out of their strong defensive position. Foot soldiers of the municipal militias of the Lombard League successfully defended the Carroccio, a war wagon surmounted by the league's battle banner, against attacks by Frederick Barbarossa's cavalry forces in the Battle of Legnano in 1176. Foot soldiers greatly outnumbered knights in most battles fought in the High Middle Ages.

Verbruggen's analyses of battles stretching from the Carolingian period to the early fourteenth century demonstrated that able medieval military commanders were capable of planning and implementing sophisticated battle tactics. They could also enforce discipline. King Richard I, "the Lionheart," for example, marched an army eighty-four miles along the Levantine coast from Acre to Arsuf under constant harassment by Saladin's horsed archers. This fighting march, an example of the successful integration of infantry, mounted cavalry, and naval forces, is arguably Richard's most impressive military feat, even more so than his victory in battle at Arsuf. Richard organized his troops into a rectangular marching formation. The van- and rearguards were manned by Templars and Hospitallers, his best mounted forces. The baggage

---

43. J. F. Verbruggen, *The Battle of the Golden Spurs: Courtrai, 11 July 1302*, ed. K. DeVries and trans. D. R. Ferguson (Woodbridge, UK: Boydell, 2002).

44. See Chapter 4 in this volume, by John France.

train and horses were flanked on both sides by a protective screen of armored foot soldiers. The march was deliberately slow, broken up by rest days. Richard took control
of ports along the way, so that his fleet could bring supplies and water to the army
and extricate the wounded. The battle that took place at Arsuf was actually against
Richard's orders. It occurred because the Hospitallers in the rear, frustrated by their
heavy losses, charged Saladin's forces. Richard ordered his other knights to follow. The
sudden charge after weeks of stolidly ignoring the harassment caught Saladin's horse
archers by surprise. Significantly, Richard chose not to pursue the defeated Saracens
but ordered his troops to continue their march to Jaffa. This serves as a reminder that
a host was never purely feudal nor a one-dimensional fighting force.

The multidimensionalism of medieval European armies manifested itself in numerous ways. As noted above, and this bears repeating, infantry invariably outnumbered
cavalry in armies of the High Middle Ages. Likewise, although knights conceived
of themselves as horsemen, when called upon, they could also dismount and serve
as a disciplined and heavily armored core for the infantry. To categorize knights as
"cavalry," a modern troop type, ignores not only their ability to fight on foot but the
important role they play in garrisoning castles.[45]

In some ways, Smail's challenge to Oman and the myth of the feudal knight was
more radical than Verbruggen's. Whereas Verbruggen accepted the primacy of battle,
and therefore the centrality of the knight in medieval warfare, Smail disputed both in
the context of crusading warfare. In the 1950s, military history, for academic as well
as popular writers, was a chronicle of decisive battles that could be studied to identify
unchanging, universal principles of warfare. This reflected the influence of the early
nineteenth-century military theorists Carl von Clausewitz and Baron de Jomini, who
saw Napoleonic warfare as a template for military science. Set-piece engagements
lay at the heart of warfare; all other military actions were secondary, either preparing
the way for or exploiting the consequences of battle. Based on his study of crusading
warfare, Smail rejected this, observing that

> the interpretation of the events of one age in the light of the assumptions
> and prejudices of another can never produce satisfactory history, and the
> story of medieval military methods told wholly or principally in terms of
> battle is very far from complete. . . . Beyond the actions of troops in battle
> lie conditions and influences which determined those actions and, even
> more important, military history was made on countless occasions before
> battle was joined, or even when it was refused or avoided.[46]

---

45. See Stephen Morillo, "*Milites,* Knights and Samurai: Military Terminology, Comparative History, and the Problem of Translation," in *The Normans and Their Adversaries at War: Essays in Memory of C. Warren Hollister,* ed. R. P. Abels and B. S. Bachrach (Woodbridge, UK: Boydell, 2001),
167–84.

46. Smail, *Crusading Warfare,* 15.

Smail concluded that crusading warfare revolved around castle building, sieges, and ravaging, not because military commanders were unable to locate enemy armies but because their primary goal, the control of territory, was best achieved through these military actions. They understood battle to be inherently risky and thought hard before risking it: "in adverse circumstances they were prepared to refuse it. Yet even when they decided against combat, conditions in the Latin states were such that by keeping their army in being in the neighborhood of the enemy they achieved important military objects."[47]

What Verbruggen had done for battle tactics Gillingham did for strategy in the provocatively titled essay "Richard I and the Science of War in the Middle Ages." Gillingham used Richard the Lionheart's military career as evidence for a well-thought-out military doctrine, followed by all good generals of the period, which accounts for the scarcity of pitched battles noted by Oman and others. Relying on vernacular (rather than Latin) sources whenever possible, Gillingham found that in twenty-five years of military campaigning Richard fought at most three battles, two of which were on crusade.[48] Mostly, Richard engaged in sieges, which is not surprising, as pitched battles were rare in the Middle Ages. Like Oman, Gillingham asked why, but came to a radically different conclusion, one that turned Oman's thesis on its head. Richard and other good military commanders in the twelfth century, Gillingham argued, followed a specific and well-defined military doctrine that involved avoidance of battle and relied on logistics and maneuver.[49] The standard offensive strategy was to begin ravaging as soon as one crossed into enemy territory to deprive the defender of supplies and to feed one's own troops. This was followed by laying siege to the enemy's fortified cities and castles. The defensive counterstrategy was also logistically based. Its goal was to deprive the attacker of supplies either by preventing him from ravaging, or in the rare instances that the invader had supply lines back to his own territory, by cutting them. The strategy that accomplished this was to garrison and supply one's

---

47. Smail, *Crusading Warfare*, 15.

48. John Gillingham, "Richard I and the Science of War in the Middle Ages," in *War and Government: Essays in Honour of J. O. Prestwich*, ed. J. Gillingham and J. C. Holt (Woodbridge, UK: Boydell, 1984), 78–91.

49. Gillingham confirmed his thesis in studies of the military careers of Duke William the Bastard of Normandy (the future Conqueror) and the late twelfth-/early thirteenth-century exemplar of chivalry William Marshal. See "War and Chivalry in the *History of William Marshal*," *Thirteenth-Century England* 2 (1988): 1–13; "William the Bastard at War," in *Studies in Medieval History Presented to R. Allen Brown*, ed. C. Harper-Bill, C. Holdsworth, and J. Nelson (Woodbridge, UK: Boydell, 1995), 141–58. Both are reprinted in *Anglo-Norman Warfare*, ed. M. Strickland (Woodbridge, UK: Boydell, 1992); 143–60 and 194–207. It is hard not to believe that Gillingham's choices of commanders were deliberately ironic. William the Conqueror is best known as the victor of the decisive Battle of Hastings in 1066, William Marshal is famed for his prowess as a tournament knight, and Richard I is better known as the Lionheart. The clear implication is if these three were practitioners of Vegetian warfare, it is a safe bet that many of their contemporaries were as well.

major fortifications and shadow the invading army with an army large enough to prevent the invader from dispersing his forces and ravaging and plundering over a wide area.[50] The defender would also avoid battle, relying on the strength of his garrisoned fortifications, and wait for the invader to run out of supplies and retreat into his own territory.

Battle avoidance was dictated by military considerations. A strategy that emphasizes ravaging, sieges, and battle avoidance is logically dictated by a military landscape dotted with strongpoints, if the goal of war is territorial control, as it largely was in the High Middle Ages. Battles were also risky—a medieval general could be killed in combat—and victory in battle often brought little gain, since a victor needed to follow up by taking the enemy's strongpoints to secure territory. Only if a commander believed that he had overwhelming superiority would he seek battle, in which case his opponent would try to deny him the opportunity. Given the time required for a medieval army to deploy from line of march to line of battle, it was extremely difficult to force an enemy to engage. Unless an enemy army was trapped and could not escape, it could easily refuse battle.

A strategy of battle avoidance would have been impossible for Oman's feudal commanders and knights to accept. According to his reading of the sources, they would have seen it as dishonorable and cowardly. For Gillingham, however, good medieval military commanders such as Richard the Lionheart were not only rational actors who assessed the costs and benefits of battle, and most often found that the former outweighed the latter, but the military doctrine they followed might even have been the product of book learning. Gillingham dubbed the dominant military doctrine of the High Middle Ages "Vegetian strategy," observing that in its broad outlines, it echoed the military advice given by the late Roman author Vegetius. When Oman wrote, the medieval aristocracy of the late twelfth century was believed to be largely illiterate and educated only in the use of arms. More recent scholarship has revised this view. Knights in the twelfth and thirteenth centuries were taught the skills of the courtier as well as the warrior. They were not the one-dimensional warriors that Oman imagined them to be. Literacy in the vernacular was common among the higher nobility by the second half of the twelfth century. Vegetius's *Epitoma rei militaris* (*The Essence of Military Matters*), also known as *De Re Militari*, was among the most widely copied texts throughout the Middle Ages and Renaissance. It was also frequently translated from Latin into the vernacular, and there is evidence that at least some military commanders owned copies.[51] Gillingham suggests that Vegetius's work may have directly shaped the way medieval commanders thought about and approached war. Richard the Lionheart, who was highly literate and sufficiently versed in Latin to tease an

---

50. Gillingham, "Richard I and the Science of War," 85.

51. Gillingham, "Richard I and the Science of War," 82.

archbishop about his imperfect grasp of grammar,[52] may even have read Vegetius in Latin. It is likely at least that he was familiar with the work.

This does not necessarily mean that Richard or other commanders learned their military doctrine by studying it in a book. As Gillingham acknowledged, strategy emphasized ravaging, sieges, and battle avoidance: where there were few fortifications, such as in England before 1066, there were more battles. Did medieval military commanders study *Epitoma rei militaris* to learn strategy, or was the text popular because it reinforced an existing consensus about strategy? Gillingham leaves this question open. Bernard Bachrach is not nearly as coy. For Bachrach, Vegetius was studied by medieval military commanders, and the strategy that Gillingham identified is evidence of the persistence of Roman ideas about warfare in the Middle Ages.[53] Nonetheless, whether the medieval doctrine of war described by Gillingham was the result of experience or book learning, "Vegetian strategy" is a useful shorthand for it.

If medieval warfare revolved around ravaging and sieges, what becomes of the military role of the feudal knight? The main activities of medieval warfare required not mounted shock troops but garrison troops, engineers, sappers, bowmen, incendiaries, and a sufficient number of foot soldiers to surround a city and starve it into submission. The role of the knight, in this scenario, is reduced to defending the siege against attack by a relief army, shadowing invading forces to limit the range of their ravaging, and performing reconnaissance. In social and political status, the knight was superior to the foot soldier, as was reflected in the wages paid each, and in medieval artistic and literary representations of warfare, knights take center stage and foot soldiers are virtually invisible. In the actual practice of medieval warfare, things were quite different. Even in the case of battle, mounted knights did not necessarily enjoy superiority over disciplined foot soldiers on the defensive. Throughout the Middle Ages the most effective armies were those with combined tactical arms, mounted shock troops supported by archers and pikemen.[54] In an additional irony, Oman seems to have inverted the chronological trajectory of the rise of infantry and the decline of the knight as a force in battle. Stephen Morillo's close analysis of the Battle of Hastings demolished Oman's assertion that the engagement established the superiority of feudal cavalry over infantry for the next three centuries.[55] Meanwhile, Malcolm Vale concluded that technological improvements in armor and weaponry and tactical developments in the fifteenth century established heavy cavalry as the most important element in battle,

52. John Gillingham, *Richard I* (New Haven, CT: Yale University Press, 1999), 256.

53. Bernard S. Bachrach, "The Practical Use of Vegetius' *De Re Militari* during the Middle Ages," *The Historian* 47 (1985): 239–55. Cf. the skepticism of Michael Prestwich, *Armies and Warfare in the Middle Ages: The English Experience* (New Haven, CT: Yale University Press, 1996), 186–87.

54. Matthew Bennett, "The Myth of the Military Supremacy of Knightly Cavalry," in *Medieval Warfare 1000–1300*, ed. J. France (London: Routledge, 2017), 171–87.

55. Stephen Morillo, "Hastings: An Unusual Battle," in France, *Medieval Warfare 1000–1300*, 313–21.

well after the "infantry revolution" of the fourteenth century was supposed to have made the knight obsolete in war.[56] Gillingham removed the key plank underlying the myth of the feudal knight and others historians gave a final push.

Abandoning the Feudal Knight?

Gillingham's "Vegetian strategy" thesis, although not universally accepted, has become the new orthodoxy among military historians specializing in the Middle Ages. The same is not true for many modern military historians and popular writers. Their portrayals of medieval warfare continue to be shaped by Oman, although without his snide asides. This dichotomy between the experts and nonexperts parallels the response to Reynolds's book, and it is unsurprising that the same authors who perpetuate the old paradigm of medieval warfare also continue to describe it as "feudal." The rapid acceptance of Gillingham's thesis reflects changes in approaches to military history. The now-not-so-new "new military history" of the 1960s shifted the focus of study from campaigns and battles to the impact of war on society and the social, political, and economic context for the recruitment, organization, and maintenance of military forces. These academic historians were concerned with virtually every aspect of military history except actual war fighting, which remained the staple of popular military history. Of the traditional triad of military science—tactics, strategy, and logistics—only the last two interested them.

Historians' understanding of what warfare *is* also changed at this time. Battle-centric narratives made sense to military historians writing prior to the 1960s, because of an underlying assumption that "true" warfare, as opposed to guerilla actions, consisted of campaigns designed to culminate in decisive battles. That assumption had its roots in a tradition of writing military history from the perspective of generals that stretched back to antiquity and to the influence of Clausewitz in military education. There was little reason to question it, as wars had largely been fought that way from the Napoleonic era through World War II. Algeria, Vietnam, and the multiple asymmetric conflicts that followed challenged that conception of war.[57] These developments in warfare laid the groundwork for Gillingham's paradigm shift.

56. Malcolm Vale, *War and Chivalry: Warfare and Aristocratic Culture in England, France and Burgundy at the End of the Middle Ages* (Athens: University of Georgia Press, 1981), 32–99 and 100–174.

57. The counterreaction to Gillingham's thesis has begun most notably in a direct challenge to the thesis by Clifford Rogers in *Journal of Medieval Military History* 1 (2002): 1–19, supplemented by Stephen Morillo's effort to place Vegetian strategy in a global context and to identify its underlying assumptions (21–41). Gillingham responded to the criticisms in *Journal of Medieval Military History* 2 (2003): 149–58. John France implicitly challenges the thesis in his discussion of the place of battle in medieval warfare in his survey *Western Warfare in the Age of the Crusades, 1000–1300* (London: UCL Press, 1999), 150–86.

The Vegetian strategy thesis helps explain an apparent paradox first identified by the American historian C. Warren Hollister: the relative *unimportance* of feudal military service in medieval England. As we have seen, from at least 1086, the English aristocracy held their estates and lands as fiefs from the king that owed quotas of knights, their *servitia debita*, for service in the king's hosts and castle-guard. Because of this, it was assumed that most knights in royal armies and the *conrois* of magnates served out of feudal obligation. Hollister discovered otherwise. In *The Military Organization of Norman England* and a series of articles, he demonstrated what he called the "irony of feudalism, that knight service owed in consequence of holding land from a lord had never been the primary mechanism through which Anglo-Norman kings raised their armies."[58] A number of British historians further undermined this assumption by identifying the king's household knights as the core of English royal armies from the eleventh to the early fifteenth century.[59] Numbering in the dozens, these knights constituted a standing professional military force that not only was the elite element in royal armies and garrisons but, on occasion, also acted as an independent military force in small-scale operations. The numbers contributed by the royal household might seem small, but given the small size of armies in the High Middle Ages, they could constitute a significant proportion of the knights on campaign with the king.

The *servitium debitum*, the feudal military service owed by tenants-in-chief to the Crown, declined in England precipitously during the thirteenth century. In 1166, King Henry II could summon 5,000 knights on the basis of feudal obligation; in 1272 his great grandson Edward I was owed 300–500 knights from the lay nobility and an additional 132 from bishops and abbots. Ninety percent of knight service owed to the Crown had evaporated within a century. The quality of troops raised by a feudal summons also declined, as sergeants, lower in status and less well armed, increasingly replaced knights. In 1277, Edward mustered for the Welsh War 228 knights and 294 sergeants serving without pay for forty days. In 1303, the feudal component of the army that Edward took to Scotland had fallen to 15 knights and

---

58. C. Warren Hollister, "The Irony of English Feudalism," *Journal of British Studies* 2 (1963): 1–26. Cf. the response of Robert S. Hoyt in the same volume, "The Iron Age of English Feudalism," 27–30; Hollister's rejoinder, "The Irony of the Iron Age," 30–31; and Cheyette's critiques in "Some Notations."

59. J. O. Prestwich, "The Military Household of the Norman Kings," *English Historical Review* 96 (1981): 1–37; Marjorie Chibnall, "Mercenaries and the *Familia Regis* under Henry I," *History* 62 (1977): 15–23; Stephen Church, *The Household Knights of King John* (Cambridge: Cambridge University Press, 1999); Michael Prestwich, *Edward I* (New Haven, CT: Yale University Press, 1988), 147–48; Chris Given-Wilson, *The Royal Household and the King's Affinity: Service, Finance and Politics in England, 1316–1430* (New Haven, CT: Yale University Press, 1986).

267 sergeants—sergeants, lower in social status and more lightly armored—out of a total force of about 7,500.[60]

English royal summons in the thirteenth century called upon the barons to attend the king in war out of loyalty and love, with the number of knights and other men whom they brought with them appropriate to their rank. This service was "voluntary," but the failure to respond meant the loss of the king's favor—and that had serious consequences for the fortunes of a noble house. By the end of the thirteenth century, barons were bringing with them larger contingents of men-at-arms (knights and mounted sergeants) than they owed from their fiefs. The last feudal summons of troops in England was in 1327, although feudal obligations continued to be exacted in Ireland and Scotland.[61]

English and French kings were so readily willing to dispense with feudal service in the late thirteenth century because it had not been the main source for heavy cavalry in royal armies since at least the beginning of that century, and in the case of England, likely well before then. The "irony" of English feudalism, to quote Hollister, is that "feudal incidents," relief, aids, wardship, and marriage, were not in the least incidental. Military service may have been the formal raison d'être for creating knights' fees, but by the early twelfth century, their real value to kings was financial. By 1100 in England, even summonses to join the king's host had become a source of revenue, as the commutation of military service for cash, known as "scutage" (shield money), became common. The Angevin kings of England, Henry II and his sons Richard and John much preferred mercenary troops to feudal levies. They raised the money needed to pay the wages of these mercenaries by requiring their tenants-in-chief to pay scutage in lieu of the knight service they owed. That the barons regarded this as an abuse of royal power and a violation of feudal custom is clear from Article 12 of *Magna Carta* of 1215, which has King John promise that "no scutage or aid (a monetary payment demanded by a lord from an enfeoffed vassal) shall be levied in our realm except by the common council of our realm."[62]

Twelfth- and thirteenth-century rulers preferred paid troops, mercenaries and household knights because of the serious limitations on and practical drawbacks of

---

60. Michael Prestwich, *War, Politics and Finance under Edward I* (Totowa, NJ: Rowman and Littlefield, 1972), 97–98; Prestwich, *Armies and Warfare*, 72. By the early fourteenth century, the distinction between knights and mounted sergeants in England may have had more to do with legally defined social status than military function. The number of men who were dubbed knights decreased throughout the thirteenth century, as the costs associated with the rank and the local administrative duties required by the Crown grew. The Crown was sufficiently concerned to impose fines on those who qualified economically for knighthood but refused to accept the honor. By the middle of the fourteenth century, the generic term "man-at-arms" displaced "knight" to designate armored horsemen. See Prestwich, *Armies and Warfare*, 12–18 and 76–80.

61. Contamine, *War in the Middle Ages*, 79–80; Prestwich, *Armies and Warfare*, 63–66 and 68–75.

62. J. C. Holt, *Magna Carta*, 3rd ed. (Cambridge: Cambridge University Press, 2015), 383.

feudal service.[63] There was no clear consensus whether feudal obligation was limited to defense of the realm or could be called upon for foreign expeditions. A feudal army would melt away when the term of service expired after forty days, unless a commander could persuade the knights to remain for wages. There was no assurance that a baron would answer a summons with the full complement of knights he owed, or that they would be properly armed and trained. Civil wars, such as Richard the Lionheart's revolt in 1189 against his dying father, Henry II, or territorial disputes in which barons held lands from both of the warring princes, forced tenants-in-chief and their subordinate tenants, those who held knight-fiefs from them, into a calculus of self-interest, the obligation to answer a feudal summons weighed against the likelihood of losing one's lands if one did so. Royal household knights and mercenaries presented none of these problems. Neither the self-interest nor loyalty of either group was divided. Although Machiavelli established a stereotype of the mercenary as unreliable and reluctant to fight, twelfth- and thirteenth-century mercenaries had a far better reputation, at least among those who hired them. Their paymasters could depend on their continued services as long as they received their promised wages. The well-trained, disciplined, and armed knights of the royal household provided the elite core of the royal army; they were the closest thing a king had to a standing army. The foot soldiers who comprised the rank and file of the mercenary companies were well suited for the ravaging and sieges that characterized warfare in the twelfth and succeeding two centuries. With the revenues raised from scutage Anglo-Norman and Angevin kings could purchase more reliable and flexible military forces. In this, at least, Oman was right.

Feudal service in France followed a similar path. But feudal service in the states of the Latin East remained a critical source of heavy cavalry, even if the fief in question came in the form of money rather than land.

Persistent Myths

As noted above, there is more than a kernel of truth in the related myths of feudalism and the feudal knight. To my mind, they who relegate feudalism to the dustbin of historiography and demote battle waged by mounted knights to a relatively insignificant element in medieval warfare overstate their cases. Brown and Reynolds were right to warn against the danger of mistaking the construct for reality and judging the actual social, political, and tenurial relationships in a particular society, whether medieval European or not, against an abstraction. An ideal construct only approximates reality. But if we keep this in mind, the Anglo-American model of feudalism remains a useful shorthand term to describe vertical social and political relations among the

---

63. See the essays collected in *Mercenaries and Paid Men*, in particular the contributions of David Crouch, John Hosler, I. W. Reynolds, and Laura Napran.

Horace Vernet's 1827 painting of the Battle of Bouvines (July 27, 1214), in which Philip II of France defeated forces led by Otto IV with mounted charges.

aristocracies of England and France from the mid-eleventh through thirteenth centuries (and of Germany in the thirteenth century).

Feudal service owed by landholders was never the sole mechanism for raising troops of knights in the Middle Ages. In the cases of England and France, it did not remain even the most important, if it had ever been. But the feudal relationship remained relevant to military history in the form of what historians have misleadingly called "bastard feudalism." Aristocratic society was bonded in late medieval England and France by a system of patronage in which personal loyalty and military service were secured by the payments of annuities rather than the granting of landed fiefs. Money-fiefs were not new; they can be found in twelfth- and thirteenth-century England and were regularly used in the states of the Latin East. But it was in the fourteenth and fifteenth centuries that they replaced the landed fief as the nexus between lords and their men. The affinity of a lord was created through contracts of indenture and proclaimed by the livery worn by a lord's retainers.

The duties of "bastard feudal" retainers were varied, as were the types of men retained. Indentured retainers could be called upon to serve as local officials, accompany the lord to tournaments or court, support him politically, and follow him to war. In exchange for loyalty and service, a retainer received "maintenance," which comprised not only the payment of an annuity but also the promise of "good lordship." A key element of maintenance was support in legal suits and in the retainer's disputes with neighbors and officials. The bodies of retainers of the greatest magnates were virtually private armies.[64] The royal armies of the Hundred Years' War were largely

64. K. B. McFarlane, "Bastard Feudalism," *Bulletin of the Institute of Historical Research* 20 (1943–45): 161–80; J. M. W. Bean, "Bachelor and Retainer," *Mediaevalia et Humanistica*, new series 3

raised on the basis of indentures between the upper nobility and the Crown, and the magnates who contracted with the king raised the agreed-on troops from their retainers. In this sense "bastard feudalism" became a mechanism for the recruitment of troops in the Late Middle Ages.

The role of the knight in medieval warfare in part depends on what one believes the role of battle to have been. I accept in its broad outlines Gillingham's Vegetian strategy thesis. Where I part ways from him is in his narrow definition of battle. Although major battles on the scale of Hastings in 1066, Bouvines in 1214, or Crécy in 1346 were rare, skirmishes and lesser engagements were common occurrences in medieval warfare. Most were chance encounters, and many arose in conjunction with sieges. But it is a mistake to believe that knights could only demonstrate their prowess in tournaments. As John France observed, "The actual experience of battle, of close-quarter fighting in small units, must have been common amongst the arms-bearers of medieval society."[65] There is also little doubt that an earlier generation of military historians insufficiently appreciated the importance of foot soldiers in European warfare in the eleventh through thirteenth centuries. Infantry may have gained in training and discipline in the fourteenth century, but they played a critical role in warfare in the preceding centuries. One can, however, both appreciate this and still accord knights a critical role in the warfare of the High Middle Ages. Most of these knights served in the retinues of lords. In that sense, we can call them "feudal." Whether that service arose from the holding of a knight's fee is far less certain.

(1972): 117–31; Bean, *Lord to Patron: Lordship in Late Medieval England* (Manchester, UK: Manchester University Press, 1989), 121–53; David Crouch, "Debate: Bastard Feudalism Revised," *Past and Present* 131 (1991): 165–77.

65. France, *Western Warfare*, 150.

4. Military Revolutions: An Academic Party Game

John France

> The language of revolution satisfies the inherent human desire for drama.
> —*John A. Lynn*[1]

A "military revolution" is a development in warfare so important and complex that it has wider effects in politics and society far beyond the conduct of war. By contrast it is possible to envisage a "revolution in military affairs" [RMA], a change which has substantial effects on military conduct, yet with no broader effect on society as a whole.[2] These definitions have the virtue of brevity, but readers will recognize problems here. The word "revolution" implies something that happens suddenly, interrupting and diverting the smooth flow of affairs. The Communist Revolution of 1917 was just such an event, yet it had deep roots going far back into Russian history. So, when does evolution become revolution? These inherent difficulties will become apparent as we consider particular events.

And a Word of Caution

Words have a life of their own quite apart from what they mean. "Revolution" conjures up a vision of excitement, turbulence, and violence: colors fly, soldiers march, and thrones topple at its very utterance. So any suggestion of a military revolution needs very careful scrutiny, especially as it is likely to have been employed by professional historians who have very good reasons for using such an exciting term. Good titles sell books, or at least are believed to. The scholarly kudos for inventing a widely used term like "Industrial Revolution" is enormous. No less than three military revolutions

---

1. John A. Lynn, "Forging the Western Army in Seventeenth-Century France," in *The Dynamics of Military Revolution, 1300–2050*, ed. M. Knox and W. Murray (Cambridge: Cambridge University Press, 2001), 35.

2. For a fine example of the distinction, see Clifford J. Rogers, "'As if a new sun had arisen': England's Fourteenth-Century RMA," in Knox and Murray, *Dynamics of Military Revolution*, 15–34.

have been posited in Greek history between the eighth and the third century BCE.[3] The sheer multiplication of suggested military revolutions is perhaps a warning. We should look critically at the notion that a military development or complex of military developments launched changes sufficiently radical to deserve the name of revolution. Inventing revolutions must not be allowed to become an academic party game; our notions of the past and how it worked is a serious matter and cannot be founded on arbitrary inventions designed to promote careers or sell books.

The Military Revolution

The general notion of an early modern military revolution was first suggested in 1955 by Michael Roberts. He was deeply impressed by the work of Maurice of Nassau and Gustavus Adolphus, who devised tactical formations for subdividing great armies into units that harnessed the firepower of musketeers and protected them with pikemen. This seemed to give a new importance to infantry and to reduce the role of cavalry.[4] In 1976, Geoffrey Parker moved the start date of the revolution backward to 1530 and suggested a different reason for the increase in numbers. When the French invaded Italy in 1494–98 they brought with them advanced cannon, like the surviving Neuchâtel guns of 1488, with a length-to-bore ratio of 40:1 and a much lighter structure. Integral trunnions anchored them in carriages with large wheels that made them much easier to move. These were highly successful in battering down the thin medieval walls of some Italian fortifications, causing immense consternation across a Europe where fortifications had long dominated warfare and acted as a brake on even the most successful campaigns.[5] However, Parker pointed out that very quickly defenders responded with a new kind of fortification, the *trace italienne*. In the new style fortifications were furnished with relatively low thick walls made of compounded earth whose sloping faces were covered with stone. On these were mounted heavy guns which could outrange those of the attacker.

As in the medieval world, such fortifications occupied strategic points and could not be bypassed. As a result, sieges once more became long and complex. They certainly involved much more technical expertise, notably in the calculation of ranges. But above all they demanded huge numbers of troops with consequent logistic demands on an enormous scale.

---

3. Kurt A. Raaflaub, "Archaic and Classical Greece," in *War and Society in the Ancient and Medieval Worlds*, ed. K. A. Raaflaub and N. Rosenstein (Cambridge, MA: Harvard University Press, 1999), 129.

4. Michael Roberts, "The Military Revolution, 1560–1660," *Essays in Swedish History* (Minneapolis, MN: Weidenfeld and Nicolson, 1967), 195–225.

5. Geoffrey Parker, "The 'Military Revolution, 1560–1660'—A Myth?" in *Spain and the Netherlands 1559–1659: Ten Studies* (London: Collins, 1979), 86–103.

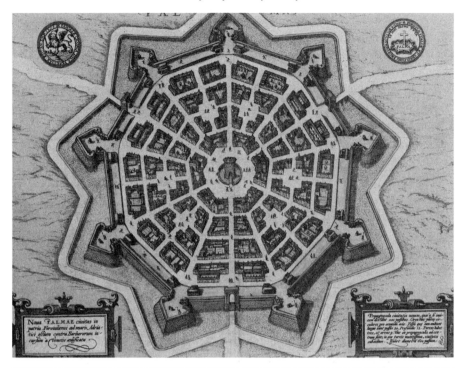

A 1593 rendering of the Italian city of Palmanova. Shown here is the manner of the *trace italienne* (or bastion fort), whose design brought changes in siege tactics, famously conceived by Sébastien Le Prestre de Vauban.

While Roberts and Parker differed in detail, they both agreed that these military changes produced new and bigger armies. Whereas medieval armies had been relatively small and depended on elite heavily armed and armored cavalry, the knights, now infantry became the dominant force. Moreover, the need to maneuver troops and to combine artillery with cavalry and infantry meant that armies became more coherent. Medieval monarchs had relied on their great subjects to supply the bulk of a large army which formed around a core of troops, often including mercenaries, who were especially the ruler's own. The result was composite armies with very uncertain chains of command because senior positions went to rank rather than competence.

This had enormous effects on society as a whole. The crippling cost of bigger armies with complex weapons could only be supported by sovereigns who could gather substantial taxes. They used their power to overawe recalcitrant nobles, to override representative institutions, and to establish centralized monarchies. This involved the creation of large bureaucracies and the displacement of nobles by professional advisers. In this way absolute monarchies were created. One might say, based on these ideas, that without the purported military revolution there would have been no Louis XIV. Hence military development changed the structure of European government and was truly revolutionary. In essence this "military revolution" was caused by the invention of new gunpowder weapons, whose expense and complex organizations needed complex state organizations to control and administer them.[6]

Criticism of the Military Revolution

There was always a certain looseness about applying the term "revolution" to such a complex process which was spread out over quite a long period of time, marked, at the very least, by the chronological differences between Roberts and Parker. And gunpowder was at the very heart of their ideas. It had been invented in China and appears to have been transmitted to Europe in the thirteenth century, a time when the Mongol Empire imposed a peace on the Asian landmass that facilitated long-distance contact. The Franciscan Roger Bacon recorded its makeup in 1267, and by the end of the century formulas suitable for use in guns were emerging.[7] The earliest European depiction of a gun is found in the Milemete manuscript of 1326.[8] There is considerable evidence for their use in the early fourteenth century, even perhaps at the Battle of Crécy in 1346.[9]

The "Medieval Military Revolution"

It was by no means true that war before 1500 was entirely dominated by mounted knights. At Legnano in 1176 the Milanese infantry in their camp fought off the German cavalry. Examples could be multiplied, for it had long been recognized as highly dangerous for cavalry to take on steady infantry especially if they were protected by ground. And in any case knights were not simply cavalrymen, for they were fully prepared to fight on foot.[10] Andrew Ayton and J. L. Price, in their *Medieval Military Revolution*, suggested that to some extent the developments embodied in the concept of the military revolution were rooted in the medieval past. Medieval kings relied on their nobles to bring contingents to their armies which were, therefore, composite forces not certainly under the control of the commander. However, in the fourteenth

---

6. By far the best introduction to the subject is Clifford J. Rogers, *The Military Revolution Debate: Readings on the Military Transformation of Early Modern Europe* (Boulder, CO: Westview, 1995).

7. Bert S. Hall, *Weapons and Warfare in Renaissance Europe* (Baltimore: Johns Hopkins University Press, 1997), 41–43.

8. M. A. Michael, "The Iconography of Kingship in the Walter of Milemete Treatise," *Journal of the Warburg and Courtauld Institutes* 57 (1994): 35–47.

9. Kelly DeVries and Robert Douglas Smith, *Medieval Military Technology*, 2nd ed. (Toronto: Toronto University Press, 2012), 138–40.

10. Stephen Morillo, "The 'Age of Cavalry' Revisited," in *The Circle of War in the Middle Ages*, ed. D. J. Kagay and L. J. A. Villalon (Woodbridge, UK: Boydell, 1999), 45–58.

century the emergence of the English longbowmen working in tandem with dismounted men-at-arms produced spectacular victories over French knightly forces, who were obliged to alter their tactics accordingly. Ayton's book demonstrated that by the sixteenth century systematic infantry tactics were emerging, at least in some armies, and the mounted knight was a component rather than the main striking force. Moreover, gunpowder weapons had a long history and sometimes armies were very large.[11] The notion of a medieval military revolution might be an overstatement, but clearly these considerations blurred the notion of a sharp change in the sixteenth century, helping to make the case for evolution rather than revolution in warfare.

But the most rigorous analysis of medieval military development is that of Clifford Rogers. He observed that English armies in the Hundred Years' War, like those of the sixteenth century, were raised by contract between the monarchy and its great men. The victories of the Flemish foot over French cavalry at Courtrai (1302), of the Scots over the English at Bannockburn (1314), the Swiss over the Hapsburgs at Mortgarten (1315) and Laupen (1339), and the English over the French at Crécy (1346) have been seen as an "infantry revolution." In addition, Rogers posited a medieval "artillery revolution" in the fifteenth century.[12] Rogers has also suggested that we need to think in terms of a "punctuated equilibrium evolution," which is "long periods of gradual incremental evolution punctuated by episodes of short, sharp, radical change" lasting from the fourteenth to the seventeenth century.[13] This idea points to change over a long period of time. But medievalists have not been the only people to criticize the idea of the military revolution.

The Nature of Armies

Fundamental to the ideas of Robert and Parker is the notion that the new weapons created more orderly and disciplined armies which replaced the heterogeneous composite forces of medieval times. The very acme of the truly modern army of the sixteenth century, which Parker brilliantly analyzed, was that of Spain.[14] However, more recent research has attacked this notion of centralized armies, which is so central to the idea of this military revolution. I. A. A. Thompson has suggested that far from being centralized, the Spanish army was increasingly run by great nobles, military

11. Andrew Ayton and J. L. Price, *The Medieval Military Revolution* (London: I. B. Tauris, 1998), especially the introduction, 1–17.

12. Clifford J. Rogers, "The Military Revolutions of the Hundred Years' War," *Journal of Military History* 57 (1993): 247–57 and 258–76.

13. Clifford J. Rogers, "Military Revolutions and 'Revolutions in Military Affairs': A Historian's Perspective," in *Toward a Revolution in Military Affairs: Defense and Security at the Dawn of the 21st Century*, ed. T. Gongora and H. von Riekhoff (Westport, CT: Greenwood, 2000), 21–36.

14. Geoffrey Parker, *The Army of Flanders and the Spanish Road* (Cambridge: Cambridge University Press, 1972).

contractors, and others, at the expense of central power.[15] Moreover, a similar picture of the French army has emerged. Precisely this kind of compromise, it has been suggested, underlay the magnificent and highly effective armies of Louis XIV.[16] David Parrott has posited that the French army flourished in the seventeenth century precisely because the monarchy worked with vested interests rather than trying to impose central authority upon them.[17] And Jeremy Black suggested that it was only with the rise of the socket bayonet that the nature of armies really changed. This apparently simple invention meant that armies could do away with masses of pikemen, whose task was to protect the slow-firing musketeers. As a result, armies were based on a single type of infantry who could be drilled and manipulated much more easily, giving rise to the characteristic tactics of eighteenth-century armies.[18] All this fundamentally challenges the idea of a revolution and points in the direction of military evolution.

Overseas Expansion

Integral to Parker's thinking was the idea that military developments, and especially ship-mounted cannon, enabled Europeans to dominate the world. But it was a very long time before European armies could rival the forces of the eastern empires in military effectiveness. The Ottomans arose from the Turkish dominance in the Middle East, and they were the greatest power in the Mediterranean from the fourteenth to almost the eighteenth century.[19] The Ming, who threw off the Mongol dominion, ruled over the richest economy in the world and maintained a formidable army and navy. China remained a great power capable of repulsing any foreign intervention well into the nineteenth century.[20] The Mughal Empire was established in India in 1526 by a dynasty from the southern steppe. In 1689, the British East India Company tried to expand its power around its base in Bombay but was brought to heel by a Mughal fleet that besieged the city.

These eastern powers were, however, tested by European sea power. Cannon were heavy and clumsy and therefore difficult to manipulate in land battle. But European shipping had developed remarkably in the late Middle Ages, and by the late fifteenth century it was recognized that the merchant ships that could face the rigors of the

---

15. I. A. A. Thompson, *War and Government in Hapsburg Spain* (London: Athlone, 1976).

16. Guy Rowlands, *The Dynastic State and the Army under Louis XIV: Royal Service and Private Interest, 1661–1701* (Cambridge: Cambridge University Press, 2001).

17. David Parrott, *Richelieu's Army: War, Government and Society in France, 1624–1642* (Cambridge: Cambridge University Press, 2001).

18. Jeremy Black, "A Military Revolution: A 1660–1792 Perspective," *Journal of Military History* 57 (1993): 241–78.

19. John France, *Perilous Glory: Understanding Western Military Power* (London: Yale University Press, 2011), 163–76.

20. See especially Tonio Andrade, *The Gunpowder Age: China, Military Innovation, and the Rise of the West in World History* (Princeton, NJ: Princeton University Press, 2106).

't Engels Comptoor op Bombaÿ.

An anonymous painting of the English fort in Mumbai, India. For the Mughal emperor, Admiral Sidi Yakut Khan besieged it on February 15, 1689, and eventually defeated its British East India Company garrison.

Atlantic were ideal platforms for cannon. Portuguese merchants, backed by their monarchy, explored the African coast and broke into the Indian Ocean. Their motives were truly mixed; at least in part they were on crusade seeking to outflank Islam. But the riches of the Far Eastern trade were a great draw, and the Portuguese quickly set out to exclude the Muslim merchants who had hitherto dominated this business. In 1509, the Portuguese defeated a Muslim coalition in the naval battle of Diu and so forced their way into the Indian Ocean and its trade. The broadsides of cannon were the key to this process, for no Eastern power had developed cannon in the same way as Europe. However, this situation was soon remedied, and though the Portuguese retained very important fortified bases they could not entirely cut out Muslim traders.[21]

---

21. William H. McNeil, "The Age of Gunpowder Empires," in *Islamic and European Expansion*, ed. M. Adas (Philadelphia: Temple, 1993), 103–41.

In China their effort to intimidate the Ming ended in defeat at Canton in 1522, for the Chinese quickly adopted cannon.[22] However, the Portuguese established a network of bases across the East and were quickly followed by the Dutch and later the English and French.

While military technology helped, the limited European success arose from essentially political developments. The Chinese, the Mughals, and the Persian Empire of the Safavids were relatively little interested in seaborne trade. The Ottomans did create a great fleet and enjoyed considerable success in the Mediterranean, but naval power in this inland sea was always supplementary to land-based military power. And the Ottomans were long preoccupied by the struggle with the Safavids, which limited their access to the Gulf and points east. So once the Europeans had developed the necessary maritime technology, they were pushing into a partial vacuum. And as time went on and the Atlantic economy developed in the seventeenth century, they could draw on new resources to sustain their fleets, but it is very notable that even then they were confined to coastal lodgments, unable to penetrate inland against resistance from the local powers. The scattering of bases that they did establish remained just that—marginal to the life of the area. Their significance has been magnified by later events in the eighteenth century when the inner decay of some Eastern regimes opened the way to conquest.[23]

The Myth of the Military Revolution?

In the light of the debate among historians, the revolution is rather difficult to pin down. There can be little doubt that between the late thirteenth and the late seventeenth centuries European warfare changed dramatically. But this was a very long period, and some of its developments were in progress even before that. So the real question is how appropriate is the term "revolution" to such a slow process—can we regard the military revolution as a myth? Well, European war changed relatively little before the thirteenth century in that it was largely a matter of clashes between masses of men, mounted or on foot, armed with edged weapons and fighting at close quarters, in which missiles generally played a minor role. It was this reality that gave fortifications their dominating role. Gunpowder had the potential to change that, but it was realized very slowly. Making the powder was expensive and difficult, while explosive power made enormous demands upon contemporary metallurgy. Integrating the new weapons, with all their limitations, into tactics took a very long time. But if we look at military history in the period from about 1300 to 1700, there is little doubt that the sixteenth century saw an acceleration in change, though this drew so heavily upon earlier developments that the term "revolution" seems like mythologizing. It

---

22. Andrade, *Gunpowder Age*, 125–31.
23. France, *Perilous Glory*, 205–9.

is, however, difficult to envisage a figure like the mathematician, engineer, and philosopher Simon Stevin (1548–1620) in any earlier age. He took a strong interest in matters military, and his writings and ideas had an enormous influence on Maurice of Nassau (1567–1625), who was famed for his systematic approach to military problems, especially siege.[24] So the sixteenth century saw an increase in the rate of change in military development, but the notion of a revolution perhaps sprang from the limited and often stereotyped knowledge of the medieval world among modernists.

However, this idea of a military revolution has, nonetheless, been extremely valuable. It has stimulated thinking about military matters. But far more importantly, Roberts and Parker understood and clearly articulated the way in which military development was central to the rise of the modern state.[25] This, of course, was a complex process to which many historical trends contributed. But war was always central to the governmental structures of medieval Europe; indeed, it was often seen as its main purpose. In the twelfth-century *Dialogue of the Exchequer*, the author instructs that "money is no less indispensable in peace than in war," going on to outline the main subjects of expenditure in both—but note that he assumes anybody can see that war costs money![26] The notion of the military revolution demonstrated how far concern with war helped to generate the new states of early modern Europe. Of course, there were other factors at work, but this idea of the military revolution stimulated debate about European state building. So while the military revolution per se is something of a myth, it is an idea that has proved enormously fruitful.

The French Revolution

There is no doubt that the French Revolution of 1789 had an enormous influence on the conduct of war, but to call it, as some have, a military revolution, is surely stretching the term beyond meaning.[27] The Revolution was intended to solve the problems of French government. In the process it created mass politics centered on national identity, which enabled government to mobilize society as never before and to project power in the form of huge armies.

---

24. Jozeph T. Devreese and Guido Vanden Berghe, *"Magic Is No Magic": The Wonderful World of Simon Stevin* (Southampton, UK: WIT Press, 2008); Geoffrey Parker, "The Limits to Revolutions in Military Affairs: Maurice of Nassau, the Battle of Nieuwpoort (1600), and the Legacy," *Journal of Military History* 71 (2007): 331–72.

25. On wider aspects, see Steven Gunn et al., "War and the State in Early Modern Europe: Widening the Debate," *War in History* 15 (2008): 371–88.

26. Richard FitzNeale, *Dialogus de Scaccario*, ed. C. Johnson et al. (Oxford: Clarendon, 1983), 2.

27. MacGregor Knox and Williamson Murray, "Thinking about Revolutions in Warfare," in *Dynamics of Military Revolution*, 6 and 8–9.

Louis-Léopold Boilly's 1808 painting, "Departure of the Conscripts, 1807." The *Levée en masse*, or national conscription in France, is thought to have brought about revolutionary change in how wars were fought.

This was the root of the spirit that Carl von Clausewitz, who had witnessed the destruction of his own Prussian army at Jena in 1806, so admired in a passage more prophetic than accurate:

> Suddenly war again became the business of the people. . . . The people became a participant in war; instead of governments and armies as heretofore.[28]

But while it is true that the Revolution fostered a spirit of nationalism, it would be naïve to believe that French military success simply rested upon enthusiasm. When France provoked war in Europe there was a rush of volunteers to defend the new republic. But by the time the famous and stirring *La Marseillaise* was written in 1792, volunteers had deserted at the prospect of contact with the enemy. Then 1793 saw the introduction of conscription, the instrument of the monarchies of Prussia and Austria that revolutionaries so despised, with all its inequities and its apparatus of enforcement.[29] There was much rhetoric of national enthusiasm, but conscription was not

---

28. Carl von Clausewitz, *On War*, ed. and trans. M. Howard and P. Paret (Princeton, NJ: Princeton University Press, 1989), 592.

29. French conscription resembled the coercive recruitment methods of the monarchies who opposed it, as noted by Hew Strachan, *European Armies and the Conduct of War* (London: Routledge, 2004), 108.

popular. When the young Napoleon took over the army of Italy in 1796, his appeal to the troops rested on the rather more traditional incentive of loot:

> Soldiers! You are hungry and naked; the government owes you much but can give you nothing. I will lead you into the most fertile plains on earth. Rich provinces, opulent towns, all shall be at your disposal; there you will find honour, glory and riches. Soldiers of Italy! Will you be lacking in courage or endurance?[30]

Napoleon inherited conscription, but he preferred to keep men with the colors for long periods of time so that they became experienced soldiers. What really gave his army its coherence and cutting edge was that the Revolution swept away the system of noble preferment and opened the highest ranks of the army to talent. F. J. Lefebvre joined the royal army in 1763, rising to the rank of sergeant by 1789. But by 1793 he was a brigadier-general and in 1804 became one of Napoleon's Marshals, ultimately receiving the title of Duke of Dantick, which he retained after Napoleon's fall.[31] He had risen from obscurity to become one of the "Swords around the Throne," epitomizing the opportunities that inspired French officers in this period, and made them not merely gallant but efficient.[32] Napoleon believed in discipline and training, and these men were ready to drill and lead their soldiers in pursuit of their own ambitions.

However, as casualties mounted after 1807, Napoleon relied more and more on raw recruits and levies drawn from client states, diluting the quality of his army. Moreover, the Revolutionary and Napoleonic armies inherited the standardized artillery of the ancien régime, along with new ideas about tactics, in particular skirmishing and attacks in column. To cope with larger armies the French divided their armies into corps, which were big enough to fight and yet could forage for themselves without relying on clumsy logistic trains. They were managed by a large staff around Napoleon, but each was commanded by a general who knew his mind. None of this was entirely new, but it became systematized through the genius of Napoleon, who made it work brilliantly.[33] But in the end Napoleon was defeated by traditional armies led by men who copied his methods but were horrified by the genie of nationalism and in 1815 devised a peace intended to bottle it up.

---

30. John A. Lynn, "Nations in Arms, 1763–1815," in *The Cambridge History of Warfare*, ed. G. Parker (Cambridge: Cambridge University Press, 2005), 200. There is some doubt as to whether Napoleon ever made this speech in quite this form, which was designed to exaggerate the poor state of the army of Italy.

31. *Biographie nouvelles des contemporains* (Paris: de Plassan, 1820), 159.

32. Phrase taken from a study of the marshals of Napoleon: John R. Elting, *Swords around a Throne: Napoleon's Grande Armée* (London: Weidenfeld and Nicolson, 1989).

33. Such ideas had been explored by French reformers, notably Count de Guibert, some of whom are translated into English in Beatrice Heuser, *The Strategy Makers: Thoughts on War and Society from Machiavelli to Clausewitz* (Santa Monica, CA: Greenwood, 2010), 147–70.

The True Military Revolution

We have become so accustomed to the application of science to warfare that it is difficult to appreciate the enormous and sudden impact of the changes in warfare in the later nineteenth century. Up to then men advanced to battle in close-order mass formations, in which each man could aid his fellows and provide psychological support for the supreme violence of close-quarter fighting. Before firearms the limitations of edged weapons meant that all fighting, on foot or horseback, was essentially like this—in close order at close quarters. Gunpowder made only limited impact on this basic reality of war. The muskets of eighteenth-century soldiers were very slow to load and very inaccurate, so that infantry warfare focused on close-order maneuver and a discharge of weapons at something like fifty to sixty meters: volley fire compensated for slow loading and inaccuracy. But edged weapons remained important: muskets were long because once mounted with a bayonet they formed pikes. Artillery could devastate such close formations, but it was heavy, slow-loading, and vulnerable to counterbattery attack. The application of science changed this style of war, and changed it with such revolutionary speed that it outpaced popular and even professional understanding of war.

The development of science and its application to war was no sudden invention of the nineteenth century. The monarchies of eighteenth-century Europe established academies to train officers. In England the Royal Military Academy began in 1741, while Napoleon was educated at a French equivalent at Brienne-le-Château.[34] An obvious landmark in military science came with the publication of Benjamin Robins's *New Principles of Gunnery* which enjoyed an astounding Europe-wide success.[35] The new precision that Robins's ideas offered was made possible by improvements in casting and boring cannon developed by the Swiss engineer Jean Maritz (1680–1743).[36]

But by the early nineteenth century, industrial development was accelerating and increasing the supply of metals for weapons and of textiles for uniforms. In 1809, a Frenchman, Nicolas Appert, invented a means of preserving food in bottles, and a few years later the tinning process was developed in Britain, where its main use was feeding troops. The railway enabled soldiers to be moved rapidly without exhausting them and their animals. Better metallurgy led to the production of new weapons, notably the rifled musket exemplified by the British Enfield of 1853 and the American Springfield of 1855. Rifling increased range and made these rather more accurate than their smoothbore predecessors, while ignition by percussion cap made them more reliable and somewhat quicker to load. Cannons largely remained smoothbore, but the US 12-pounder Napoleon Model 1857 was very reliable, relatively light, and

---

34. Andrew Roberts, *Napoleon: A Life* (London: Penguin, 2014), xvi.

35. Benjamin Robins, *New Principles of Gunnery* (London: Richmond, 1972).

36. William H. McNeill, *The Pursuit of Power: Technology, Armed Force, and Society since AD 1000* (Chicago: Chicago University Press, 1982), 166–67.

mobile. It had a range of over a mile and could fire a variety of munitions so it was highly suitable for deployment in battle.[37]

Convergent with these new technical developments was the legacy of the French Revolution. The 1848 revolutions broke the resistance of European governments to nationalism, the fruit of the French Revolution, which was now increasingly unleashed. In the name of the nation, states could call all suitable young men to the ranks, making possible mass armies. What this meant was illustrated by the American Civil War. This saw whole societies mobilized for war using the very latest devices of industrial society like the Morse telegraph system invented in 1844. After their defeat at Chickamauga by the Confederates on September 18–20, 1863, the Northern commanders moved twenty thousand men and their equipment by rail from Virginia to Chattanooga in eleven days, a feat not equaled until the twentieth century. European powers were much impressed by the logistical support provided for the Northern armies. At Hampton Roads in 1862, the *Virginia* and the *Monitor* fought out the first battle between ironclads, though two years before the British had launched the steam-driven iron ship, the HMS *Warrior*. A Prussian observer of the land war, Justus Scheibert, noted the new firepower and its effect on armies: "From the chaos . . . infantry tactics developed clear and sharp. Both sides adopted them. They deserve our attention."[38] The war accelerated weapons development. Rifled cannon came into increasing use, and the Spencer repeating rifle was adopted by the US cavalry. Most ominous of all was the development of a primitive machine gun, the Gatling, whose inventor thought this mechanical weapon would dispense with the need for large armies and so reduce casualties.[39]

If the rate of military change between the fourteenth and eighteenth centuries can be reasonably described in Roger's terms as "punctuated equilibrium evolution," after 1850 it can only be described as fugal. Breech-loading rifles were adopted by all the European powers in the 1860s, while by the 1870s breech-loading cannon, like the French Reffye 85 mm, were becoming common. Cheap steel, which was the basic stuff of the Second Industrial Revolution, replaced iron and bronze in weapons because it could be worked to fine tolerances. A key development was the invention by the French in 1884 of Poudre B, a smokeless explosive. Gunpowder burns with great clouds of smoke, clearly revealing the position of its firer and obscuring his vision. Equally importantly, it leaves heavy solid deposits on weapons, making smooth operation difficult. The new steel and powders enabled the European powers in the 1890s to build a generation of magazine rifles that would serve them until the 1950s, increasing infantry firepower on the battlefield enormously. In 1914, a British army sergeant-instructor

37. Philip R. N. Katcher, *American Civil War Artillery 1861–65 (1): Field Artillery* (Oxford: Osprey, 2001).

38. *A Prussian Observes the American Civil War: The Military Studies of Justus Scheibert,* ed. F. Trautman (Columbia: University of Missouri Press, 2001), 34.

39. Paul Whal and Don R. Toppel, *The Gatling Gun* (New York: Arco, 1965), 12.

using the Lee-Enfield magazine rifle in one minute fired thirty-eight rounds into a twelve-inch target at three hundred yards. But the most significant consequence of the invention of smokeless powder for small arms was the machine gun, invented by Hiram Maxim in London in 1884.

The idea of using recoil to load and fire was not new, but it was made practical by smokeless powder. It was generally considered to provide the firepower of twenty infantrymen. The British were early adopters because they considered it a useful force multiplier for their small army in colonial wars.[40]

Small-arms development was matched by improvements in artillery. Steel could be finely machined

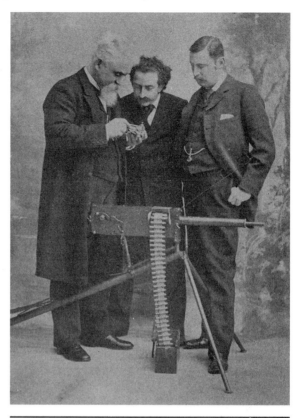

Inventor Hiram Stevens Maxim with his machine gun. Firing nearly six hundred rounds a minute but requiring a team of men to move and operate, it was the first recoil-operated weapon put into general use.

so that guns were stronger and lighter and employed sophisticated breach-loading mechanisms. Smokeless powder made cannon more efficient. The science of optics improved range finding and, therefore, accuracy. But the key problem was recoil: every time a gun was fired it had to be relayed on its target. In 1896, the French adopted a new field gun, the Puteaux 75 mm, the famous *soixante-quinze*, which incorporated a lightweight hydraulic recoil mechanism and used self-contained cartridges that were ejected by opening the breech. It was equipped with its own sight, an automatic fuse setter to determine the range at which the shell would explode, and a nickel-steel shield to protect the crew. The weapon could fire twenty shots per minute in its famous *rafale* ("gust of wind," a progressive fire system). Little wonder that it was revered as "God the Father, God the Son, and God the Holy Ghost." But in the close country of Western Europe, fortifications were formidable and as a result

40. Strachan, *European Armies and the Conduct of War*, 113–14.

immense siege guns were developed, using indirect fire to destroy trenches and concrete emplacements.[41]

By the 1860s, European soldiers understood that radical changes in tactics were needed. A French military thinker, Ardant du Picq, perceived that the day of close-order battle was over, noting that "ancient combat was fought in groups close together . . . the surveillance of leaders was easy."[42] He argued for open and flexible formations in the face of increased firepower. The Prussian Helmuth von Moltke the Elder developed this into a doctrine of war later called mission tactics (*Auftragstaktik*), under which subordinate officers, even down to platoon level, were instructed in the intentions of the overall commander, but left to find their own way of achieving this end:

> Diverse are the situations under which an officer has to act on the basis of his own view of the situation. It would be wrong if he had to wait for orders at times when no orders can be given. But most productive are his actions when he acts within the framework of his senior commander's intent.[43]

Although all armies accepted the need for such change, it seemed to generals that breaking down formations into small groups would nullify the force and impact of attack. In addition, commanders disliked the idea of trusting juniors to this extent, and this slowed the adoption of such tactics. But the impact of the new firepower forced soldiers to examine their tactical ideas, and even to debate them in public.

And the pace of change was relentless. In 1896, Marconi patented his radio communication system, which promised a new method of controlling forces, though installations were big and clumsy. In 1903, the Wright brothers tested the first heavier-than-air flying machine.[44] Although it was not immediately apparent, this opened the way for three-dimensional warfare. In 1905, the Russo-Japanese war tested virtually all of the tool kit of industrial killing, which the world would witness on a larger scale in 1914. At the siege of Port Arthur the Japanese attacked machine guns in concrete emplacements behind barbed wire. Both sides used searchlights at night and radio and even radio interception. Firepower inflicted terrible casualties, and it was the employment of 28 cm (eleven-inch) Krupp howitzers that finally overcame the Russian defenses.[45] But perhaps the best illustration of the revolutionary speed of

---

41. "Artillery," in *The Oxford Companion to Military History*, ed. R. Holmes (Oxford: Oxford University Press, 2001), 92–98.

42. Ardant du Picq, *Battle Studies: Ancient and Modern Battle*, in *Roots of Strategy 2*, ed. S. Brooks (Mechanicsburg, PA: Stackpole, 1987), 124, 128, 196, and 253.

43. R. R. Davis, "Helmuth von Moltke and the Prussian-German Development of a Decentralised Style of Command: Metz and Sedan 1870," *Defence Studies* 5 (2005): 84.

44. Walter J. Boyne, *The Influence of Air Power upon History* (Gretna, LA: Pelican, 2003), 21–46.

45. "Port Arthur," in *Oxford Companion to Military History*, 732.

development of weaponry in the later nineteenth century was at sea. In 1897, the first practical submarine, the *Holland VI* powered by petrol-electric engines, was launched in New Jersey opening the way for three-dimensional naval warfare. In 1854, Britain went to war against Russia with a fleet of "wooden walls." In 1906, she launched HMS *Dreadnought*, a steel battleship of 17,900 tons capable of 21.6 knots and carrying ten twelve-inch guns with ranges of over 12,000 meters. The science of hydraulics, which governed the movement of her guns, and optics, which made it possible to aim them, barely existed a hundred years before.[46]

Perceiving the Revolution

The scale and importance of military development in the later nineteenth century were, to a degree, concealed from contemporaries. They certainly recognized that huge changes had taken place. The railway now dominated European strategy, while it was obvious that close order for battle was doomed by the new firepower, and the increasing weight and accuracy of artillery was a challenge to fortifications. But this was an optimistic age, and for Europe as a whole the new weaponry seemed part of the miraculous scientific development growth that characterized the Industrial Revolution. This new equipment underlined the world supremacy of the European powers, which was possible because of the decay of the Eastern empires of the Ottomans and Manchu China. They could bask in the worldwide "civilizing mission of colonialism," which their new weapons so facilitated. In Europe itself the Schleswig-Holstein Conflict (1864) and the Austro-Prussian (1866) and Franco Prussian Wars (1870–71), which made possible a united German Empire, seemed to have solved European problems without undue threats to the stability of the continent.[47] But, in fact, the new developments had far-reaching effects on society, creating a true military revolution.

Very quickly the impact of growing militarization of European society became disquieting. The French Revolution had proclaimed the rights of the citizen and his duty to defend the community of citizens. After the revolutions of 1848 nationalism seemed to offer opportunities to expand armies, and German unification pointed to the rewards of doing so. As a result, conscription was widely introduced after 1870, so that collectively France, Germany, Italy, Russia, and Austro-Hungary doubled their numbers of soldiers. By 1914, the French and the Germans each had 800,000 men, and the Russians 1,300,000 under arms.[48] These huge standing forces were backed up by immense numbers of reservists who were kept in part-time military training

---

46. David K. Brown, *Warrior to Dreadnought: Warship Development, 1860–1905* (London: Caxton, 2003).

47. Dennis Showalter, *The Wars of German Unification* (London: Bloomsbury, 2004).

48. Strachan, *European Armies and the Conduct of War*, 108.

and could be called up as needed. To support these forces states constructed complex bureaucracies and imposed taxes on their citizens. The enormous fabric of the modern state was being built, and liberal-thinking people began to see juggernauts arising that threatened freedom. Society was, indeed, being militarized. More subtly, states offloaded the costs of research and development.

In 1849, the Prussian "Cannon King" Alfred Krupp delivered an all-steel breach-loading cannon to the Prussian army, only for it to be left out in the rain to rust for nearly two years. But he exhibited it at the London Great Exhibition in 1851, evoking international admiration. Thereafter the Krupp enterprise at Essen dominated the manufacture of arms in Germany. In France there were state arsenals, but the vast private business of Schneider at St. Etienne became the vital developer and supplier of weapons to the French forces. In Britain the Woolwich arsenal continued, but the biggest manufacturer of military hardware was Armstrong on the Tyne—later Vickers-Armstrong. In the United States private firms like Colt, Smith and Wesson, and Winchester were major innovators and producers of weapons. The result of this was huge numbers of people, shareholders and workers, with a vested interest in the arms trade. These were the first military-industrial complexes, creating an intimate link between business, the military, and the bureaucracy created to support it.[49]

The internal politics of the European powers created a range of tensions. National leaderships were challenged by the new ideologies of socialism. Industrial growth needed an educated workforce and created the means to achieve this. But increasing prosperity and greater education fostered discontent. Broadly socialist ideas and organizations spread and were perceived by governments as a threat to the status quo. As a result, governments unleashed storms of nationalist propaganda, in which they were able to use the mass newspapers, a powerful phenomenon of the late nineteenth century. Violent nationalist propaganda directed against the left was especially notable in Germany, where the largest social democratic party, the SPD, was for a long time banned.[50] In 1907, Karl Liebknecht was charged with treason because he published *Militarism and Anti-Militarism*.[51] Patriotic societies raised the temperature all over Europe, and such propaganda tended to highlight the enemies both within and without.

The tensions within and between these well-armed powers aroused considerable apprehension. Germany feared French revanchism and, envious of Britain, wanted

---

49. World War I created a violent reaction against what had come to be called the "merchants of death": H. C. Engelbrecht and F. C. Hanighen, *Merchants of Death: A Study of the International Armament Industry* (New York: von Mises, 1934). On evolving attitudes, invoking the notion of the military industrial complex, see Robert H. Ferrill, "The Merchants of Death, Then and Now," *Journal of International Affairs* 26 (1972): 29–39.

50. Gary P. Steenson, *"Not One Man! Not One Penny!" German Social Democracy, 1863–1914* (Pittsburgh, PA: Pittsburgh University Press, 1981).

51. Karl Liebknecht, *Militarism and Anti-Militarism* (Cambridge: Rivers Press, 1973).

a share of the wider world. Italy resented continued Hapsburg control of parts of the peninsula. Russia encouraged nationalist movements in the polyglot Hapsburg Empire and among the people of the Ottoman Empire, whose demise seemed imminent. The vast militarization of European societies and the obvious risks of war between them provoked a peace movement that was highly variegated.[52] At one level it became intimately associated with the broadly socialist movements. This had the perverse effect of embittering patriots, aided and abetted by governments, against them and deepening internal divisions. On the other hand, attempts to limit the likely horrors of war enjoyed great support among the upper and middle classes. The Red Cross, founded in 1859, had already achieved the Geneva Convention of 1864, and this was reinforced by the Hague Conventions of 1899 and 1907.[53]

Jan S. Bloch's *La guerre future* of 1898, translated into many languages, was immensely influential in bringing about the Hague Conventions. Bloch argued that defensive firepower had become so intense that any war between modern states would simply result in a bloody stalemate. Moreover, he thought the world was so interdependent that the disruption of trade and finance would impoverish states and produce collapse if they persisted in seeking to end it. Yet, perversely, even this argument for peace was in a sense counterproductive.

Senior officers of all nations were aware that firepower could turn war into stalemate, so they planned for a war which, although bloody, would at least be quick. Count Alfred von Schlieffen, chief of the Imperial General Staff from 1891 to 1905, understood clearly the terrible risks of deadlock. Commenting on the Russo-Japanese War he remarked:

> Out there in Manchuria they may face each other for months on end in impregnable positions. In Western Europe we cannot allow ourselves the luxury of waging war in this manner. The machine with a thousand wheels, upon which millions depend for their livelihood, cannot stand still for long. . . . We must try to overthrow the enemy quickly and then destroy him.[54]

To avoid a war of attrition Schlieffen argued for rapid flanking movements that would avoid fortified zones and punch through enemy lines. All the European military chiefs came to much the same conclusion. In 1914, France, Germany, and Russia implemented sweeping offensive plans designed to win quickly. All failed and produced the war of attrition that Bloch had prophesied.[55]

---

52. Martin Ceadel, *Semi-Detached Idealists: The British Peace Movement and International Relations, 1854–1945* (Oxford: Oxford University Press, 2000).

53. Stephen C. Neff, *War and the Law of Nations* (Cambridge: Cambridge University Press, 2007).

54. Quoted in Gerd Hardach, *The First World War, 1914–1918* (Berkeley: University of California Press, 1977), 55.

55. Strachan, *European Armies and the Conduct of War*, 130–39.

What Bloch had not foreseen was the sheer resilience of the modern state and its ability to sustain the war of attrition beyond all expectation. This involved the exploitation of all possible resources and immense control over populations in a conflict in which production was paramount. Total mobilization of the populations of the competing powers to produce the means to fight and sustain armies was made possible by propaganda and the assumption of immense directing powers by the organs of the state. War was now three dimensional, with the deployment of airplanes and submarines. New weapons were developed, notably gas and the tank, while at the front every effort was made to improve tactics. But ultimately this was a war of attrition. Under its immense weight Russia collapsed in 1917, and Germany in 1918. These were the fruits of the military revolution of the late nineteenth century. Abrupt and unprecedented military development could only be supported by increasingly militarized states capable of exerting enormous control over their populations. The military revolution engendered and formed the dictatorships that dominated Europe after the First World War.

Toward World War II

After 1919, it was apparent to the participants, as they considered the lessons of the conflict, that war had become three dimensional and that success rested on the coordination of all arms, for which communication was key. The result was a new focus on radio out of which arose, by the early 1930s, radar, which was seen as vital in an age when airplanes were increasing in speed, size, and lethality. The tank was clearly vital on the battlefield, and it was a real turning point when in 1923 the British Vickers Tank reached 20 mph. The dependability of the internal combustion engine was vital for tanks and also for transport and logistics. The toolbox for World War II was very much a development of existing technologies. There was no military revolution between the wars, but in one vital respect the working through of the consequences of the late nineteenth century had made itself felt.

The trend of military thinking in the eighteenth century had been to isolate the civilian population from war. This was never perfect. In 1704, Marlborough savagely ravaged Bavaria in an attempt to force its duke out of the war, while French armies often plundered appallingly during the revolutionary and Napoleonic Wars. But broadly the notion of separating soldier and civilian continued and was a central plank of the thinking that produced the Hague Conventions. But the claims of the modern state to enroll all its citizens in supporting war undermined this separation. In the great conflict of attrition, 1914–18, the woman rolling ammunition became as vital to the overall effort as the soldier at the front line. The full logic of that was realized by the German Zeppelin and, later, bomber raids on Britain, which made producers, like soldiers, targets in the struggle. The British naval blockade of Germany had much the same effect, starving civilians and soldiers alike.

In this context it is important to understand that there are three modes of war: battle, siege, and devastation—economic warfare that strikes at the mass of the population. The effects of the nineteenth century military revolution were to make war continuous battle and to make battle closely resemble siege. But historically the most common mode has always been devastation because it is easier and less risky (bullying peasants is safer than fighting soldiers) than the others. The eighteenth century had attempted to minimize economic warfare and to separate military personnel and civilians. The military revolution sharply reversed this process because the link between factory and front line became very apparent.

In the 1920s and 1930s, the development of airpower intensified this reversal, and the idea grew that civilian life would be targeted because it generated the means by which armies, navies, and air forces were sustained. Devastating air attack, it was believed, would not merely destroy material things, but break the will to war of the enemy. Britain and the United States saw in this new extent of airpower the means to fight enemies without the extraordinary bloodshed of World War I and devoted huge resources to strategic air forces. Their purpose in World War II was not always terror, but even when specific military targets were intended, the means to hit them were so crude that civilian casualties were inevitable. It is generally calculated that some 30,000 French civilians died in the bombing that backed up the Normandy landings of 1944.[56] This inevitably blunted the perception of cruelty, and it penetrated popular culture, leading to the broad acceptance of the consequences of violence. The atomic bombs dropped on Japan in 1945 have often been hailed as introducing a new military revolution, but can also be seen as the ultimate form of indiscriminate attack on "enemy" targets. Giulio Douhet, in a work of 1921, argued that air attack in itself was revolutionary because it created a new dimension of warfare that would relegate armies and navies to secondary forces, and he had numerous disciples, notably in the British and US air forces.[57] But this was not a revolution, for devastation and its accompanying terror were as old as war itself—all that was new was the means. And, of course, he was wrong. Airpower alone has not won wars.[58]

A Nuclear Revolution

This great revolution arose from pure scientific research in nuclear fission. The possibility of releasing extraordinary amounts of energy from the atom became apparent

---

56. Richard Overy, *The Bombing War: Europe, 1939–1945* (London: Penguin, 2014); Steven Borque, *Beyond the Beach: The Allied War against France* (Annapolis, MD: Naval Institute Press, 2018).

57. Giulio Douhet, *Command of the Air*, trans. D. Ferrari (Washington, DC: Air Force History and Museums Program, 1998); for Douhet's influence, see David MacIsaac, "Voices from the Central Blue: The Air Power Theorists," in *Makers of Modern Strategy: From Machiavelli to the Nuclear Age*, ed. P. Paret et al. (Princeton, NJ: Princeton University Press, 1986), 624–47.

58. See Chapter 5 in this volume, by John Curatola.

in the late nineteenth century, and it fairly quickly raised the prospect of application to weapons. H. G. Wells, in his 1914 novel *The World Set Free*, suggested a new kind of bomb arising from this kind of work. Research reached fruition in the American Manhattan Project. Very quickly, as Japan capitulated after the nuclear destruction of Hiroshima and Nagasaki on August 6 and 9, 1945, people began to see that this marked a revolution in human affairs, a true "military revolution."

After 1945, the world divided between the USSR and "the West"—principally the United States—and both sides acquired nuclear weapons. The prospect of mankind destroying itself became real. By the 1960s, the idea of mutually assured destruction (MAD) created an extraordinary military situation. Both sides feared to resort to open war for fear of annihilation. There was, however, no peace because all over the world there were proxy battles, in the Middle East, South America, South Africa, and, most obviously, in Vietnam. Although these conflicts were seen in terms of the superpower/ideological confrontation, local matters were at stake with which the United States and the USSR had to come to terms. Both great powers felt enormous political pressures in different ways. In the democratic countries aligned to the United States, public anxiety manifested itself in protests which, in the United States itself, reached a peak in the Vietnam War. In the USSR, the economy creaked and ultimately collapsed under the pressures of sustaining weapons and political support. Nuclear fission, although it had not produced a nuclear war, had produced a military revolution that, acting with a great complex of factors, had created a new world order.

And that order has yet to change fundamentally. There are now more nuclear players than ever before, but the prospects of MAD remain a deterrent to using this armory. The nuclear deadlock has made room for the emergence of new forces like militant Islamic groups that aim to take over states. The great powers use semi-independent agencies whose actions are "deniable." Blackwater (now, Academi) is seen as acting for the United States, while the Wagner Group plays a similar role for Russia. The world's dependence on digital technology means that attacks on infrastructure can be launched and denied with relative ease. The Russian Business Federation is one such group close to the Russian state and is suspected of massive interference across the internet. In Hainan, the Chinese People's Liberation Army is suspected of the same.

In 1991, the world hailed a revolution in military affairs as the United States swept to victory in the Gulf War by deploying "smart bombs" dropped by "stealth" aircraft. Underlying this was the digital technology that enabled all weapons to hit their targets with unprecedented accuracy, and directed troops in complex maneuvers. The sheer scale of the US military establishment seemed to betoken a world domination, to show the way ahead for all powers. But on 9/11 four airliners were hijacked and three crashed into the World Trade Center and the Pentagon using nothing more advanced than box cutters. The world's greatest military power invaded Afghanistan in 2001 and Iraq in 2003, but despite all the advantages of missiles, radar, and aircraft has not enjoyed decisive victory. In the hands of guerilla groups, improvised explosive devices (IEDs) and cheap drones are proving deadly weapons. Yet all these are made possible by the nuclear deadlock. If that should be broken, the world will be on the edge of a new military revolution.

Summary

To an absurd extent the cannons and arquebuses of sixteenth-century armies have been credited with creating a military revolution. They have even been seen as establishing a new world order in which Europe rose to commanding heights. This Eurocentric perspective is a terrible distortion: the reality was that Europe was catching up in governmental sophistication and consequent military competence. What began as a stimulating new idea has atrophied into a convenient myth that can be used for a whole host of purposes. These changes in human society arose from a long evolution and, above all, the development of the state. As a modern scholar has remarked, "One does not safely bet against continuity in history."[59]

There have been only two military revolutions with shockingly profound effects on society and politics. In the later nineteenth century, technological development suddenly accelerated. In about fifty years the technological, strategic, and tactical basis of the industrial warfare of 1914–18 and 1939–45 was created with such profound effects that it can only be regarded as a military revolution that changed entire societies. During World War II, research consciously devoted to military ends then produced the nuclear bomb, and that brought in its train new forms of delivery systems. This created a new world order with which we are living to this day.

---

59. Thomas N. Bisson, "The Feudal Revolution," *Past and Present* 142 (1994): 9.

5. STRATEGIC AIR POWER: AN ELEGANT IDEA FALLEN SHORT

John Curatola

[A] more gigantic waste of effort and personnel there has never been in any war.
—*Marshal Hugh Montague Trenchard, "Father of the Royal Air Force"*[1]

With the advent of powered flight, arguably no innovation has had such an effect on modern warfare as the airplane. While extended-range artillery, automatic weapons, and armored vehicles/tanks, along with other technologies, could lay claim to the same effect, the use of airplanes and application of airpower significantly changed the entire calculus of war. Although many saw limited military utility for airplanes before World War I, that global conflagration provided ample opportunity for aviation to prove its role as an effective weapon. Echoing this sentiment, before the war Field Marshal Ferdinand Foch of France held airplanes in little military regard and quipped, "Aviation is fine as a sport, but as an instrument of war, it's worth zero."[2] While Foch's statement is obviously erroneous and truly lacked vision, the idea of aerial strategic bombardment is a concept that has yet to truly fulfill its promise. Even when the Royal Air Force initiated such operations during the World War, Hugh Trenchard initially placed little faith in the application.[3]

Despite these initial beliefs, the idea that strategic bombing could bring about capitulation of the enemy has been a persistent myth of airpower advocates for decades. While winning a war by bombing factories, cities, and infrastructure indeed has utility, in various applications this concept has fallen short. As a result, the idea that strategic bombing can ensure a victory through use of this form of airpower is more myth than manifestation.

---

1. Quoted in Christopher Clark, "Air Power Finds Its Ascendency at Last," in *Imponderable but Not Inevitable: Warfare in the 20th Century*, ed. M. Murfett (Santa Barbara, CA: ABC CLIO, 2010), 110; Communique to All Personnel of the Independent Force, 11 Nov. 1918, The British National Archive, AIR 1/2085 as referenced in Richard Overy, *The Birth of the RAF*, 1918 (London: Random House, 2018), 76.

2. Steven Budiansky, *Air Power: The Men, Machines, and Ideas That Revolutionized War from Kitty Hawk to Iraq* (New York: Penguin, 2004), 47.

3. During the interwar years, Trenchard would eventually change his mind and become an advocate of strategic bombing for the Royal Air Force.

Powered flight grew out of the technological innovations that emerged from the Industrial Revolution in the waning days of the nineteenth century. Leading economies during the Gilded Age increasingly accepted technological advancement as a way to solve problems and advance the human condition. In this regard, the United States was, and still is, a nation that embraces technology and innovation. One of the first countries to leverage the telegraph, railroads, assembly line production, atomic energy, and space travel, America has a strong history of mechanical infatuation. As the country entered the new millennium, Americans increasingly saw technology as representing the optimistic forward march of civilization.[4] In this light, aviation too served to excite Americans about the future and humanity's progress as it entered the twentieth century.[5]

Part of the conceptual beginnings of strategic bombing came as an alternative to the static trench warfare so characteristic of World War I's Western Front. Using the third dimension for more than just artillery and observation, aviation was a way to re-introduce maneuver on the battlefield while overcoming the deadly slog of crossing "No Man's Land." In this manner the concept offered a new form of warfare that might prevent a repeat of the horrors of World War I and potentially make other forms of warfare obsolete.

Many also saw the concept as "victory on the cheap." Not only did the idea appear inexpensive in terms of manpower, but as aviation technology grew, airplanes and their deadly payloads offered the promise of considerable firepower at great speed and flexibility, at a relatively cheap cost.[6] The economy of airpower was an especially attractive attribute during the interwar years and after 1945, when defense budgets were limited and anti-military sentiment prevailed.

Not only did airplanes have a utility on the battlefield, but the allure of flight and the casting of World War I pilots as "knights of the air" provided a romantic, albeit inaccurate, portrayal of air combat.[7] In the 1920s and 1930s, aviation and airpower captured the public imagination as air races and aviation-record-setting events were popular, with planes and pilots pushing the limits of the new technology. During World War II the feats of the US Army Air Forces (USAAF), especially their bombing assaults on Germany and Japan, were front-page news with the press supporting the

---

4. Lynn Dumenil, *Modern Temper: American Culture and Society in the 1920s* (New York: Hill and Wang, 1995), 6.

5. John Whiteclay Chambers II, *The Tyranny of Change: America in the Progressive Era 1890–1920* (New York: St Martin's, 1992), 124.

6. John Buckley, *Air Power in the Age of Total War* (Bloomington: Indiana University Press, 1999), 78.

7. David Courtwright, *Sky as Frontier: Adventure, Aviation, and Empire* (College Station: Texas A&M Press, 2005), 53–55.

effort.[8] This sort of popularity continued after 1947 as the newly designated US Air Force (USAF) made deliberate efforts to publicize the efficacy of airpower.[9] Movies, such as *Strategic Air Command*, *A Gathering of Eagles*, and *Bombers B-52*, extolled a brave new future with air-centric military defenses. Consequently, the theory of strategic bombardment, which was aimed at destroying or crippling an enemy's war-waging infrastructure and morale, became part of military orthodoxy for many, inasmuch as it combined ever-evolving aeronautical innovations with the elegant idea of waging war with powerful, yet aesthetically pleasing aircraft and heroic aviators.

Despite its apparent attributes, strategic bombardment has yet to entirely fulfill its promise. Applied in both world wars and in smaller limited conflicts following 1945, the concept of strategic bombing has a history of falling short of expectations. Although some military theorists believed in strategic bombing's ability to bring about victory with minimized losses, cheaper costs, and with more efficiency than other military means, the concept has historically proven to have serious shortcomings and has not lived up to its hype.

Early Attempts

Even before launching the Schlieffen Plan in 1914, the Germans had already developed ideas regarding strategic bombardment. The building of hydrogen-filled zeppelins during the turn of the century piqued the interest of the German military, with several already in service on the eve of the war. The extremely flammable zeppelins operating over England participated in the first sustained strategic bombing attacks in history. The motivation behind these attacks was twofold.[10] The deputy chief of the German Naval Staff, Paul Behncke, believed dropping bombs over Great Britain would create only minimal physical damage but speculated such attacks might yield a panic in the British mind, "which may possibly render it doubtful that the war could be continued."[11] This idea showed merit when attacks created localized panics in targeted areas. Ensuing concern over such raids resulted in an anxiety referred to as "zeppelinitis," generating a multitude of false reports reflective of public concerns.[12]

---

8. US Army Air Forces (USAAF) will be used to identify the US air arm before it officially became the US Air Force in 1947.

9. Steve Call, *Selling Airpower: Military Aviation and American Popular Culture after World War II* (College Station: Texas A&M Press, 2009), 3.

10. John Buckley, *Air Power*, 59.

11. Richard Overy, "Strategic Bombing before 1939," in *Case Studies in Strategic Bombing*, ed. R. C. Hall (Washington, DC: Air Force History and Museums Program, 1998), 14.

12. Thomas Fegan, *The "Baby Killers": German Air Raids on Britain in the First World War* (Barnsley, UK: Pen and Sword, 2012), 12 and 45; Buckley, *Air Power*, 59.

Alternatively, Captain Peter Strasser, commander of the German Naval Airship Division, firmly believed that the war might end quickly if the nation built a large fleet of airships that attacked British home infrastructure.[13] For Strasser, such a fleet might bring "a prompt and victorious ending of the war . . . [if Great Britain] could be deprived of the means of existence through increasingly extensive destruction of cities, factories, complexes, dockyards, harbor works."[14] While the first German raids were precedent-setting, losses began to mount as the British developed effective countermeasures. The fleet of zeppelins, as well as Strasser himself, fell prey to British fighters, with German aircrews suffering unacceptable loss rates.[15] Naval zeppelins were soon replaced in 1917 by army Gotha G.V. and the Zeppelin-Staaken R.VI aircraft, which conducted raids primarily over London. The

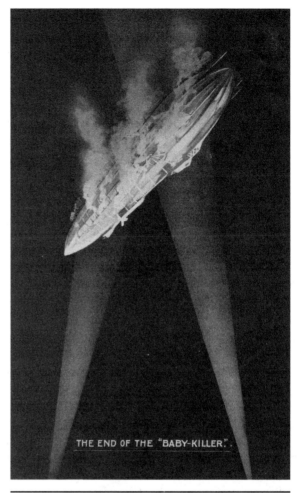

THE END OF THE "BABY-KILLER".

The first German Zeppelin (SL-11) shot down by Captain William Leefe Robinson of the Royal Flying Corps on September 3, 1916. This marked the beginning of the end of the zeppelin.

results were similar to those of the zeppelin raids, creating local panic and creating short-term work stoppages but ultimately failing to break British morale or significantly reduce the overall war effort.

---

13. Eric and Jane Lawson, *The First Air Campaign, August 1914–November 1918* (Cambridge, MA: Da Capo, 1996), 65; Fegan, *Baby Killers*, 30.

14. Overy, "Strategic Bombing before 1939," 14; Lawson, *First Air Campaign*, 79.

15. Robin Higham, "Airpower in World War I, 1914–1918," in *The War in the Air 1914–1994*, ed. A. Stephens (Maxwell AFB, AL: Air University Press, 2001), 9; Buckley, *Air Power*, 59.

The British responded in kind with their own strategic effort under the command of General Hugh Trenchard. Looking for vengeance against German cities, the British planned to attack "densely populated industrial centers . . . to destroy the morale of the operatives."[16] Despite commanding the strategic effort, Trenchard himself was skeptical of the entire concept and feared such an effort would undercut air requirements needed for tactical campaigns and troop support. Designated "Inter-Allied Independent Air Force," the effort was hamstrung with aircraft having both limited range and capability for strategic bombing missions. Despite the introduction of the large Handley Page O/400 in 1918, the Allied strategic effort remained focused largely on tactical targets with most raids against enemy airfields and supply rail lines with only a small percentage against industrial targets.[17] While an increased strategic effort was planned for 1919, the war ended in November 1918. As far as the British were concerned, strategic bombing had no real opportunity to prove its utility. However, there were those who yet believed that the concept held promise for the future.

Interwar Development

Following World War I and the Treaty of Versailles, many nations looked to avoid another military quagmire. Air-minded advocates thought the next conflict would be an opportunity to prove the efficacy of airpower, especially strategic bombing. Supporting this supposition, the interwar years' feats of Charles Lindberg, Roscoe Turner, Amelia Earhart, and other aviators, combined with ever-increasing airframe capabilities, helped elevate the allure of airplanes and airpower. Like previous decades, the interwar years were a time when technological innovations, such as the radio, telephones, and automobiles, enthralled the American public. Airplanes became commercial assets as well, moving people, mail, and cargo as part of the nation's transportation network. Established airlines provided scheduled passenger services with reliable aircraft like the Ford Trimotor, the DC-2/3, and the Boeing 247. Aviation was increasingly establishing itself as part of the nation's cultural, economic, and technological mosaic.[18]

Strategic bombing doctrines emerged on two continents. In the early 1920s, Italian artillery officer Giulio Douhet published the first treatise regarding the utility of strategic airpower. Entitled *Command of the Air*, Douhet's work emphasized the bomber as the primary weapon of the future. Based on the limited experiences of World War I, he believed that fleets of "battle planes" attacking population centers would create such horrors that civilian populations would demand an end to the

---

16. Overy, "Strategic Bombing before 1939," 20–21.
17. Overy, "Strategic Bombing before 1939," 23.
18. Overy, "Strategic Bombing before 1939," 18, 94, and 99–100; Buckley, *Air Power*, 107–8.

hostilities as "normal life could not be carried on."[19] According to the Italian, "the battlefield can no longer be limited; it will be circumscribed only by the frontiers of the nations at war. Everyone becomes a combatant, for all are directly menaced."[20] Breaking national morale and the killing of thousands of civilians in the course of a few weeks was a better alternative for Douhet than the deaths of millions over the span of a few years. With this thinking emerged the modern notion of "total war." While certainly a bleak outlook, Douhet warned against sentimentalism, given the nature of mechanized war.[21]

In America, however, both General Billy Mitchell and the faculty at the Air Corps Tactical School (ACTS) had a more nuanced approach to strategic bombardment. As far as Mitchell was concerned, wanton killing of civilians was not necessary, as he wrote:

> In the future the mere threat of bombing a town by an air force will cause it to be evacuated, and all work in munitions and supply factories to be stopped. . . . Air forces will attack centers of production of all kinds, means of transportation, agricultural areas, ports and shipping; not so much people themselves.[22]

This same sentiment was expressed at the school, which eventually framed the American concept of daylight precision bombardment used in World War II.[23]

In 1935, ACTS clearly outlined the idea of precision strategic bombing and formally reported that "the principle and all important mission of airpower when its equipment permits is the attack of those vital objectives in a nation's economic structure to the attainment of the ultimate objective of war, namely the disintegration of the will to resist."[24] According to the strategic doctrine that the school developed, destruction of enemy morale was based upon bombing the infrastructure that was essential to the enemy's war effort.[25] In their lesson plans, instructors taught that attacking civilian populations was largely ineffective because such applications created only "temporary effects and that [these attacks]

---

19. Buckley, *Air Power*, 75; Phillip S. Meilinger, *Airwar: Theory and Practice* (London: Frank Cass, 2003), 15 and 175.

20. Giulio Douhet, *La Guerre del' Air* (*Air Warfare*), trans. L. Ailes and D. Benedict (Washington, DC, 1933 mimeograph), 24.

21. Douhet, *Command of the Air*, 181–82; as referenced in Ronald Schaffer, *Wings of Judgment: American Bombing in World War II* (New York: Oxford University Press, 1985), 23.

22. William Mitchell, *Winged Defense* (New York: Putnam and Sons, 1925), 6 and 16.

23. Buckley, *Air Power*, 79.

24. Air Corps Tactical School, "A Study of Proposed Air Corps Doctrine," based on a memorandum dated December 21, 1934, furnished by the War Plans Division, General Staff, January 31, 1935; quoted in Frank Futrell, *Ideas, Concepts, and Doctrine: Basic Thinking in the United States Air Force 1907–1960* (Maxwell AFB, AL: Air University Press, 1989), 77.

25. Robert Finney, *History of the Air Corps Tactical School* (Washington, DC: Office of Air Force History, 1992), 66.

are not necessarily cumulative."[26] Even on the eve of World War II, the first commander of the US Eighth Air Force, Ira Eaker, co-authored a treatise with General Henry "Hap" Arnold, the USAAF chief, arguing that attacking civilian populations was an unwise strategy and that the best method of forcing an enemy to surrender was attacking national infrastructure. More specifically they wrote, "Human beings are not priority targets except in certain special situations."[27]

Additionally, in 1937, the Air Corps also fielded its new four-engine strategic bomber, the B-17. A leap in aviation technology, the "Flying Fortress" provided the performance required to conduct strategic bombing operations as envisioned by the ACTS. The B-17's elegant shape developed in parallel with the American doctrine with both helping to foment the other. The development of both airframe and doctrine was advanced further with the development of the Norden Mk XV bombsight. American aircraft were thought to now have both the performance and accuracy to conduct precision strikes. Deducing from their interwar bombing experiments, the Air Corps assumed a heavy bomber at 20,000 feet could hit a 100 × 100 foot target with an average circular bombing error of 555 feet.[28] This marriage of doctrine and technology promised victory and an attractive alternative to the lengthy and bloody ground campaigns of World War I. Even President Franklin Roosevelt, who usually displayed loyal affection for the naval services, placed great faith in airpower stating, "This kind of war [strategic bombing] would cost less money, would mean comparatively few casualties, and would be more likely to succeed than a traditional war by land and sea."[29]

Much like civilian aviation, the Air Corps, too, looked to leverage popular support of aviation and staged events promoting the service and its growing capabilities. These actions often placed it in direct competition with traditional military combat arms. While defense dollars were in short supply during the Great Depression, publicity was a way to advocate the emergence of airpower. These events, combined with the nation's fascination with technology, helped pave the way for the belief in strategic bombing.

The Combined Bombing Offensive

Once the United States entered the war, the USAAF had the opportunity to prove the efficacy of strategic airpower and was eager to execute its new concept. However, before the Americans even began, the Royal Air Force (RAF) had already conducted strategic bombing operations over Germany since May 1940. Finding that operating

---

26. Air Corps Tactical School Lecture, March 28, 1939, file 248.2019A, Albert F. Simpson Historical Research Center (ASHRC), Maxwell AFB, AL.

27. H. Arnold and I. Eaker, *Winged Warfare* (New York: Harper, 1941), 134.

28. Stephan L. McFarland, *America's Pursuit of Precision Bombing, 1910–1945* (Tuscaloosa: University of Alabama Press, 1995), 102.

29. As referenced in Michael Sherry, *The Rise of American Airpower: The Creation of Armageddon* (New Haven, CT: Yale University Press, 1987), 79.

bombers over Germany in the daylight was too costly, the RAF switched to the cover of night.[30] Unlike their USAAF counterparts, the RAF never fully embraced the idea of precision bombardment in the manner the Americans had and instead practiced area attacks on German urban centers. As the US Eighth Air Force began to arrive in England, RAF representatives encouraged American air crews to follow their example.[31] In an effort to resolve their differences, at the Casablanca Conference in January 1943 the two air forces drafted what became known as the "Casablanca Directive." This document laid out the respective bombing methodologies for the Combined Bomber Offensive (CBO). According to General Haywood S. Hansell, a key framer of the American interwar doctrine:

> The directive endorsed both American and British grand strategy for air power. . . . The Eighth Air Force and RAF Bomber Command could operate as coordinate members of a team progressing toward a common destination. . . . RAF Bomber Command was free to continue its chosen air strategy . . . [and] the Eighth Air Force was free to pursue its doctrine of destruction of selective targets by daylight.[32]

As a result, the two air forces began the "round the clock" bombing effort over Germany with the Americans operating by day and the British by night. According to the Americans who developed Air War Planning Document-1, which established the Air Force's blueprint for execution, the entire effort when fully mature, equipped, and focused on strategic targets would take only six months.[33]

The Eighth Air Force's learning curve was steep as bomber and aircrew losses grew excessive. On average during the first months of the bombing offensive, American loss rates for a given mission ranged from 8 to 10 percent. Given that aircrews were required to fly twenty-five missions before rotating home, statistically an individual airman would survive only until his eleventh mission. Among the Eighth Air Force alone, 44,472 men were lost in action over the course of the war.[34] This number exceeds the list of the 24,511 killed serving in the US Marine Corps during the "island hopping" campaign in the Pacific.[35]

---

30. Buckley, *Air Power*, 157.

31. Buckley, *Air Power*, 158.

32. Haywood S. Hansell Jr., *The Strategic Air War Against Germany and Japan: A Memoir* (Washington, DC: Office of Air Force History, 1986), 73.

33. Hansell, *The Strategic Air War Against Germany and Japan*, 36.

34. Number includes killed in action and missing in action. For the entire CBO the number of men lost is 79,625. USSBS, *Statistical Appendix to Over-All Report (European War)* (Washington, DC: US Government Printing Office, 1947), Personnel Lost in Action, 3.

35. "US Military Casualties in World War II," National WWII Museum, accessed August 15, 2019, https://www.nationalww2museum.org/students-teachers/student-resources/research-starters/research-starters-us-military-numbers.

Moreover, the results of the bomber offensive were less than what the framers expected. Near the end of the war President Roosevelt commissioned a study (at the behest of the USAAF) to analyze the campaign's performance. Entitled *US Strategic Bombing Survey*, the effort was a painstaking, in-depth look at the effect of strategic bombing on the Axis nations. The survey found that German aircraft production rates rose exponentially during the height of the bombing effort![36] Additionally, while withstanding over 1.7 million tons of bombs dropped on occupied Europe, German combat munitions (including aircraft, ammunition, tanks, and naval construction) rose close to a factor of two until just before the last months of the war.[37] This doubling of production was hardly what the strategic bombing advocates expected. Conversely, once the CBO began focusing on the German gas and oil industry in summer 1944, synthetic fuel production dropped significantly and continuously until the end of the war.[38] While important, these attacks on petroleum came two years after the campaign's inception and at a time when Germany was already on the strategic defensive.

Although it appeared Germany's industry was "thriving on bombs," what American intelligence analysts had failed to realize was that German production capacity did not fully mobilize until 1942. In order to balance both "guns and butter," the Nazi state had sufficient production capacity in reserve and could surge when required. Furthermore, once Albert Speer took charge of German armaments production in February 1942, processes were streamlined, shortcuts created, and systems maximized, with youth and slave labor impressed. In other words there was sufficient slack with the German industrial base to compensate for the Allied aerial onslaught.[39]

Additionally, the precision bombing concept the USAAF embraced also fell short in execution. In 1943, only about 20 percent of bombs fell within 1,000 feet of the designated targets, and only 50 percent of the bombs dropped by the heavy bomber fleet landed within some 3,400 feet of the designated target.[40] However, as the war progressed and German airpower began to dwindle, USAAF crews grew in proficiency with their accuracy increasing by the end of the war.[41] Even a direct hit, however, did

---

36. USSBS, *Statistical Appendix to Over-All Report (European War)* (Washington, DC: US Government Printing Office, 1947), German Aircraft Production, Chart No. 7, 92.

37. USSBS, *Statistical Appendix to Over-All Report*, Combat Munitions (Includes Aircraft, Ammunition, Weapons, "Panzer," and Naval Construction), Chart No. 15, and Panzer Production, Chart No. 26, 112, and 140.

38. USSBS, *Statistical Appendix to Over-All Report*, German Gasoline and Rubber Index, Chart No. 18, 122.

39. USSBS, *Summary Report (European War)* (repr., Maxwell AFB, AL: Air University Press, 1987), 8.

40. USSBS, *Bombing Accuracy, USAAF Heavy and Medium Bombers in the ETO* (Washington, DC: US Government Printing Office, January 1947), Exhibits H and I.

41. USSBS, *Bombing Accuracy*, Exhibit I.

not always guarantee destroying a factory's production capacity, with the survey's analysts reporting that constant reattack was always required.

More important was the topic of German morale. While morale is a difficult value to measure, the survey addressed the issue and concluded that, despite the fact that the German population toiled under a totalitarian regime,

> [German workers] showed surprising resistance to the terror and hardship of repeated air attack, to the destruction of their homes and belongings, and to the conditions under which they were reduced to live. Their morale, their belief in ultimate victory or satisfactory compromise, and their confidence in their leaders declined, but they continued to work efficiently as long as the physical means of production remained. The power of the police state over its people cannot be underestimated.[42]

This was the case, despite absenteeism in German factories being reported as high as 25 percent.[43] Highlighting these was a response from a Luftwaffe Flak sergeant, who as a teen was pressed into service in 1942 and crewed an 88 mm flak gun. When queried as to why she did not quit her duties with the defeat of the Nazi state imminent, her response was both simple, yet thoughtful: "What else could I do?"

Despite the numbers, true believers in the idea of strategic bombardment argue that the aircraft, men, and materials diverted to the defense of the Reich as a result of the CBO assisted the ground campaign and overall war effort. German fighters, flak, troops, and ammunition used in a defensive posture against American bombers and formations were diverted from operations against Allied ground and naval forces. Given this consideration, advocates claim the Allies' strategic bombing offensive directly assisted the larger campaign by pressing German resources at a time it could ill afford.[44] Going further, despite their increase in aircraft production, the Germans had to limit combat operations due to fuel shortages. Additionally, Luftwaffe units suffered from a lack of new, fully trained replacement aircrews compared to that of their Allied counterparts.[45] There is indeed merit to these arguments. However, the strategic bombing campaign in the European theater failed to live up to its full expectations, as the concept framed in the interwar years fell short.

Publicly, support for the bombing campaign was widespread because Americans believed it provided just retribution for the horrors of Nazism. Papers and news outlets were largely supportive of the strategic bombing offensive. In a March 1944 Gallup Poll survey, 74 percent of Americans approved of bombing historic religious

---

42. USSBS, *Summary Report (European War)*, 39.

43. Buckley, *Air Power*, 166.

44. Philip S. Meilinger, *Air Power Myths and Facts* (Maxwell AFB, AL: Air University Press, 2003), 42–44.

45. USSBS, *Statistical Appendix to Over-All Report (European War)*, Chart No. 10 German Air Force Training, 100; Buckley, *Air Power*, 161.

buildings if necessary.[46] Defense contractors and other manufacturers leveraged the campaign by advertising their products as part of the bombing offensive. General Electric, AC Delco, Studebaker, Texaco, Yale Locks, and a host of other companies all publicized how their wares were used in the aerial endeavor. The press, too, was supportive and ran articles that largely lauded the effort with very few counter-narratives. When peace activist Vera Brittain decried the Allied bombing effort, the *New York Times* editorial page replied, "We should leave tactics and strategies to the generals hoping they can be as merciful as they can . . . but let us not deceive ourselves into thinking the war can be made humane."[47]

USAAF Chief Arnold fully endorsed publicity for strategic bombing and saw it as a way to validate a postwar independent Air Force. Arnold's professional agenda of establishing a separate air service helped promote and endorse a positive public portrayal of strategic bombing. For Arnold, the combined bomber operations were a way to show the contribution of airpower during the war while ensuring the service received credit through publicity.[48] While not necessarily looking to create more death and destruction, Arnold did advocate for more effective raids, even if it came at a cost.

Firebombing Campaign

As strategic bombing in Europe was in its final phases, the United States was starting another campaign in the Pacific to undermine the Japanese war effort. This was an entirely different operation with a wholly new aircraft bombing the home islands of Honshu and Kyushu. Executed by crews flying the new B-29 "Superfortress" bomber, these raids were distinctly different from their European counterparts and deliberately departed from established Air Force doctrine.

The new B-29 was yet another leap in aviation technology, much like its B-17 predecessor. Designed to fly at thirty thousand feet with a payload of ten tons, the new bomber also had a range of over three thousand miles and was therefore well suited for the long distances required in the Pacific theater. The Superfortress was the single biggest expense for the United States during the war, and Arnold staked his professional reputation on it. While its first missions were flown out of China, these raids were logistically unsupportable and yielded little strategic impact. Conceding the logistics problem in China, the Air Force moved the B-29 effort to the Mariana Islands in mid-1944. However, the new commander of the XXI Bomber Command,

---

46. George Gallup, *The Gallup Poll Public Opinion, 1935–1971: Volume 1* (New York: Random House, 1972), 441.

47. Editorial, "The Bombing of Germany," *New York Times*, March 8, 1944.

48. Conrad Crane, *Bombs, Cities, and Civilians* (Lawrence: University of Kansas Press, 1993), 34, 38, and 59.

General Curtis LeMay, saw his force suffering from a number of obstacles preventing the aircraft from reaching its full potential. Weather, engine problems, and other related issues precluded the results expected of the new and expensive airframe.[49]

The USAAF also believed that the Japanese had a wholly different approach to industrial production. While the Germans constructed large factories, American intelligence surmised that cottage industries, with home-based production, served as a foundation for the Japanese war effort. Reportedly, Japanese city dwellers individually operated tool and die equipment in their homes then forwarded their products to assembly plants located in urban areas. Furthermore, while European buildings were largely composed of brick and mortar, Japanese cities were mostly constructed of wood and paper. As a result, American planners understood that Japanese urban landscape was much more susceptible to incendiary area bombing.

Given the considerations of Japanese infrastructure and manufacturing methods, combined with the command's operational problems, LeMay turned American bombing doctrine on its head. Instead of high-altitude, daylight precision bombing, on the evening of March 9, 1945, LeMay launched a nighttime raid, with B-29s flying at low level (approximately 4,900 to 9,200 feet), and dropping incendiary bombs in a four-by-three-mile area in Tokyo.[50] Taking great risk by single-handedly changing bombing tactics, LeMay gambled with his crews and planes. While waiting for the results that evening, he recalled feeling "anxiety I'd not wish to experience again."[51] However, in that single night the XXI Bomber Command killed over 80,000 Japanese and razed over sixteen square miles of urban landscape. The fires burned so hot in the targeted area that water in canals reached the scalding point, bodies were melted together, and glass and concrete liquefied. Flying at such low altitudes, crews arriving over the target in later waves resorted to breathing bottled oxygen as the stench of burning flesh rose with the embers making airmen nauseous. After receiving the news regarding the Tokyo fire raid, USAAF Chief Arnold wired LeMay: "Congratulations. This mission shows your crews have the guts for anything."[52]

The results of the Tokyo raid spawned similar attacks on Nagoya, Kobe, Osaka, and Yokohama. By the time Japan surrendered, 40 percent of sixty-six Japanese cities had been destroyed by incendiaries.[53] While these raids certainly affected Japanese production capacity, the bombing survey found other factors contributing to the empire's ultimate defeat. Japanese industrial output was only 10 percent that of the United States. In view of its wartime requirements for occupying both China and Manchuria, Japan was already rationing the sinews of life by December 1941. Given Japan's lack

---

49. The B-29 was the single biggest expense of the United States during the war, costing some $3 billion. Its expense was rivaled only by the Manhattan Project with a price tag of *only* $2 billion.

50. Alvin D. Coox, "Strategic Bombing in the Pacific, 1942–1945," in Hall, *Case Studies*, 319.

51. Coox, "Strategic Bombing in the Pacific," 318.

52. Coox, "Strategic Bombing in the Pacific," 319–21.

53. USSBS, *Summary Report (Pacific War)* (repr., Maxwell AFB, AL: Air University Press, 1987), 86.

of natural resources, her newly acquired territories provided raw materials needed for the war effort and everyday life. Getting these materials to the Japanese home islands, however, required a capable and robust merchant fleet. Consequently, from the very beginnings of the Pacific war, the US Navy deliberately targeted Japanese merchant vessels. In a highly effective interdiction campaign, American submarines and surface vessels sank most of the Chrysanthemum Throne's merchant fleet.[54] Unable to replace it, the Japanese had no way to transport required raw materials back to their island nation. Regarding both the Air Corps' and Navy's efforts, the survey found:

> Even though the urban attacks and attacks on specific industrial plants contributed a substantial percentage of the over-all decline in the Japanese economy, many effects were duplicative. Most of the oil refineries were out of oil, the alumina plants out of bauxite, the steel mills lacking ore and coke, and the munition plants low on steel and aluminum. Japan's economy was in large measure destroyed twice over, once by cutting off imports, and secondly by air attack.[55]

In brief, strategic bombardment's ability to destroy Japanese industry cannot be analyzed without considering the interdiction campaign waged against her merchant fleet. Moreover, after the aerial assault, 97 percent of Japan's stock of guns, shells, explosives, and related supplies remained intact in underground storage.[56] While impressive, and it was destructive, the firebombing campaign by itself failed as a war winner.

Atomic Applications

Even before the bombing survey tabulated much of its findings, the concept of strategic bombing received a sudden infusion that changed its very nature. With the atomic events at Trinity site, Hiroshima, and Nagasaki, the United States not only acquired a monopoly on atomic weapons but also had the means to deliver them. With atomic fission, the concept of strategic bombing was in essence "made anew." No longer required were hundreds of planes, massed in formation, looking to drop thousands of tons of bombs on a relatively small area. Now one plane could fly a single mission, with precision less a concern, and destroy an entire city and possibly a multitude of factories and industries at one time.

Once the survey finally analyzed the atomic bombings in Japan, it determined that one atomic-equipped B-29 carried as much explosive firepower as 220 Superfortresses with payloads of 1,200 tons of incendiary weapons, 400 tons of high-explosive

54. Buckley, *Air Power*, 184.
55. USSBS, *Summary Report (Pacific War)*, 90.
56. USSBS, *Summary Report (Pacific War)*, 87.

bombs, and 500 tons of anti-personnel fragmentation bombs.[57] In this regard atomic strategic bombing certainly provided a cost savings in terms of men, planes, and associated expenses. As expected, and much in line with the USAAF doctrinal precepts, the populations in the targeted areas of Hiroshima and Nagasaki reacted with great fear and terror as 29 percent of those surveyed claimed the bomb convinced them a Japanese victory was impossible.[58] If breaking the morale of the enemy populace was the intent, the people of Hiroshima and Nagasaki succumbed to the doctrinal dictates that the ACTS had articulated. However, word regarding the atomic attacks was largely restricted to the targeted cities with most Japanese unaware and lacking an understanding of atomic munitions.[59]

The American narrative regarding the two atomic bombs is that the Japanese sued for peace yielding to an atomic "rain of ruin." This version of history offers a validation of strategic bombing while also providing an attractive alternative to invading the home islands. Veterans of the war saw the atomic attacks as a godsend, which spared their lives and hundreds of thousands of would-be Japanese civilian fighters. The bombs appeared to provide a clean and abrupt ending to the conflict. As a result, strategic bombing provided not only a simple answer to why the Japanese surrendered, but also a validation of the Manhattan Project, the B-29, and their associated expense.

There is some truth to this perspective, but it ignores the fact that on the same day "Fat Man" was dropped over Nagasaki, the USSR fulfilled its promise made at the Yalta Conference and initiated operations against the Japanese. Starting their assault in occupied Manchuria, the Soviets committed more than one million troops, thousands of tanks and self-propelled artillery, and over 3,700 aircraft to the defeat of the Japanese Kwantung Army. Having already been soundly defeated by the Soviets at the Battles of Khalkhin Gol in 1939, the Japanese feared another USSR offensive.[60]

The Japanese had looked to leverage their neutral relationship with the USSR, hoping the Soviets could mediate a negotiated peace with the Americans. Seeking to hold what they gained militarily, the Japanese were interested in a limited war that established the Chrysanthemum Throne as hegemon for greater Asia. Once the Soviets shed their neutrality and sought access to Manchuria for postwar positioning, their attack on Japanese forces left the island nation few options.[61] Attacked on both sides, lacking industrial capacity, along with an inability to ship materials to the home

57. USSBS, *Summary Report (Pacific War)*, "The Effects of the Atomic Bombs," 102–3.

58. USSBS, *Summary Report (Pacific War)*, 103.

59. USSBS, *Summary Report (Pacific War)*.

60. Ronald Spector, *In the Ruins of Empire: The Japanese Surrender and the Battle for Postwar Asia* (New York: Random House, 2007), 27; James Sheridan, *China in Disintegration: The Republican Era, 1912–1949* (New York: Free Press, 1975), 271.

61. Tsuyoshi Hasegawa, *Racing the Enemy: Stalin, Truman, and the Surrender of Japan* (Cambridge, MA: Harvard University Press, 2005), 40–41; Ward Wilson, "The Bomb Didn't Beat Japan . . . Stalin Did," *Foreign Policy*, May 30, 2013.

The *Los Angeles Times*, August 7, 1945. Conventional bombing continued with the B-29 assault on Honshu's arsenal.

islands, the Japanese found themselves in an untenable position. Like the Navy's campaign against the Japanese merchant fleet and the strategic air effort, the effect of the atomic bombs and the entry of the USSR in the Pacific are two events that cannot be considered separately from one another. They are inextricably linked.

Once the war was over, the United States found itself the preeminent power on the globe and in sole possession of atomic weapons. As the only nation with a strategic bomber force that possessed fission technology, the United States expected an

"American Pax Atomica." The Air Force was now envisioned as the most important of the military services. Supporting this assertion was a pointed comment by Air Force general Frank A. Armstrong who quipped:

> You gentlemen had better understand the [Army] Air Force is tired of being a subordinate outfit and is no longer going to be a subordinate outfit. It was the predominate force during the war and it is going to be a predominate force during the peace and you might as well make up your minds whether you like it or not, and we don't care whether you like it or not, the [Army] Air Force is going to run the show. . . . You [Navy types] are not going to have anything but a bunch of carrie[r]s which are ineffective anyway, and they will probably be sunk in the first battle.[62]

This idea dominated military thinking after the war, as illustrated in a February 1949 Gallup Poll finding most Americans were willing to pay more taxes for the Air Force than for any other service.[63] Regarding this particular issue, George Gallup added, "Airpower became a major 'love' of the American people, even before military experts were willing to admit the importance of its role in warfare."[64]

Furthermore, in sole possession of fissionable weapons, the United States could depend upon its arsenal of atomic bombs to deter or at least offset the Soviet Red Army. While the United States demobilized much of its standing military after V-J Day, the Soviet Union maintained a sizeable military of 4.5 million men.[65] In this regard, atomic strategic bombing provided a potent deterrent for Soviet aggression at a relatively small cost and force structure.[66] The economy of the concept again had positive attributes as America looked to return to a peacetime economy.

Despite its newfound status, studies conducted during the postwar period called into question the efficacy of atomic strategic bombardment. In December 1948, Air Force general Hubert R. Harmon, along with an accompanying staff, studied the effectiveness of an American war plan code-named Trojan. The plan called for the use of 147 atomic weapons while attacking seventy Soviet cities focusing on petroleum

62. Drew Pearson, "End of the Marines?" Summary of Remarks from General Frank Armstrong, *Washington Post*, March 20, 1947, in AAF Information Program B-36 Folder, CNO; Organizational Research and Policy Division (OP-23) 1932–1949, box 174, Naval History and Heritage Command (NHHC), Washington, DC.

63. Gallup, *Public Opinion 1935–1971*, 897.

64. Murray Green, draft of "The B-36 Controversy in Retrospect," box 102, LeMay Papers, Manuscripts Division, Library of Congress, Washington, DC.

65. Lawrence Wittner, *Cold War America* (New York: Praeger, 1974), 9; "'Caldron' War Plan, 2 Nov 1946," in *Pincher Campaign Plans Part 1*, ed. S. Ross and D. A. Rosenberg (New York: Garland, 1989), 112.

66. John Curatola, *Bigger Bombs for a Brighter Tomorrow: The Strategic Air Command and the American War Plans at the Dawn of the Atomic Age, 1945–1950* (Jefferson, NC: McFarland, 2015), 100, 105, and 118.

and other war-related industries.[67] Upon review of the plan, the Harmon Committee reported that 30 to 40 percent of Soviet industry would be reduced; however, the results would be only temporary due to Soviet recuperative powers. Estimates had the assault producing some 2.7 million deaths, over 4 million other casualties, with 28 million "severely affected."[68] While the Harmon Committee agreed that the psychological shock would be devastating, it also determined that such an offensive "would not per se bring about the capitulation, destroy the roots of Communism, or critically weaken the power of Soviet leadership."[69] On the larger strategic imperative, Harmon concluded that the aerial offensive would "produce certain psychological and retaliatory reactions detrimental to the achievement of allied war objectives and its destructive effects will complicate post-hostility problems."[70] Harmon envisioned that the devastating effect of such an attack would only embolden Russian resistance. Given the German Wehrmacht's experience from 1941 to 1945, Russian resistance seemed an abundant commodity. With this evaluation, strategic bombardment apparently again fell short of the larger objective.

Less than a year later, another evaluation analyzed Trojan's succeeding war plan, code-named Offtackle. The plan's goal was to reduce Soviet power and influence outside her borders, wrestle political control from the Communist Party, and destroy Russian ability to conduct offensive operations.[71] The new plan was a four-phased effort targeting twenty-six Soviet war-making industries with 220 atomic bombs (with seventy-two planned reattacks) on 104 urban areas.[72] In fall 1949, the Weapons System Evaluation Group (WSEG), a multiservice permanent organization

---

67. Kenneth Condit, *Joint Chiefs of Staff and National Policy Volume II, 1947–1949* (Washington, DC: Office of Joint History, 1996), 158.

68. "Evaluation of the Effect on Soviet War Effort Resulting from the Strategic Air Offensive (Harmon Report)," in *Containment: Documents and American Policy and Strategy 1945–1950*, ed. T. Etzold and J. Gaddis (New York: Columbia University Press, 1978), 362.

69. "Evaluation of the Effect on Soviet War Effort," 324; David Kunsman and Douglas Lawson, *Sandia Report, RAND 2001-0053: A Primer on US Nuclear Policy* (Albuquerque, NM: Sandia National Laboratories, 2001), 23.

70. Etzold and Gaddis, *Containment*, 361–63; Condit, *Joint Chiefs of Staff*, 168–69.

71. "Brief of Joint Outline Emergency War Plan (OFFTACKLE) JSPC 877/59, May 26, 1949," in Etzold and Gaddis, *Containment*, 327.

72. "Brief of Joint Outline Emergency War Plan," 332–33; *Proceedings of the Strategic Air Command Commanders (SAC) Conference, Ramey Air Force Base 25-26-27 April 1950*, National Archives and Records Administration (NARA), Record Group 341, RG 341, Headquarters US Air Force, Office of the Chief of Staff, Vice Chief of Staff Executive Service Division, General Files 1950–1953, box 1, George Washington University, National Security Archive, accessed December 2, 2014, http://www.alternatewars.com/WW3/WW3_Documents/AIRFORCE/SAC_Commanders_Conference_Apr_50.htm, 18; JCS 1952/11 Weapons Systems Evaluation Group, Evaluation of Effectiveness of Strategic Air Operations, February 10, 1950, in *America's Plans for War Against the Soviet Union 1945–1950, Evaluation the Air Offensive, WSEG-1 Study*, Vol. 13, ed. Steven Ross and David Alan Rosenberg (New York: Garland, 1989), 163.

established under the auspices of Secretary of Defense James Forrestal, conducted an analysis of Offtackle. In January 1950, the WSEG presented its results; while they believed that most of the bombers would hit their respective targets, the Air Force's Strategic Air Command (SAC) would experience a loss rate that exceeded even that of the dark days of World War II bombing operations in Europe.[73] While the plan looked to land a "knockout" blow to the Soviet military in the opening weeks of a conflict, the evaluators estimated that high aircraft losses precluded bomber operations in later phases of the plan.[74] In addition to the bomber and aircrew losses, the report also pointed to serious shortfalls in logistics, forward basing, fuel, targeting and air defense intelligence, and maintenance support. While the initial phase of the operation might be successful, the strategic plan would again fall short of its intended objectives.

The Soviet Union exploded its own fission-based atomic weapon in August 1949 followed by a fusion one (a hydrogen, or thermonuclear, bomb) in 1953. But even when the United States had a monopoly on strategic nuclear bombardment, the concept of a strategic air attack was found lacking. The idea of affecting a nation's morale by attacking its infrastructure and military capacity via aerial bombardment had once again come up short, albeit only theoretically. Regardless, such studies highlighted the deficiencies of strategic bombing.

The Fiscal Year 1951 budget called for an exponential increase in defense spending as a result of the Soviet success and the establishment of the People's Republic of China in October 1949. With this, Truman broke from his parsimonious military allocation and increased defense spending from $14 billion to $44 billion. Once Dwight Eisenhower assumed the presidency, he looked to reduce the defense budget and conducted his own review of national military strategy. The resulting policy, NSC-162/2, economized future military spending by emphasizing nuclear application through airpower with the Air Force's SAC gaining primacy.[75] The "New Look," as it was termed, not only provided a deterrent effect, but again offered a cheaper military option.

Korea

In June 1950, as SAC focused on a potential war with the Soviet Union, the North Koreans attacked across the thirty-eighth parallel. In response, Far East Air Forces (FEAF) Bombing Command posited that it should inflict "the maximum damage to

---

73. JCS 1952/11, 193.

74. Philip S. Meilinger, *Bomber: The Formation and Early Years of Strategic Air Command* (Maxwell AFB, AL: Air University Press, 2012), 164.

75. Buckley, *Air Power*, 207.

the enemy with the reservation that the situation does not at this time warrant the mass destruction of population centers."[76] With this guidance, Commanding General George E. Stratemeyer specifically looked not only to sidestep attacking urban areas and avoid potentially unpopular press, but more importantly to avoid expanding a localized conflict into a global one.

The problem of strategic bombing in North Korea was twofold. There were too few strategic targets worthy of attacking, and the area of operations was largely limited to the geographical area of Korea. At the start of the war, North Korea was hardly an economic giant, as it had little industrial output. Dependent upon material assistance from its communist allies, North Korea received its supply and equipment from the Soviet Union and China. Furthermore, given Korea's proximity to the USSR and newly established People's Republic of China (PRC), FEAF operations were limited to attacks south of the Yalu River that divided Korea from Manchuria, China. Looking to avoid any expansion of the war, FEAF specifically prohibited B-29 crews and tactical jets from entering the airspace of adjacent communist nations.[77]

Despite the lack of North Korean manufacturing, early Bomber Command targets included industries in the major cities of Hungham, Wonsan, Pyongyang, and Konan and their associated infrastructure. However, General Douglas A. MacArthur, commander in chief of UN forces in Korea, avoided attacking the North Korean hydroelectrical plants in the far north in order to use them as a potential bargaining chip in peace negotiations. After the amphibious landings at Inchon in September and the subsequent approval by the United Nations to allow allied forces to attack above the thirty-eighth parallel, by October 19, UN forces captured the North Korean capital of Pyongyang. Days later, FEAF Bomber Command suspended operations, reporting: "no targets were available on the Korean side of the Yalu."[78] Having destroyed what production North Korea had, groups of FEAF B-29s returned home to the continental United States.[79]

Communist China entered the fight unexpectedly in late October, overrunning General MacArthur's offensive drive toward the Yalu. Despite intelligence that indicated the entry of Chinese forces, the UN commander's hubris precluded an appreciation of the developing situation. Embarrassed by his blunder, MacArthur ordered Bomber Command to "destroy every means of communication and every installation, factory, city and village."[80] However, MacArthur forbade attacks on the city of Rashin, as it bordered the USSR, and continued the restriction on attacks against

76. Thomas Hone, "Strategic Bombardment Constrained: Korea and Vietnam," in Hall, *Case Studies*, 473.

77. Conrad Crane, *American Airpower and Strategy in Korea, 1950–1953* (Lawrence: University of Kansas Press, 2000), 70–71.

78. Hone, "Strategic Bombardment Constrained," 477.

79. Crane, *American Airpower in Korea*, 44 and 63.

80. Hone, "Strategic Bombardment Constrained," 478; Crane, *American Airpower in Korea*, 47.

B-29 strikes of October 27, 1951, against rail bridges at Sinanju, North Korea. Such attacks degraded North Korean lines of supply and communication but could not sever them.

the Yalu hydroelectric dams.[81] MacArthur's targeting guidance directed FEAF to start bombing targets in north and then work southward. Eventually, everything in North Korea became a target. While Bomber Command looked to apply discriminate bombing as the conflict began, months later it began carpet-bombing much of North Korea. Since Korean architecture was similar to that of Japan, the use of incendiaries was again authorized. To increase pressure on the Chinese, expanded targets lists eventually included the hydroelectric plants on the Yalu that had previously been off-limits.

Since North Korea received its vital materials from its allies, the only mission left for Bomber Command was one of "interdiction." In trying to cut off the flow of supplies, one Air Force officer complained, "We are somewhat in the position of trying to starve a beggar by raiding his pantry when we know he gets his meals from his rich relatives up the street."[82] Bombing operations in 1951 focused on road networks,

---

81. Crane, *American Airpower in Korea*, 64.
82. Crane, *American Airpower in Korea*, 127.

115

rail lines, bridges, and various mountain passes. These targets do not necessarily fit the definition of "strategic," as they were not centers of manufacturing, production, or the government. These targets were more "operational" in that they were in direct support of enemy forces and/or troops in the field. However, as the United Nations bombed thoroughfares and existing supply depots, the North Koreans adapted by using human transport with backpacks and "A-frames" while moving supply bases underground. Such expedient methods were effective in countering the aerial effort.[83] One frustrated aviator flying interdiction missions in an overtly racist tone quipped, "The gooks are just too smart for us."[84]

Mindful of the limitations on the UN air campaign, both the North Koreans and Chinese based their new MiG-15 fighters from the Soviet Union just north of the Yalu River at Antung. The swift, swept wing communist fighter was a surprise for the West and inflicted such damage to B-29s that FEAF command shifted to night-time radar bombing. Because the Antung airfield was out of bounds, frustrated UN fighter pilots were prohibited from attacking the MiG base.[85] While some renegade pilots did pursue communist jets north of the Yalu, the MiG dilemma reflected the same problem the strategic campaign had: How do you affect enemy operations when they have sanctuary and supply in prohibited areas?

Korea was yet another failure for strategic bombing. While much post–World War II military thought was focused on atomic applications, a limited war like Korea posed a problem with the emerging paradigm. Although the US Joint Chiefs of Staff drafted plans for the potential use of nuclear weapons in the Korean conflict, nuclear bombs played no role in the execution of the campaign. Their potential use, how-ever, served as a backdrop during armistice negotiations. Additionally, despite the widespread destruction of North Korea by bombing, once again enemy morale failed to break as the communists continued their wartime efforts.[86] With most of the enemy's material produced in facilities located outside of the country, the strategic campaign was severely limited. As the commander of SAC during the conflict, Curtis LeMay agreed that the bombing effort was merely an interdiction campaign, stating: "We never did hit a strategic target."[87] However, LeMay's remark may be disingenuous for, as seen, FEAF attempted to reduce morale by destroying infrastructure, produc-tion, and transportation networks. Given the conflict's political considerations and the larger mandate to prevent expansion of the war, the bombing effort clearly failed. This situation would again repeat itself.

---

83. Robert Pape, *Bombing to Win: Air Power and Coercion to Win in War* (Ithaca, NY: Cornell Uni-versity Press, 1996), 150.

84. Crane, *American Airpower in Korea*, 114.

85. Some UN pilots did violate the standing order and pursued fleeing jets over the border in "hot pursuit." While officially a violation, such actions were tacitly approved.

86. Pape, *Bombing to Win*, 73.

87. Hone, "Strategic Bombardment Constrained," 517.

Vietnam

Much like its Korean counterpart, the Vietnam War was also an exercise in frustration for advocates of strategic bombing. Many of the same considerations relevant in Korea were applicable to North Vietnam. American planners and political leadership tried to keep the war limited, while enemy production facilities and resupply flowed in from the same outside entities—namely China and the USSR. Like Korea, the air campaign in Vietnam was also an operation that gradually escalated in bombing intensity only to become unrestricted near the end. However, by the time the United States resorted to unrestricted bombing, the American people had lost the desire for victory and sought only a withdrawal of its forces.

Starting in February 1965, the United States initiated an air campaign to deter North Vietnam's effort to infiltrate South Vietnam and undermine its government. Conceived as an eight-week program, Operation Rolling Thunder lasted over three years.[88] Designed to cut supply lines from Hanoi, the campaign focused on destroying railways, roads, bridges, water transport, and radar and communication nodes.[89] As in Korea, some consider Rolling Thunder an interdiction effort as opposed to a strategic operation. However, given the mandate and goals of the campaign, it certainly had strategic intent with representative targeting.

Intended to reduce North Vietnamese military capabilities and infrastructure, the campaign also had a diplomatic role. Rolling Thunder not only showed American resolve in supporting an ally, but sought to use military pressure as a way to communicate with the communist government.[90] In a twofold effort, the United States hoped to exercise a carrot-and-stick policy in Southeast Asia. The Johnson administration envisioned that increasing air strikes in the north would elicit positive responses: if the communists in the north relented and reduced their military actions, the United States would reduce its aerial offensive and provide respites for potential negotiations. With this approach, the Johnson administration ordered bombing pauses at various times to diplomatically entice the North Vietnamese. However, the temporary reprieves only provided North Vietnam a respite to repair and recover from the aerial attacks.[91] As a result, each break resulted in enhanced enemy defense, including new surface-to-air missiles (SAMs), rebuilt infrastructure, and repairs done by forty thousand Chinese construction workers combined with millions of civilians pressed into service.[92]

---

88. Ronald Frankum Jr., *Like Rolling Thunder: The Air War in Vietnam 1964–1975* (New York: Rowman and Littlefield, 2005), 19; U. S. Grant Sharp, *Strategy for Defeat: Vietnam in Retrospect* (Novato, CA: Presidio, 1978), 63.

89. Frankum, *Like Rolling Thunder*, 20; Pape, *Bombing to Win*, 192.

90. Pape, *Bombing to Win*, 174 and 177.

91. Frankum, *Like Rolling Thunder*, 28; Sharp, *Strategy for Defeat*, 82.

92. Hone, "Strategic Bombardment Constrained," 496.

While intended to be a form of diplomatic communication, targets were initially carefully selected through a lengthy, weeklong process. The process concluded when the proposed target list was finally approved by a small cadre of Johnson advisors with no military members present.[93] Key tenets of airpower are its inherent flexibility and offensive nature. Given the approval methods and oversight at the highest levels of the federal government, air commanders in Vietnam were hamstrung, left with little flexibility or initiative in reacting to enemy military action.

Initially focused on targets in the southern half of North Vietnam, the strikes did very little to disrupt communist military operations and eventually moved northward.[94] As bombing operations crept north, the list of approved targets also expanded. By 1965, the Joint Chiefs of Staff submitted plans to attack additional North Vietnamese infrastructure, including the mining of Haiphong Harbor. Secretary of Defense Robert McNamara rejected the recommendation.[95] However, as the campaign continued, the aerial assault increased in tempo and intensity by an implicit policy of gradualism. Targets expanded again by 1967, including supply routes coming out of China, trucks and trains, airfields and power plants, and oil storage facilities, along with the mining of canals.[96] Many in Congress were frustrated by an apparent lack of progress. In August 1967, congressional hearings found that the doctrine of gradualism prevented the maximum results that airpower promised to produce.[97]

Hampering the strategic effort was the fact that a number of high-value targets were located in restricted or prohibited areas, safe from bombing operations. The prohibited area included a ten-mile radius from the center of Hanoi and a four-mile radius from central Haiphong.[98] No targets could be attacked in the prohibited area unless specifically approved by Washington. In addition, a restricted area was designated thirty-nine miles around Hanoi, another a ten-mile area around Haiphong, along with a twenty-five-mile one along the Chinese border.[99] Attacks in the restricted areas were less controlled, but still required approval by the Joint Chiefs of Staff.

While thousands of North Vietnamese initially left the cities for the safety of the countryside, eventually many returned, having realized that the Americans avoided targeting populated areas.[100] In response to the bombing, the North Vietnamese dispersed much of their supplies and provisions, and like their North Korean predecessors,

93. Hone, "Strategic Bombardment Constrained," 500–501; Sharp, *Strategy for Defeat*, 86–87.
94. Frankum, *Like Rolling Thunder*, 26; Pape, *Bombing to Win*, 185.
95. Hone, "Strategic Bombardment Constrained," 496.
96. Hone, "Strategic Bombardment Constrained," 500; Frankum, *Like Rolling Thunder*, 36.
97. Sharp, *Strategy for Defeat*, 197.
98. Sharp, *Strategy for Defeat*, 100.
99. Sharp, *Strategy for Defeat*, 100; Frankum, *Like Rolling Thunder*, 33 and 44.
100. Hone, "Strategic Bombardment Constrained," 496.

moved a considerable amount underground.[101] Furthermore, leveraging the Americans self-imposed limitations, communist forces stored weapons and other materials within the prohibited/restricted areas. One of the more important locations that remained untouched by the American campaign in the early years was the Phuc Yen airfield north of Hanoi, home to many of the North Vietnamese fighter planes of Russian design. Fear over killing Russian (or Chinese) advisors was a key element in target limitations both in Hanoi and Haiphong.

Despite the increasing level of bombardment, the morale of the North Vietnamese remained intact.

A group of USAF F-105 "Thunderchiefs" bombing in support of Rolling Thunder with an EB-66 (center) providing radar/electronic support.

Communist forces enjoyed generally widespread support from the north's population. Although North Vietnam was a totalitarian regime, many North Vietnamese continued to fight against what they saw as another occidental power looking to colonize them, with strategic bombing making little difference. Again the targeting of morale failed.

Perhaps more importantly, strategic airpower applications envisioned the destruction of an enemy's ability to prosecute war. With important areas off-limits, combined with the insurgent nature of the Viet Cong, strategic bombing had little effect on the enemy.[102] Before the Tet Offensive in January 1968, Viet Cong units comprised most of the communist forces in the south. During this period enemy contact was generally limited to once a month and was largely guerilla in nature. Given this paucity of combat and its limited scale, enemy logistics requirements were minimal. Given this small logistical footprint, no amount of bombing would have affected Viet Cong offensive action and its prosecution of war.[103]

---

101. Hone, "Strategic Bombardment Constrained," 503.

102. Mark Clodfelter, *The Limits of Airpower* (New York: Free Press, 1989), 208–10.

103. Clodfelter, *The Limits of Airpower*, 205.

The Tet Offensive that began on January 31, 1968, was a dismal failure for the communist cause. But it essentially ended Lyndon Johnson's presidency, and with it the bombing north of the twentieth parallel halted. In the end, Rolling Thunder failed to elicit the response the administration had hoped. While the aerial campaign did in part weaken the North Vietnamese military effort, the communists in the north continued to supply their allies in the south. As a result North Vietnam's source of external supply remained intact. Rolling Thunder also failed as an interdiction, strategic, and/or diplomatic campaign. Regarding the campaign's failure to communicate diplomatically, one analyst of the effort quipped, "If you want to 'send a message,' call Western Union."[104]

With the incoming Nixon administration and the policy of "Vietnamization," US strategic imperatives changed.[105] Looking for "peace with honor," Americans hoped to extract themselves from the conflict. US airpower was key to defeating the Easter Offensive in 1972, and in other tactical operations, it also played a larger role in the American effort to disengage. A new air campaign called Linebacker commenced in May 1972 with expanded target lists and more permissive engagement criteria. The primary goal was again to destroy war materials in the north and interdict supplies and men moving south. Major oil facilities, transportation nodes, and railways and bridges, all of which were key in aiding enemy forces in the south, were targeted, including the mining of Haiphong Harbor. More importantly, most sorties were scheduled without presidential approval, but collateral damage was to be minimized, with B-52 strikes requiring the approval of the Joint Chiefs of Staff.[106] One Air Force observer claimed that "Linebacker achieved more in its first four months of operation than Rolling Thunder had in three years."[107]

Again using bombing as a diplomatic tool, Nixon hoped that B-52 strikes would bring the North Vietnamese to the bargaining table while also buying time for his Vietnamization policy. Only when the bombing increased during Linebacker II during the 1972 Christmas season did the North Vietnamese finally agree to reenter negotiations. Featuring expanded target lists, increased tempo, and removal of restrictions, Linebacker II unleashed the full fury of American airpower.[108] By January 8, 1973, the North Vietnamese entered negotiations and Nixon ordered a cease-fire a week later.[109]

---

104. Benjamin Lambeth, *NATO's Air War for Kosovo: A Strategic and Operational Assessment* (Santa Monica, CA: RAND, 2005), 249, as referenced in Colin Gray, *Airpower for Strategic Effect* (Maxwell AFB, AL: Air University Press, 2012), 223.

105. Vietnamization aimed to turn the war over the South Vietnamese forces through a deliberate training and enhanced equipment program. Hoping this would allow US forces to withdraw, the South Vietnamese were to fight the north on their own with new US arms and training.

106. Frankum, *Like Rolling Thunder*, 157 and 161.

107. Hone, "Strategic Bombardment Constrained," 508.

108. Frankum, *Like Rolling Thunder*, 163.

109. Frankum, *Like Rolling Thunder*, 165.

While formal negotiations began in May, by January 27, an agreement was reached, with Secretary of State Henry Kissinger remarking that the bombing, indeed, made the Paris Accords possible.

While the Linebacker raids are often touted by airpower advocates as exemplifying the power of strategic bombing, they occurred long after America lost the war and was merely a tactic employed by an administration looking for a way out. Furthermore, by 1972 the nature of the conflict changed to more of a conventional fight.[110] In other words, strategic bombing operations only had an effect once the North Vietnamese began conducting conventional military operations over their previously practiced guerilla actions. Airpower proponents argue that had the United States started the strategic campaign in accord with the Joint Chiefs' 1965 recommendation, the war would have been won years earlier. Given the guerilla tactics used by the enemy during the early part of the war, claims of victory through bombing are only conjecture. Concerns of a larger war with the USSR or with China overshadowed bombing operations, with American anxiety over publicity of wanton destruction always a consideration. Pro-bombing viewpoints regarding an unrestricted Rolling Thunder operation ignore the more intangible aspects of war, while embracing simple formulaic methods of military power.

Post-Vietnam/Cold War Efforts

After Vietnam, the American military conducted a wholesale review of its doctrines, equipment, and focus. Eventually the Pentagon developed the concept of "Air-Land Battle" that revamped many of its basic war-fighting doctrines. Among these new doctrines, Air Force colonel John Warden developed a modified air campaign theory known as the "Five Rings." In this concept, inner concentric rings symbolized key enemy nodes and capabilities, with the most important targets in the interior circles and rippling outward in descending importance. At the core of the model was enemy leadership, followed in the larger outer rings by system essentials, infrastructure, population, and military forces.[111] However, critics saw the Five Rings model as merely a repackaging of the old doctrine that ACTS developed and trumpeted in the 1930s, again promising an air-centric victory and minimizing the effects of ground and naval forces.

In response to the 1990 Iraqi invasion of Kuwait, Warden designed a corresponding air campaign plan based upon his ideas. Warden fully believed that his plan could

---

110. Frankum, *Like Rolling Thunder*; Pape, *Bombing to Win*, 209.

111. Richard G. Davis, "Strategic Bombardment in the Gulf War," in Hall, *Case Studies*, 535–36; Meilinger, *Airwar: Theory and Practice*, 178.

easily bring about victory in a matter of days.[112] Looking to avoid the mistakes of Rolling Thunder, the Warden plan, entitled Instant Thunder, sought to destroy Saddam Hussein and his Ba'athist leadership's ability to command and control its forces. The plan called for hitting eighty-six targets with some 5,700 sorties in a short span of a few days.[113] Dismissing the ground component, during his briefing to Lieutenant General James Horner, the Central Command Air Force commander in Saudi Arabia, Warden casually commented, "Ground forces aren't important to this campaign."[114] Horner bristled not only at Warden's response but at this apparent outsider telling him how to do his job. Given Warden's impolitic quip and attitude, he was returned home only hours later. General Horner chided Warden's plan and remained unconvinced that Warden's six-day campaign would succeed. Horner derisively noted, "There is no way the Iraqis are going to turn tail and head home after six days of bombing!"[115]

Yet, the concept looked good on paper. Like the World War II CBO plan, however, Instant Thunder rested upon the assumption of accurate targeting data, identification of system essentials, and a presumption that aerial bombardment would have a negative effect on morale in a totalitarian state.[116] Additionally, the term "strategic" again became a semantic argument as the Iraqi Republican Guard troops as well as transportation networks feeding into Kuwait were added to the list of primary targets.[117] Under Warden's model, troops and infrastructure were in the lesser rings of five and three respectively, but now troops and transportation networks were labeled as "strategic." Interdiction of supplies, attacking transportation networks, as well as the ground forces themselves now became "strategic" targets.

Despite his dismissal, much of Warden's initial targeting list remained intact. However, the attacks on the leadership and command and control failed to decapitate the Iraqi leadership and its ability to direct and lead the army. Looking to communicate with the Iraqi masses, Instant Thunder hoped "to convince the Iraqi people that a bright economic and political future would result with the replacement of the Saddam Hussein regime."[118] Despite the supposed importance of the first ring, only a small number of sorties were dedicated to the effort. While the targeting did reduce Iraqi command and control abilities, it never fully severed the relationship between Hussein

112. Thomas A. Keaney and Eliot Cohen, *Gulf War Air Power Survey (GWAPS) Summary Report* (Washington, DC: US Government Printing Office, 1993), 35–37; Pape, *Bombing to Win*, 219–20.

113. Davis, "Strategic Bombardment in the Gulf War," 542; Budiansky, *Air Power*, 414; Keaney and Cohen, *GWAPS*, 37; Pape, *Bombing to Win*, 222.

114. Budiansky, *Air Power*, 416.

115. Pape, *Bombing to Win*, 224.

116. Davis, "Strategic Bombardment in the Gulf War," 544; Budiansky, *Air Power*, 428–29; Meilinger, *Airwar: Theory and Practice*, 178.

117. Keaney and Cohen, *GWAPS*, 46–47; Budiansky, *Air Power*, 418; Pape, *Bombing to Win*, 224.

118. Keaney and Cohen, *GWAPS*, 44–45.

and his people.[119] In fact, the people had little motivation to rise against Hussein. As one war correspondent observed, "I found the Iraqis, on the whole, remarkably tolerant of the allied bombs that had destroyed their homes or killed civilians."[120] Another reporter found that Iraqis did not fear coalition strikes and quickly figured out that the bombs were not aimed at them, but only at military targets.[121]

Perhaps the biggest distraction to the strategic effort was the unfortunate incident regarding Al Firdos bunker on February 13, 1991. Hundreds of civilian men, women, and children were killed while seeking shelter in the bunker, with the world press publicizing the tragedy. After Al Firdos, the Air Force directed a dramatic drop in the targeting of Ba'athist leaders, as now the Central Command commander in chief, General Norman Schwarzkopf, personally reviewed any targets planned for downtown Baghdad.[122] The *Summary Report of the Gulf War Air Power Survey* (GWAPS) claimed the twenty-four-hour news cycle coverage of collateral damage and the perception of the excessive use of airpower caused anxiety in the Bush administration.[123] As a result of a sensitivity regarding aerial slaughter at the hands of coalition air forces, world opinion forced a truncated use of strategic power.

Given that reality, Allied interdiction and close air support focused on Iraqi ground forces with significant effect, making outstanding contributions to the defeat of enemy formations.[124] However, the strategic campaign failed to cut off the enemy from supply and equipment. The post-conflict survey found that the Iraqi Army never suffered from lack of equipment, never running out of tanks, vehicles, artillery, or supplies, as had been envisioned in the strategic elements of the air campaign.[125] The strategic effort also failed in its original intent as none of the senior Iraqi leadership was killed and Hussein retained control of his Republican Guard.[126] Even after weeks of attacks, in mid-February communication links between the Iraqi leadership and the army remained intact.[127] While segments of the Iraqi population did rebel after the conflict with limited success, the lack of American material support allowed the regime to maintain power. Once again, strategic efforts failed to produce the expected results when faced with the vagaries of war.

119. Keaney and Cohen, *GWAPS*, 67; Gray, *Airpower for Strategic Effect*, 213.

120. Milton Viorst as referenced in Richard Hallion, *Storm over Iraq: Air Power and the Gulf War* (Washington, DC: Smithsonian Institute, 1992), 199.

121. Hallion, *Storm over Iraq.*

122. Kearny and Cohen, *GWAPS*, 69; Pape, *Bombing to Win*, 231–32.

123. Kearny and Cohen, *GWAPS*, 250–51.

124. Pape, *Bombing to Win*, 274.

125. Pape, *Bombing to Win*, 248; Kearny and Cohen, *GWAPS*, 117.

126. Pape, *Bombing to Win*, 231.

127. Kearny and Cohen, *GWAPS*, 70; Pape, *Bombing to Win*, 221, 230, 236, and 239.

Operation Allied Force

Before the end of the decade, strategic bombardment had yet another chance at validation, but this time in an international effort. During Operation Allied Force, starting on March 24, 1999, the North Atlantic Treaty Organization (NATO) looked to remove Serbian forces from Kosovo and end the atrocities of ethnic cleansing. With UN backing, the NATO-led air operation was a key campaign that validated the alliance's cohesion in the face of adversity and its first extended use of military force. Successful in deterring the Soviet Union during the Cold War, NATO's combined military forces had yet to be fully tested in combat. Would there be the cohesion that is such an important factor in any military operation? With the United States flying the bulk of the missions, what was supposed to be a four-day air campaign to coerce Slobodan Milosevic to withdraw his forces ended up taking seventy-eight days.[128] While ultimately successful, observers of the campaign claimed that the execution of the aerial offensive was a piecemeal effort, lacking full coordination, with restrictive rules of engagement, and targeting scrutinized with cumbersome approval methods.[129] Furthermore, clever dispersion of Serbian forces with mobile launchers, inclement weather, and hilly terrain were among the other factors that hampered NATO's attempt to degrade the enemy's capabilities.[130]

Individual national goals for and perceptions of the international effort differed slightly. Coalition partners often employed national caveats and interjected interpretations of the effort that affected execution. On his part, President Bill Clinton envisioned the campaign as a demonstration of NATO's position against Milosevic and his forces and as an effort that would damage Serbian military capabilities, while avoiding a ground commitment.[131] In this landlocked conflict, with the explicit avoidance of ground forces, airpower served as the sole means of coercive military power. Although the air campaign was expected to be short, as in prior conflicts, escalation would again characterize the aerial effort. As Milosevic and the Serb forces held out, sortie generation grew with targeting lists expanded.[132]

---

128. Benjamin S. Lambeth, *NATO's Air War for Kosovo* (Santa Monica, CA: RAND, 2001), xiii; Gray, *Airpower for Strategic Effect*, 222; Meilinger, *Airwar: Theory and Practice*, 191.

129. Dag Henriksen, *NATO's Gamble* (Annapolis, MD: Naval Institute Press, 2007), 20–22; Lambeth, xiii; Gray, *Airpower for Strategic Effect*, 222; Budiansky, *Air Power*, 430; Tony Mason, "Operation Allied Force 1999," in *A History of Air Warfare*, ed. J. A. Olsen (Washington, DC: Potomac, 2010), 237.

130. Lambeth, *NATO's Air War*, xvi–xvii; Mason, "Operation Allied Force," 234–35; William Sayers, "Operation Allied Force," *Air Force Magazine*, May 2019, 76.

131. Robert Gregory, *Clean Bombs and Dirty Wars: Airpower in Kosovo and Libya* (Lincoln: University of Nebraska Press, 2015), 34 and 118; Henriksen, *NATO's Gamble*, 86–87; Mason, "Operation Allied Force 1999," 229; Sayers, "Operation Allied Force."

132. Lambeth, *NATO's Air War*, xxii; Gregory, *Clean Bombs*, 72; Sayers, "Operation Allied Force."

Execution of the campaign was difficult given the nature of the environment combined with the international caveats imposed by various NATO members. Added to these was the ever-increasing scrutiny of aerial attacks by the world press, which raised the bar on accuracy. NATO aircrews were held accountable for almost every drop in near-real time, as the twenty-four-hour news cycle continuously monitored execution.[133] Nightly news coverage of strike footage from Operation Desert Storm combined with the Allied Force effort created the impression that accuracy was no longer a problem. Using precision-guided munitions (PGMs) against Serbian structures, the campaign did an excellent job of keeping collateral damage to a minimum, resulting in only a few hundred civilian deaths, with no NATO casualties.[134] Up to a third of the weapons dropped were guided, and outside of a few errors, were largely successful in hitting their targets. Embarrassingly, when a B-2 bomber mistakenly hit the Chinese Embassy on the night of May 6th, NATO responded by claiming that of the 1,900 targets attacked with a total of 9,000 bombs and missiles, only 12 had gone amiss.[135] In this regard, technology had finally caught up with doctrine, as PGMs provided a degree of accuracy that the ACTS faculty would have marveled at back in the 1930s. This use of PGMs started a precedent for future air operations, as misdrops and collateral damage appeared more the exception than the norm.

By May, Milosevic's main ally, Russia, began to side with NATO, and days later the Serbian leader was indicted by the International War Crimes Tribunal. Losing a powerful ally was a blow to the regime as Serbia could never stand alone against NATO's fractured, but collective power. The air campaign continued in intensity as NATO went from flying fewer than a hundred sorties a day in March to over seven hundred daily sorties by June 1st.[136] Additionally, the publicized cruelty of the Serbian atrocities garnered the attention of the world press, and alongside Milosevic's indictment, resulted in the loss of international support. Furthermore, the destruction of Serbian infrastructure and imposed economic constraints had potential economic consequences for the Yugoslavian elite.[137] When governmental buildings and infrastructure took a large number of hits, the financial value of privately owned facilities became a concern. Moreover, the opposition Kosovo Liberation Army (KLA) began massing along the border and causing Serbian troops to do the same. As a result, the assembled Serbian army formations became susceptible to aerial attack, as they were no longer dispersed and employing cover and concealment tactics. Additionally, NATO patience regarding the air campaign was coming to an end with ground action a growing possibility. As

---

133. Mason, "Operation Allied Force 1999," 251; Gregory, *Clean Bombs*, 87, 103, and 113.

134. Lambeth, *NATO's Air War*, XX.

135. Mason, "Operation Allied Force 1999," 242.

136. Mason, "Operation Allied Force 1999," 243.

137. Lambeth, *NATO's Air War*, xiv; Sayers, "Operation Allied Force," 75.

the air campaign continued with no sign of abating, Milosevic was running out of options as Russia pulled its support, international opinion was against him, and the country's financial state was in peril.[138]

In the end, Milosevic capitulated. Superficially, this could count as validation of strategic bombardment. USAF chief of staff Michael Ryan firmly believed that airpower was finally the decisive element and said as much when he stated:

> The lights went down, the power went off, petroleum production ceased, the bridges were down, communications were down, the economics of the country were slowly falling apart and I think he [Milosevic] came to the realization, in a strategic sense, he wasn't prepared to continue this.[139]

However, given the number of other factors that led to the Serbian withdrawal, the "win" for the strategic concept at least requires an asterisk.

The Global War on Terror

With the fall of the World Trade Center buildings on September 11, 2001, and the suspicion that Saddam Hussein colluded with Al-Qaeda, the US military again executed strategic air campaigns in two separate regions of the world. One was a technologically backward, loosely conjoined region; the other a contiguous nation-state with modern infrastructure. Afghanistan became the first target of American military power as the Taliban, an ultra-fundamentalist Sunni Islamic emirate that ruled roughly three-fourths of the country, harbored those who planned and launched the World Trade Center attacks. This was followed shortly by Iraq due to two fallacious claims: its connection with Al-Qaeda and its production of weapons of mass destruction.

The strategic effort over Afghanistan in Operation Enduring Freedom was not only short-lived, but it also had few targets. Starting on October 7, 2001, five Air Force B-1s and ten B-52s launched out of the small island of Diego Garcia in the Indian Ocean and stuck targets at Herat, Mazar-i-Sharif, and Kandahar, among others. With the Taliban lacking any real strategic infrastructure or manufacturing, initial missions hit terrorist training camps and the few anti-air defenses that existed, and easily established air dominance.[140] In the nights that followed, Navy and Air Force aircraft struck cave complexes housing Taliban fighters and what little equipment they had. As early as

---

138. Lambeth, *NATO's Air War*, xiv–xv; Meilinger, *Airwar: Theory and Practice*, 201; Mason, "Operation Allied Force," 244.

139. General Michael E. Ryan, in Air Force Policy Letter (August 1999), as referenced in Mason, "Operation Allied Force," 244.

140. Benjamin Lambeth, "Operation Enduring Freedom 2001," in Olsen, *History of Air Warfare*, 259–60.

the tenth day of the air campaign priorities shifted to targets of opportunity.[141] Given these sorties, this "strategic" air operation did much to bring down the Taliban in the early days of the conflict, but it fell short in winning the larger war.[142] Most of the subsequent operations in Afghanistan required mainly tactical air support for ground forces, who were transported and supported by helicopters. "Taliban plinking" and close tactical air support became the most important role for airpower, eclipsing the relevance of strategic bombardment.

While B-1s, B-2s, and B-52s continued missions in Afghanistan, the use of precision guided munitions from these types of aircraft serve largely as weapons platforms assisting in the tactical fight. The use of bombers in Operation Anaconda in March 2002 in Afghanistan met with lukewarm success. The use of B-1s, B-2s, and B-52s serve an important role as their range allowed continuous support to ground troops. However, as in Korea and Vietnam, strategic bombing had no effect on Taliban sources of supply, as they received aid and support from outside their country. Although strategic bombers were effective in servicing tactical level targets and disrupting Taliban formations, this effort did not disrupt overall enemy morale. Fighting for more than nineteen years after the start of the conflict, aerial bombardment did not break the enemy's will, as Taliban forces defied the theory behind the effort.

In the opening phases of Operation Iraqi Freedom in 2003, coalition forces faced a more capable, but still overmatched, enemy.[143] Unlike the buildup for Desert Storm, in Operation Iraqi Freedom strategic airstrikes took place in concert with the ground assault from Kuwait. Looking to provide "shock and awe," strategic bombing operations focused on both the regime's leadership and the will of the Iraqi people. Similar to Warden's Five Rings model, coalition air and naval forces looked to decapitate Iraqi leadership and deliberately targeted Saddam Hussein and other members of his regime.[144] None of these strikes was successful, including a pre-conflict strike aimed directly at Saddam Hussein. Despite the attempt to strike the regime's system essentials of command and control, one Iraqi commander claimed, "The early air attacks hit only empty headquarters and barracks buildings . . . we used schools and hidden command centers in orchards for our headquarters—which were not hit."[145] Given the dubious status of existing Iraqi command and control abilities, and combined with the poor quality of the regime's military, had these strikes been successful it

---

141. Lambeth, "Operation Enduring Freedom," 261.

142. Gray, *Airpower for Strategic Effect*, 251.

143. Williamson Murray and Robert Scales, *The Iraq War: A Military History* (Cambridge, MA: Belknap, 2003), 83–84, 87, and 102.

144. Murray and Scales, *Iraq War*, 155–56 and 167; John Keegan, *The Iraq War* (New York: Alfred A. Knopf, 2004), 143.

145. Williamson Murray, "Operation Iraqi Freedom, 2003," in Olsen, *History of Air Warfare*, 289.

is questionable that they would have made any difference in Iraqi performance.[146] Concurrently, the Iraqi industrial base supporting its military was severely lacking or nonexistent. Most of its equipment was of old Soviet vintage with little improvement since 1991. Combined with that, Iraqi military units had substantial equipment shortages.[147]

Furthermore, much of the Iraqi populace was already disgruntled with Ba'athist rule, needing no further motivation to withdraw support from that totalitarian regime.[148] Ba'athist support was largely based upon ethnic lines, as the ruling Arab Sunnis dominated the Kurdish and Shi'a populations. Even among the Sunni population support for the regime was split along rural and urban lines.[149] While the Iraqi people were cautious with their response to the coalition advance, a lack of support for the Hussein regime already existed.

As a result, the major foundations for conducting a strategic bombing campaign were moot before the conflict even began. The Iraqi military was already in poor shape, with little or no production capacities to support it. Motivation of the civilian populace to support the regime was already at low ebb, rendering futile attacks aimed at Iraqi civilian morale. Furthermore, the strategic bombing efforts to decapitate the Ba'athist leadership and disrupt its command and control capabilities were abject failures. Given these circumstances, the majority of air operations for the remainder of the operation were tactical in flavor, providing timely and effective support to troops on the ground or the movement of needed supplies during times of high-density fighting against insurgent forces.

Conclusion

The history of strategic bombing covers a relatively short period, but spans the bloodiest era of warfare. From its hopeful beginnings as a way to ameliorate the suffering and death of protracted wars to its measured responses in limited conflicts, the execution of strategic air campaigns has a checkered past with debatable results. In the parlance of the Pentagon, the concept of strategic bombing "briefs well." The idea of strategic bombing sounds logical, methodical, and well reasoned, and its advocates make a good case for the concept. However, the execution of strategic bombing campaigns is much more complex, dependent on various factors, and subject to the vagaries of human interaction. Strategic bombing campaigns fell victim to innumerable factors of the inherently illogical, inconsistent, and specious

---

146. Anthony Cordesman, *The Iraq War: Strategy, Tactics, and Military Lessons* (Washington, DC: Center for Strategic and International Studies Press, 2003), 483.

147. Cordesman, *Iraq War*, 45.

148. Keegan, *Iraq War*, 164; Cordesman, *Iraq War*, 43.

149. Cordesman, *Iraq War*, 43.

nature of humans. Similarly, war is a human endeavor, and as such it is subject to the failings of its participants. Results of strategic bombing campaigns often reflect those very factors and shortcomings.

While World War II strategic bombing did contribute to victory, the European theater's combined bomber strategy and the firebombing campaign against Japan equally either fell short of intent or were duplicative. After the war, various plans to deploy nuclear attacks were shown, albeit theoretically, to be unfeasible and destined to fail in their primary objectives. To be fair, as an act of deterrence, the strategic capabilities of the superpowers could claim success in preventing a nuclear holocaust. However, in the limited wars of Korea and Vietnam, strategic bombing and interdiction were largely the same phenomenon separated only by semantics. Whatever this type of bombing is classified as, it proved far less than 100 percent effective.

After the experience of Vietnam, the American military entered a renaissance, with many reflecting on the military failure in Southeast Asia. However, strategic bombing in post-Vietnam conflicts reflected some of the same characteristics of previous campaigns. While Operation Allied Force was indeed a victory of sorts for airpower advocates, Operation Instant Thunder fell victim to some of the same constraining factors of previous limited engagements: public perception of collateral damage; misdrops, lack of definitive proof of effectiveness during air operations; and perhaps most important, the images of dead women and children as a result of bombing shown around the world. These considerations following 9/11 provided new challenges for the concept. Limited wars, counterinsurgent-dominated conflict, and increased concern over collateral damage and civilian casualties have all contributed to the marginalization of the theory of strategic bombing.

But why does the myth persist? Why is strategic bombing such an attractive idea? The answer is manyfold. First, as noted earlier, technological solutions are part of America's collective DNA and are foundational to the nation's growth and experience. America is a nation fascinated with technology. The use of sophisticated aircraft manned by highly trained crews fits our national paradigm. Second, from a moral point of view, historian Michael Sherry offers the insight that the technology inherent with strategic bombing potentially distances people from the ugly consequences of their actions. While aircrews, and even drone pilots, may suffer from posttraumatic stress syndrome, strategic bombing provides an appearance of cleanliness in application despite the consequences of large-scale destruction and death largely unseen by protagonists.[150] It gives the impression of sanitized warfare, providing the illusion of the "clean kill," while delivering a quick alternative to the messiness and chaos in other forms of combat.

Third, strategic airpower is economically attractive. Since one plane with one or a few crew can carry thousands of pounds (or megatons) worth of explosive power,

---

150. Michael Sherry, *The Rise of American Airpower* (New Haven, CT: Yale University Press, 1987), 251–55.

it appears cheaper than battalions of troops or fleets of ships. The inherent power of aerial bombs and strategic missiles far exceeds that of small arms, artillery, or naval gunfire, thus providing more "bang for the buck." This idea regarding economic savings first manifested in the interwar period during the Great Depression and surfaced again under Eisenhower's policies in NSC 162/2. The fiscal considerations are a key component during peacetime preparations, when budgetary concerns are often the priority.

Fourth, strategic airpower also allows a nation to conduct warfare, enforce its will, and pursue political aims with fewer personnel serving in a combat environment. Both Vietnam and Korea embodied this presumed attribute. While ground forces are required to hold terrain and provide a sustained presence, strategic bombardment provides quick, powerful, and flexible options that reduce, but do not eliminate, the need for "boots on the ground." While killing of enemy civilians and noncombatants occurred in the examples provided, American lives were spared. With a few hundred aircrew in harm's way during a given strategic mission, thousands of enemy citizens and soldiers were in peril. As a result, from the standpoint of manpower, bombing provides a cost savings in military personnel while endangering the larger enemy population.

Furthermore, its speed of response is attractive. Bombers, missiles, and drones all move relatively quickly in the third dimension and are flexible in application. Deployment in a few hours by aircraft is much more responsive as opposed to several weeks or months for surface forces. This is a very appealing prospect regarding global emergencies. As the world becomes smaller and speed of response requires immediate action, airpower is uniquely equipped to act expeditiously, but not necessarily comprehensively. Even Douhet identified the inherent attribute of airpower to respond quickly before the employment of other forms of warfare. Its rapid offensive nature is an attractive characteristic that often appears to negate other military services.

Lastly, and certainly arguably, airpower has an attraction, an allure that evokes romantic notions of combat and heroic deeds.[151] Although other mediums of warfare have their own attractive attributes, sleek advanced combat airplanes, piloted by highly skilled and brash aviators, continue to have a special place not only in the pantheon of warfare but also in American popular culture. Movies such as *Twelve O' Clock High*, *The War Lover*, *Strategic Air Command*, combined with the latest manifestations of *Top Gun*, *Iron Eagle*, *Memphis Belle*, *Pearl Harbor*, and *Unbroken*, perpetuate this cultural iconography.

Throughout its history, strategic bombing as a single application has failed to achieve the results its framers envisioned. While airpower is a key component in any modern military victory, the application of strategic bombardment is hardly

---

151. Martin van Creveld, *The Age of Airpower* (New York: Public Affairs, 2011), inside cover.

the panacea many believed. While a nation cannot win a war through airpower alone, it also cannot win without it. A carefully orchestrated combination of airpower integrated with all efforts and levels of warfare provides the best results not only for conflict resolution but also for victory. Yet as an independent action absent the other forms of warfare, strategic bombing remains a concept still wanting.

6. NEW ASYMMETRIC WARFARE: SOMETHING OLD, SOMETHING NEW, SOMETHING BORROWED

William Kautt

> The time has come for the Islamic movements facing a general crusader
> offensive to internalize the rules of fourth-generation warfare. They must
> consolidate appropriate strategic thought, and make appropriate military
> preparations. . . . In addition to the religious obligation, this has become
> an integral part of the means to triumph in fourth-generation warfare. Old
> strategists, such as Clausewitz and Mao Zedong, have already indicated this.
> —*Abu 'Ubeid al-Qurashi, aide to Osama bin Laden*[1]

Conceptions of war have undergone dramatic shifts over the last twenty-five years.
The attacks of 9/11 and the subsequent American wars in Afghanistan and Iraq
featured dramatic instances of so-called asymmetric warfare, which, for the purposes
of this chapter, is one of the more recent terms for unconventional, guerrilla, partisan,
people's war, terrorism, and other similar means of waging war. The more technical
definition is that asymmetric warfare is where one attacks an enemy's vulnerabilities
with markedly disparate means to nullify the enemy's military advantages to unequal
effect.[2] This simply means using unconventional attacks to strike an enemy's weak-
nesses, while avoiding strengths, to achieve a greater result out of proportion to the
force used. Many people have asked over the past twenty-five years whether asymmetric means have changed warfare itself, especially how wars will be fought in the future.
Indeed, some observers believe that recent insurgencies—which employ political and
diplomatic, economic, sociocultural, informational, and military means simultaneously against their enemies—are proof of a new form of war. They are not, in fact,
and asymmetrical warfare is nothing new. The more recent applications of it are only
the adaptation of an ancient form of resistance evolved to meet modern conditions,
particularly in regard to technology. While some tactics and means are somewhat
new (such as exploitation of communications technology, especially social media), the

---

1. "Bin Laden Lieutenant Admits to September 11 and Explains Al-Qa'ida's Combat Doctrine,"
The Middle East Media Research Institute, Special Dispatch No. 344 (February 10, 2002).
2. AJP-01: *Allied Joint Doctrine* (Brussels: NATO Standardization Office, 2017), LEX 3; AJP-3.2:
Allied Joint Doctrine for Land Operations (Brussels: NATO Standardization Office, 2016), LEX 2.

process employed is not. Claims of its recent origins propagate a myth due to social, ideological, and economic reasons, but particularly because the technological and political elements that form what is today called asymmetrical warfare are far older than proponents realize.

Probably the most famous pre-nineteenth-century examples of this type of conflict come from antiquity. In 9 CE, Publius Quinctilius Varus famously marched three legions across the Rhine and was ambushed and slaughtered in the Teutoburg Forest in present-day Saxony by massed Germanic tribes under Arminius Germanicus achieving asymmetric effects.[3] Later in the Roman province of Judea, there arose the Zealots and an extremist offshoot group, the Sicarii (the "dagger men"). The Sicarii conducted assassinations of prominent Jews whom they believed were collaborating with the Romans. These groups were partly responsible for the Jewish War (66–73 CE) against the Roman Empire.[4] By medieval times, there were many conflicts that could fit into this genre of war; the Welsh Rebellions[5] of the twelfth century and the Scottish Wars of the fourteenth century are most demonstrative. These wars were both against the English and quite successful in their way. While the Welsh ultimately lost their fight against English dominance, the Scots were more successful, using a combination of asymmetric and conventional warfare to bring the English forces to their knees.[6] The early modern era differentiates its warfare with multiple periods within, starting with the Wars of Religion after the Reformation. One of the most telling wars of that era was the Dutch Revolt (1566–1648), in which the Netherlands fought Habsburg Spain for some eighty years to gain independence.[7]

Thus, this form of warfare was hardly unknown but became more pronounced when militias and regulars in the British North American colonies began to copy Indian ways of fighting.[8] Probably the best example of this method occurred during

---

3. A. Murdoch, *Rome's Greatest Defeat: Massacre in the Teutoburg Forest* (Cheltenham, UK: History Press, 2008).

4. W. D. Morrison, *The Jews under Roman Rule* (London: Palala, 2016); M. Goodman, *The Ruling Class of Judaea: The Origins of the Jewish Revolt against Rome, A.D. 66–70* (Cambridge: Cambridge University Press, 1993).

5. G. Brough, *The Rise and Fall of Owain Glyn Dŵr: England, France and the Welsh Rebellion in the Late Middle Ages* (London: I. B. Tauris, 2017); M. Davies, *The Last King of Wales: Gruffudd ap Llywelyn c. 1013–1063* (Cheltenham, UK: History Press, 2012).

6. D. Santiuste, *The Hammer of the Scots: Edward I and the Scottish Wars of Independence* (Barnsley, UK: Pen and Sword Military, 2015); C. Brown, *King and Outlaw: The Real Robert the Bruce* (Cheltenham, UK: History Press, 2018).

7. Geoffrey Parker, *The Dutch Revolt* (Ithaca, NY: Cornell University Press, 1977), and *Spain and the Netherlands 1559–1659* (Waukegan, IL: Fontana Press, 1990).

8. Patrick M. Malone, *The Skulking Way of War: Technology and Tactics among the New England Indians* (New York: Madison, 2000).

the French and Indian War (1754–63),[9] which saw the New Hampshire colonial militia establish "Rogers's Rangers," the inspiration for the modern US Army Rangers. Yet, even Rogers's force was inspired by Gorham's Rangers of the Massachusetts Militia that fought in King George's War (1744–48) and Father Le Loutre's War (1749–55).[10] During the American Revolution (1775–83), the exploits of the "Green Mountain Boys" in what became Vermont and Francis Marion, the "Swamp Fox" of South Carolina, are legendary.[11] The combination of guerrilla and conventional tactics worked, especially in the southern colonies, where hybrid forces maneuvered Lord Cornwallis into the position at Yorktown Peninsula, where he ultimately surrendered in 1781.[12]

Asymmetry and Nineteenth-Century Developments in Military Technology

The timeless aspects of warfare are that armies have to mobilize soldiers and materiel, train them, supply them, move them to the engagement, and fight. In the early modern period, gunpowder weapons were so inaccurate that large numbers of soldiers had to stand shoulder to shoulder to inflict enough damage on the enemy to win. Armies, both regular and irregular, therefore needed large numbers of men, necessitating leaders to drum up popular support. Under such limitations, would-be revolutionaries struggled to win supporters to their side. This acted as a sort of relief valve that prevented some conflicts due to low numbers.

Two nineteenth-century advances in military technology, both stemming from the development of high explosives, changed this formula. The first was smokeless powder, and the second was the high-explosive bomb. Both resulted from Alfred Nobel's creation of dynamite in 1867, the first stable and practical high explosive.

The high-explosive innovation dramatically influenced firearms development. Prior to Nobel, the effective range that a handheld gunpowder weapon could shoot a projectile was five hundred meters at best. Almost as important, gunpowder created debris in the barrel of the weapon, which built up to the point that, after about two dozen rounds, many weapons could not shoot anymore. Thus, inventors sought

---

9. David L. Preston, *Braddock's Defeat: The Battle of the Monongahela and the Road to Revolution* (Oxford: Oxford University Press, 2015).

10. John F. Ross, *War on the Run: The Epic Story of Robert Rogers and the Conquest of America's First Frontier* (New York: Bantam, 2009).

11. John Buchanan, *The Road to Charleston: Nathanael Greene and the American Revolution* (Charlottesville: University of Virginia Press, 2019); Scott D. Aiken, *The Swamp Fox: Lessons in Leadership from the Partisan Campaigns of Francis Marion* (Annapolis, MD: Naval Institute Press, 2012).

12. Burke Davis, *The Cowpens-Guilford Courthouse Campaign* (Philadelphia: University of Pennsylvania Press, 2002).

a good replacement propellant, and high-explosive compounds provided this.

Once firearms manufacturers recognized that they could use high explosives as propellants, weapon designs began to change to take advantage of the differences between gunpowder and the so-called smokeless powder. High-explosive propellants produced considerably higher velocities, increasing range and the damage caused. This permitted designers to decrease the size of bullets without reducing the killing power of the weapon. Smaller bullets also allowed soldiers to carry more ammunition. Another benefit of the smokeless powder was that it was cleaner, thus reducing the

Alfred Nobel (1833–96), the Swedish inventor. Aghast at the use of his inventions for war and a popular reputation as "the master of death," he later bequeathed his fortune for the creation of the Nobel Peace Prize.

amount of fouling in the barrel and the mechanical parts. This permitted greater tolerances in the machining, which meant that the weapons became more accurate, and with the increased velocities came increased range—out to 1,500 meters.

The L-shaped bolt mechanism in rifles was forty years old by the 1880s, and magazine-fed rounds were in use by the 1850s, so marrying the two concepts to increase the reliability, accuracy, and efficiency of the rifles was only natural and permitted an experienced shooter to fire rapidly and accurately.[13] In the late nineteenth century, American Hiram Maxim invented and fielded a weapon that only required one pull of the trigger, which would fire, reload automatically, and continue firing and reloading until the trigger was released—a machine gun, or automatic weapon. Then, weapons designers developed the semiautomatic pistol that would reload automatically after each shot. Finally, during World War I, the Germans needed a light, handheld machine gun that one man could carry and fire. In 1918, the German Army issued the Bergmann MP-18 to storm units on the Western Front for the ill-fated Spring

13. Spencer Jones, *From Boer War to World War: Tactical Reform of the British Army, 1902–1914* (Norman: University of Oklahoma Press, 2012), 9, 94, and 96; Army Council, *Musketry Regulations, 1909*, Part 1 (London: His Majesty's Stationary Office, 1909), 258–61.

Offensive. The weapon was successful in combat (although the offensive ultimately was not).

The advent of modern firearms had an equal effect on irregular conflicts as with conventional combat: they favored the defensive. This strengthening of the defensive posture was significant. Indeed, it changed the character of war. Instead of requiring dozens or even hundreds of men to hold a position, now just a few soldiers, in a defensible site, could hold off many times their strength. Sustained, accurate fire from concealment increased casualties far beyond what experts foresaw.

Moreover, the volume of fire these weapons produced also permitted just a few shooters to inflict damage on a scale that, in the past, had only been possible with large numbers. For example, the Thompson submachine gun, made infamous by American gangsters in the 1920s and 1930s and used in World War II to great effect by American and Allied troops, first saw combat in Ireland in the hands of Irish rebels attacking British troops on a train in June 1921.[14] It saw extensive service on both sides of the later Irish Civil War (1922–23).

The development of dynamite also enabled so-called scientific warfare.[15] The application of this new explosive capability reduced the importance of attracting popular support. The limitations of technology up to 1867 meant that without the people on their side, there was little they could accomplish. Dynamite, they thought, was the "poor man's artillery," which would now allow them to fight well above their weight.

Asymmetry and Terrorism

Yet, these technological developments were only part of the equation. Dynamite was worthless without doctrine to use it. Fortunately for the early insurgents, a doctrine of revolution had grown alongside the technology that would enable it. The stage was set for insurrectionary uses of this modern technology that further calls into question the myth of asymmetrical warfare.

We look first to France. The French Revolution (1789–99) gave rise to a period known as "The Terror" (1793–95), from which the term "terrorism" (the illegal use of violence for political gain) was coined to describe the government's use of violence against its population.[16] Further, there was a revolt against the French Republic in

---

14. Peter Hart, *The IRA and Its Enemies* (Oxford: Oxford University Press, 1998), 178–93; J. Boyer Bell, "The Thompson Submachine Gun in Ireland, 1921," *The Irish Sword* 8 (1967): 98–101; Patrick Jung, "The Thompson Submachine Gun during and after the Anglo-Irish War: The New Evidence," *The Irish Sword* 21 (1998): 191–218.

15. Niall Whelehan, *The Dynamiters: Irish Nationalism and Political Violence in the Wider World, 1867–1900* (Cambridge: Cambridge University Press, 2012), 77.

16. See David Andress, *The Terror: The Merciless War for Freedom in Revolutionary France* (New York: Farrar, Straus and Giroux, 2006).

the Vendée (1793)[17] and later against the empire in Tyrol (1809).[18] The Napoleonic period also saw the first recorded use of a vehicle-borne improvised explosive device, when conspirators attacked Bonaparte's convoy on the rue Saint-Nicaise in Paris with a wagon packed with gunpowder on Christmas Eve 1800. The devastating "small wars" in the Peninsular War (1807–14)[19] and the Russian Campaign of 1812[20] are legendary and provide excellent examples of hybrid, or combined guerrilla and conventional, capabilities, and the former gave birth to the word "guerrilla."

Revolutionaries and theorists took note of the fear with which the European monarchies reacted to the new threats. The revolutions of 1848 then led to the Second Republic (1848–51), the Second Empire (1852–70), the Paris Commune (March–May 1871), and the Third Republic (1870–1940) in France. The brutality of the suppression of the Commune, in particular, spurred on revolutionaries, particularly anarchists, elsewhere in Europe.

During the Franco-Prussian War (1870–71), the new French government called on its citizens to rise up; these irregulars (the so-called *Francs-tireurs*) caused considerable trouble for invading German forces, particularly by attacking lines of communication. The Germans responded ferociously, executing *Francs-tireurs* prisoners, whom they considered murderers.[21] This, along with the brutal postwar suppression of the Paris Commune, provided impetus to revolutionaries around Europe.[22]

Anarchism originally arose in Europe in the 1830s in response to what its adherents saw as oppressive governments. Idealistic in many ways, the anarchists, first inspired by theorist Pierre-Joseph Proudhon (1809–65), believed that government in most, if not all, forms was oppressive and that voluntary adherence to limited local governance was the only just means of organizing society. Revolutionary Italian anarchist and student of Proudhon Carlo Pisacane (1818–57) was convinced that "ideas spring from deeds and not the other way around": giving rise to the concept of "propaganda by the deed," or that the deed *is the propaganda* for the revolution. Russian anarchist Mikhail Bakunin (1814–76) echoed this, saying revolutionaries should spread their ideas "not with words but with deeds," while German anarchist Johann Most (1846–1906), writing from America, stated that "we preach not only action in

17. Reynald Secher, *A French Genocide: The Vendée* (South Bend, IN: University of Notre Dame Press, 2003).

18. Gunter F. Eyck, *Loyal Rebels: Andreas Hofer and the Tyrolean Uprising of 1809* (Lanham, MD: University Press of America, 1986).

19. Don W. Alexander, *Rod of Iron: French Counterinsurgency Policy in Aragon during the Peninsular War* (New York: Rowman and Littlefield, 1985).

20. Richard K. Riehn, *1812: Napoleon's Russian Campaign* (New York: McGraw-Hill, 1990).

21. Geoffrey Wawro, *The Franco-Prussian War: The German Conquest of France in 1870–1871* (Cambridge: Cambridge University Press, 2003).

22. Jonathan M. House, *Controlling Paris: Armed Forces and Counter-Revolution, 1789–1848* (New York: New York University Press, 2014).

and for itself, but also action as propaganda."[23] This line of thinking established one of the first concepts of modern terrorism, that of violent, evocative events.

Anarchist Louis Auguste Blanqui (1805–81) believed that the best means for revolution was for a small, highly trained, and secretive band to overthrow the government via coup d'état, establish a temporary dictatorship to enact reforms, then turn power over to the people. The Russian anarchist Sergey Nechayev (1847–82) was the first to refer to himself as a "terrorist" and believed that anything was permissible to achieve freedom from oppression. These concepts led to the organization of small groups and helped remove the idea of restraint.

Other locales stirred similarly. By the mid-1870s, the Irish American republicans, still stinging from a half dozen failed raids into Canada, established the Skirmishing Fund to take the "war" to Britain's doorstep. Soon thereafter, they established a semisecret "dynamite school" in Brooklyn. In this school, the republicans taught would-be revolutionaries to manufacture dynamite and to construct bombs.[24] From these classes, the leaders selected recruits for the first mission to the United Kingdom, which began in January 1881 with the bombing of a military barracks at Salford and ended, after seven attacks and two attempts, with the arrests of most of the plotters in April 1883. Despite the failure of the first mission, the republicans began another in October, which included twelve bombings and three attempts and lasted until January 1885. While the two missions were distinct, they had much in common. Both recruited Irish immigrants from respectable working-class backgrounds, enabling the operatives to disappear within Britain's Irish expatriate communities. After training, each man went across singly and awaited instructions. Although the longer second mission suffered some fatal accidents and some bombs were defused, most bombs detonated as planned. These attacks led the British to create the first "Irish Special Branch," a detective force dedicated to internal security against terrorism. In time, the "Irish" was dropped and such branches became part of many British possessions. Prime Minister William Ewart Gladstone and his liberals gave more attention to Ireland, first through passing agrarian and land tenure reform measures. Then the liberals introduced the First Home Rule Bill in the mid-1880s, which, had it passed, would have provided Ireland with a devolved local government for "Irish" affairs. Just how much the Dynamite War contributed to greater attention from the government is unknowable.

Although this first modern terrorist campaign failed, that the republicans saw some positive result was not lost on other revolutionaries. Elsewhere, anarchists

---

23. Carlo Pisacane, "Political Testament," (1857), Robert Graham's Anarchism Weblog, accessed October 6, 2019, https://robertgraham.wordpress.com/carlo-pisacane-propaganda-by-the-deed/; Mikhail Bakunin, "Letters to a Frenchman on the Present Crisis," (1870), Marxists Internet Archive, accessed June 25, 2019, http://marxists.org/reference/archive/bakunin/works/1870/letter-frenchman.htm; and Johann Most, "Action as Propaganda," *Freiheit*, July 25, 1885.

24. Whelehan, *Dynamiters*, 69–71, 75–85, 157–64, and 167–72.

rose to conduct revolutionary violence. In the United States, there were attacks by anarchists associated with the labor movements, the Haymarket Square bombing in Chicago in 1886 being the best known, and anarchist Leon Czolgosz assassinated President William McKinley in 1901.[25] In tsarist Russia, after three failed attempts by assassins, Alexander II finally died from a bomb blast in 1881, and revolutionaries killed many other government officials in Russia. In France, anarchists attacked random bourgeois sites in Paris in the early 1890s.[26]

The asymmetric threat seemed to be growing. During the Second South African War (1899–1901), Boer commandos inflicted heavy losses on British imperial forces using hybrid methods for reasons similar to

Tsar Alexander II of Russia. The anti-tsarist revolutionary group known as "People's Will" orchestrated his murder via bombing in St. Petersburg in 1881.

the Americans in the Philippine-American War (1899–1902)—regular soldiers were unable to see their enemy.[27] The Boers, using modern firearms, engaged British troops at long distances, over one thousand meters, from concealed positions. The Filipinos

---

25. Robert F. Coakley, *The Role of Federal Military Forces in Domestic Disorders, 1789–1878* (Washington, DC: US Army Center for Military History, 1988), 12.

26. Simon Webb, *Dynamite, Treason and Plot: Terrorism in Victorian and Edwardian London* (Cheltenham, UK: History Press, 2012); John Merriman, *The Dynamite Club: How a Bombing in Fin-de-Siècle Paris Ignited the Age of Modern Terror* (Boston: Houghton Mifflin Harcourt, 2009); Anna Geifman, *Thou Shalt Kill: Revolutionary Terrorism in Russia, 1894–1917* (Princeton, NJ: Princeton University Press, 1995).

27. Frank Pakenham, *The Boer War* (New York: Random House, 1979); *The United States and the Philippines*, ed. F. H. Golay (Englewood Cliffs, NJ: Prentice-Hall, 1966).

attacked suddenly from the dense jungles and then disappeared quickly. Still, both the American and British armies eventually won their conflicts.

The so-called long nineteenth century ended with the start of World War I in 1914, which was best known for the wholesale, industrialized, conventional devastation of stalemate on the Western Front. Elsewhere, however, the war was different. In the Middle East, T. E. Lawrence (Lawrence of Arabia) assisted with the Arab Revolt (1916–18),[28] and P. E. Lettow-Vorbeck, the "Lion of Africa," fought the British imperial forces to a standstill using guerrilla tactics in German Southeast Africa (present-day Tanzania).[29] The British found themselves fighting in the Irish War of Independence (1919–21),[30] the Northwest Frontier (the British-Afghan War of 1919), and Mesopotamia (the 1920 Iraqi Revolt). Moreover, the Mandate of Palestine was a hotbed of activity, especially with the Palestine Riots of 1929 and the Arab Revolt (1936–39). Nor were the British alone; Spaniards fought the Rif War (1920–27) in Morocco, while the French, also fighting in the "Rif," a mountainous region of Morocco populated by Berber tribes, maintained a tenuous grip on Algeria and the assigned mandates from the League of Nations. In the Western Hemisphere, Americans continued to fight a series of conflicts in Latin America collectively known as the "Banana Wars" (1898–1934).

The Second World War offers many examples of asymmetric combat. The British established multiple special operations forces, the most famous being the Special Operations Executive (SOE)[31] and the military's commando forces.[32] Many countries had resistance movements, most of which were assisted by agents from the SOE and the US Office of Strategic Services (OSS).[33] These resistance movements ranged from various French and Italian groups to the USSR's semiofficial bands to Yugoslav partisans to Chinese insurgents to American and Filipino guerrillas in the Philippines.[34]

---

28. T. E. Lawrence, "The Evolution of a Revolt," *Army Quarterly and Defence Journal* 1, no. 1 (October 1920): 55–79; *The Seven Pillars of Wisdom* (privately published, 1935).

29. Paul E. Lettow-Vorbeck, *My Reminiscences of East Africa* (London: Hurst and Blackett, 1920); Edwin P. Hoyt, *Guerilla: Colonel Von Lettow-Vorbeck and Germany's East African Empire* (London: Macmillan, 1981).

30. Charles Townshend, *The Republic: The Fight for Irish Independence, 1918–1923* (London: Penguin, 2014); D. M. Leeson, *The Black and Tans* (Oxford: Oxford University Press, 2011).

31. M. R. D. Foot, *Special Operations Executive* (London: Mandarin, 1990).

32. Charles Messenger, *Commandos: The Definitive History of Commando Operations in the Second World War* (London: William Collins, 2016).

33. See "Progress of 'Para-Military' Preparation," Memorandum No. M.I.1 (R)/I/2, July 10, 1939, National Archives of the UK (NAUK), HO 58/260.

34. "USSR NKVD (People's Commissariat for Internal Affairs)," in *The Partisan's Companion*, ed. and trans. L. Grau and M. Gress (Havertown, PA: Casemate, 2011); Patrick G. Zander, *Hidden Armies of the Second World War: World War II Resistance Movements* (Santa Barbara, CA: Praeger, 2017); R. W. Volckmann, *We Remained: Three Years Behind Enemy Lines in the Philippines* (New

The Cold War seemingly overshadowed everything and decolonization became a cause célèbre around the globe, but many such small wars spurred decolonization. The norm was either wars of independence or civil wars for the rest of the 1940s and 1950s: Greece (1946–49), Cyprus (1955–56), the Iran Crisis (1945–46), British Mandatory Palestine (1946–48), and the Costa Rican Civil War (1948). British forces fought a brutal counterinsurgency in Kenya against the Mau (1952–60) and against insurgents in Malaya (1948–60), and the French fought a vicious war against the National Liberation Front (NLF) in Algeria but ultimately lost.[35] All of this occurred against the backdrop of superpower competition.

Constructing the Myth

As mentioned above, there are theories that say the changes of the past three decades constitute an extreme shift in the conduct of war. Two of the most popular concepts that have been bandied around are so-called fourth-generation warfare (4GW) and "nontrinitarian warfare."

In the mid-1990s, several articles argued that 4GW was actually a new type of insurgency.[36] The 4GW theory posits that warfare developed in distinct historical phases, referred to as "generations." The first (1GW, circa 1740s–1905) was the use of massed manpower; the second (2GW, 1914–39) was the use of massed firepower; and the third was the advent of maneuver warfare (3GW, 1945–91/2003).[37] According to the most commonly accepted definition, 4GW is "an evolved form of insurgency" using "all available networks . . . to convince an opponent's decision-makers that their strategic goals are either unachievable or too costly."

Meanwhile, in 1991, the noted Israeli military historian Martin van Creveld espoused the nontrinitarian warfare model. Van Creveld explained his view of the West's method of war, which, he claims, is based on a state-on-state model of "regular

---

York: W. W. Norton, 1954); R. C. Hunt and B. Norling, *Behind Japanese Lines: An American Guerrilla in the Philippines* (Lexington: University of Kentucky Press, 2000).

35. Martin Evans, *Algeria: France's Undeclared War* (Oxford: Oxford University Press, 2013); Alistair Horne, *A Savage War of Peace: Algeria, 1954–62* (New York: Viking Adult, 1978).

36. See William S. Lind et al., "The Changing Face of War: Into the Fourth Generation," *Marine Corps Gazette*, October 1989, 22–26; William S. Lind, "Fourth Generation Warfare: Another Look," *Marine Corps Gazette*, September 1994, 34–7; and Thomas X. Hammes, "The Evolution of War: The Fourth Generation," *Marine Corps Gazette*, September 1994, 14; Hammes, "Insurgency: Modern Warfare Evolves into a Fourth Generation," *Strategic Forum* 214 (2005): 1–8; Hammes, "Fourth Generation Warfare Evolves, Fifth Emerges," *Military Review* 87, no. 3 (May–June 2007): 14–23; Hammes, *The Sling and the Stone: On War in the 21st Century* (St. Paul, MN: Zenith Press, 2006).

37. Lind et al., "Changing Face of War," 22–23; William S. Lind et al., "Fourth Generation Warfare: Another Look," *Marine Corps Gazette*, December 1994, 34–37.

warfare" instituted after the Treaty of Westphalia in 1648. Regular war consists of uniformed military forces fighting each other in the open. He argues that this Western model is no longer valid because the nation-state's relevance is diminishing due to non-state actors, which range from terror groups to international corporations to international NGOs (nongovernmental organizations) to communities and ethnic groups. Thus, van Creveld argues, war, having regressed to what warfare was like before 1648, is no longer the sole province of armies and governments. Although he did not expressly mention 4GW in his book, van Creveld does not object to the equation of nontrinitarian warfare, a reference to Clausewitz's model of the "fascinating trinity,"[38] and 4GW as the same phenomenon.[39] Both theories place the birth of this new sort of warfare around the year 1945.

The 4GW and nontrinitarian theories suggest that the current War on Terror is a kind of conflict different from any seen before. The enemy conducts asymmetric operations and employs tactics that require radically different responses. The theory holds that elements of 4GW began developing alongside the maneuver-based third generation, but 4GW really came into its own after World War II because of the superpower conflict between the United States and the Soviet Union, which fomented limited war.

There are several issues with these 4GW and nontrinitarian models. The first concern is the same as all models of human behavior which, of course, have utility but are not crystal balls. Second, the concept of generations of warfare is problematic because the divisions are arbitrary.[40] There are many events and developments that could easily serve as points of change in warfare: for example, the rise of infantry-centric armies in the fifteenth century "infantry revolution," or the advent of useful firearms on the battlefield, which has been called the "gunpowder revolution,"[41] or even the so-called managerial revolution of the Prussian General Staff in the mid-nineteenth century.[42] Each could serve as a point of substantial change. The theory assumes that the "generation" of massed firepower was more crucial than these.

38. Martin van Creveld, *The Transformation of War: The Most Radical Reinterpretation of Armed Conflict since Clausewitz* (London: Free Press, 1991), 49–54. Carl von Clausewitz wrote that war is like an object suspended over three magnets that represent policy, hatred and enmity, and probability and chance; see Carl von Clausewitz, *On War*, ed. and trans. M. Howard and P. Paret (Princeton, NJ: Princeton University Press, 1989), I.28.89.

39. Martin van Creveld, interview by Sonshi.com, October 2005, accessed July 29, 2019, https://www.sonshi.com/martin-van-creveld-interview.html; P. J. McCormack, "The Nature of the British Soldier: Warrior or Weapons Platform a Philosophical Framework" (PhD diss., Cranfield University, Cranfield, UK, 2014).

40. Antulio J. Echevarria, "Deconstructing the Theory of Fourth-Generation War," *Contemporary Security Policy* 26, no. 2 (2005): 9–10.

41. See Chapter 4 in this volume, by John France.

42. Walter Millis, *Arms and Men: A Study in American Military History* (New Brunswick, NJ: Rutgers University Press, 1981); Dennis E. Showalter, "The Prusso-German RMA, 1840–1871," in *Dynamics of Military Revolution*, 92–113.

Moreover, there are many historical inaccuracies. Hammes emphatically maintains, for example, that 4GW started with Mao during the Chinese Civil War (1927–49) and World War II (1939–45).[43] This connection is spurious at best. Indeed, some argue that Mao was not the originator of the strategy that became the "People's War" and that Mao himself did not actually use this strategy during either war.[44] The American scholar Crane Brinton identified revolutionary trends similar to what Mao espoused in his *Anatomy of Revolution* (1938).[45] Brinton approached the development of revolution with the metaphor of a disease, which develops from exposure to the onset of symptoms to the full-blown contagion, and found similar qualities in four historical case studies of revolutions: the English (1640–49), American (1775–83), French (1789–99), and Russian (1917–23). Following Brinton, we shall see that the Maoist origin thesis is wrong and that an earlier example exists that undermines the proposed 4GW model.

The Irish Revolution (1913–23) in Asymmetric Terms

The proponents of 4GW have based much on the chronology of 4GW and Mao, but by doing so they have misread history. Decades previously, as we have seen, Irish republicans fought a "protracted popular war."[46] There were three conflicts comprising the Irish Revolution: the Easter Rising of April 1916, the Irish War of Independence (1919–21), and the Irish Civil War (1922–23). This protracted popular insurgency in Ireland predated Mao's first exposition of his theories by almost twenty years and therefore belies asymmetry's Maoist origins. This conflict matches all the criteria the 4GW theorists list (military, economic, political and diplomatic, sociocultural, and informational).

After defeat in the 1916 Easter Rising, the republicans contested the 1918 General Elections, won a majority of the Irish seats in Parliament, and, instead of attending the Imperial Parliament at Westminster, met in Dublin and formed the Dáil Éireann (Assembly of Ireland), which declared independence and formed a provisional government. By establishing a cabinet with ministers responsible for their given tasks, the Dáil took a step closer to establishing a legitimate government with a mandate from the majority of the people in Ireland. The Dáil maintained representatives around the world, while Éamon de Valera, president of the Dáil and a US citizen, spent most

---

43. Hammes, *Sling and the Stone*, 3, 5, and 44–55.

44. Francis Grice, *The Myth of Mao Zedong and Modern Insurgency* (Basingstoke, UK: Palgrave Macmillan, 2019).

45. Crane Brinton, *Anatomy of Revolution* (New York: Prentice-Hall, 1938).

46. Bard E. O'Neill, *Insurgency and Terrorism: From Revolution to Apocalypse* (Washington, DC: Potomac, 2005), 49–56. The phrase was coined by National War College professor Bard O'Neill, who noted that nationalists also fought "people's wars."

of the War of Independence in the United States. The fledgling Soviet Union even received a loan of $20,000 from the Dáil.[47] Finally, Dáil representatives reached an international agreement with the British in 1921 in the Anglo-Irish Treaty, which created the Irish Free State, precursor to the current Republic of Ireland, and recognized the Dáil and Irish Republican Army's (IRA) legitimacy ex post facto. Another sign, if not source, of legitimacy was a functioning court system. Sinn Féin, the party in control of the Dáil, established arbitration courts for civil matters in 1919. These courts, known for their fairness, proved so popular that even pro-British citizens used them. The reason for this was the steady destruction of the existing British courts system by the IRA through violence and intimidation. The Dáil followed these courts with the Dáil Criminal Courts in 1921. Thus, the rebels had an executive, a legislature, a judiciary, an army, a police force, and conducted foreign affairs with several countries.[48]

The Irish Volunteers were founded in Dublin in November 1913, fought in the Easter Rising of 1916,[49] and commenced a guerrilla war against British forces in January 1919.[50] The Irish Volunteers eventually became known colloquially as the Irish Republican Army and established a Republican Police force from its ranks in 1920 to take over functions in those areas the police had evacuated. From 1916 to 1923, there were approximately 3,200 combat fatalities on all sides, while an additional (approximate) 1,500 civilians died. With a population of about 3.9 million, this was 120.51 per 100,000. For comparison, Iraq experienced 15.79 per 100,000 in 2008, during the height of "the Surge."[51] Clearly, the conflict was bloody by any modern standard.

The economic element in this conflict was robust and consisted of several campaigns at once: the Royal Irish Constabulary (RIC) and Belfast Boycotts, and the labor "operations" by primarily the allied Irish Transport and General Workers' Union. The boycotts were essentially the same and restricted commerce against the members of the RIC and their families, and the heavily unionist provinces of the north of Ireland.

---

47. Barry Whelan, "Éamon de Valera, a Republican Loan and the Secret of the Lost Russian Jewels," *Scoláire Staire* 3, no. 1 (2013): 25–27.

48. Mary Kotsonouris, *Retreat from Revolution: The Dáil Courts, 1920–1924* (Dublin: Irish Academic, 1994).

49. See *1916: The Long Revolution*, ed. G. Doherty and D. Keogh (Cork: Mercier, 2007); Keith Jeffery, *The GPO and the Easter Rising* (Dublin: Irish Academic, 2006); *The Sinn Féin Rebellion as They Saw It* (Dublin: Irish Academic, 1999); Fearghal McGarry, *The Rising: Ireland—Easter 1916* (Oxford: Oxford University Press, 2010); Charles Townshend, *Easter 1916: The Irish Rebellion* (Chicago: Ivan R. Dee, 2006).

50. See *The Irish Revolution, 1913–1923*, ed. J. Augusteijn (Basingstoke, UK: Palgrave Macmillan, 2002); Marie Coleman, *The Irish Revolution, 1916–1923* (Harlow, UK: Pearson, 2013); Michael A. Hopkinson, *The Irish War of Independence* (Montreal: McGill-Queen's University Press, 2002).

51. United Nations Office on Drugs and Crime, "Intentional Homicide Victims," accessed September 21, 2019, https://dataunodc.un.org/crime/intentional-homicide-victims.

The goals, however, were different: the republicans wanted Irishmen to quit the police and used a combination of economic and social exclusion to compel them to do so; the rebels wanted simply to hurt the unionists in the north financially and, by extension, the British. Only the former campaign succeeded. Police recruiting plummeted, to the point where the government brought in non-Irishmen, the infamous "Black and Tans," for the first time in the RIC's history.

The most significant labor action during the Irish War of Independence was the so-called munitions strike (May–December 1920). This was a good example of ordinary Irish "fighting" this war. Dockworkers at Kingstown, County Dublin, refused to offload ammunition in May 1920 because they did not want to assist the British in fighting other Irish people. Soon thereafter, railway employees followed suit. Both groups announced they would not load or offload or transport military or police cargo or personnel. There were numerous incidents of railway employees refusing to move trains once police or military boarded them.

Proponents of 4GW argue that information operations are critical to this supposed new style of warfare—that information is a weapon in today's world is cliché—but in truth, information has always been a weapon, and this was no less true in Ireland during this period. The US military lists electronic warfare, computer network operations, psychological operations, military deception, operations security, supporting capabilities, and required capabilities as core competencies of information operations generally.[52] The Irish Revolution contained each of these elements except, for obvious reasons, computer network operations.

Electronic warfare might seem anachronistic to the Irish Revolution, but the IRA found that it could jam British army wireless radios when several rebel radio operators transmitted signals on the same frequencies. They had to be careful because the British could triangulate their positions, but they conducted intermittent jamming operations throughout the war. The rebels also attacked the War Signal Stations along Ireland's coasts in an attempt to hurt British communications, which, while not technically electronic warfare, was an attack on electronic communications systems, as were activities to "listen in" on telecommunications.

Psychological operations were not normally considered part of military operations until World War II, but the IRA declared war on British morale in 1920.[53] In 1916, Michael Collins urged: "Sit down—refuse to budge—you have the British beaten. For a time they'll raise war—in the end they'll despair."[54] This campaign sought

---

52. JP 3-13: *Information Operations* (Washington, DC: Joint Staff, 2014), II-6.

53. In *An t-Óglác*: "No Slackers," April 1, 1920, 78–79; "A Fateful Time," June 1, 1920, 93–94; "New Measures," October 1, 1920, 125–26; "The War for Freedom" and "Sniping Barracks," April 1, 1921, 149–50; "Forward!" April 22, 1921, 1–2; "The War," May 1, 1921, 1; "The Laws of War," May 27, 1921, 1; "The Present!" June 3, 1921, 1–2.

54. Michael Collins to Sean Deasey, October 22, 1916, quoted in Rex Taylor, *Michael Collins* (Hutchinson, UK: New English Library, 1958), 51.

Michael Collins, a politician, guerilla soldier, and army leader who organized Irish revolutionary forces in the Easter Rising (1916), Irish War of Independence (1919–21), and the Irish Civil War (1922–23).

to reduce British forces' effectiveness through attacks on various targets that would decrease the morale of the troops and police. Such targets were bars, military sporting events, women who dated soldiers, soldiers going to or coming from church services, and so forth. The RIC boycott was also linked to this campaign. How effective they were in this campaign has yet to be studied, but the rebels certainly tried.

The IRA also employed excellent security practices to mask its activities. It ingeniously hid its arms smuggling, weapons manufacturing, and explosives mixing all over Dublin and all throughout Ireland, primarily in legitimate businesses.[55] Although the British captured several sites and several arms shipments, the IRA's capabilities in these realms increased throughout the war. Collins, the IRA's leading guerilla strategist, instituted processes and security procedures for communications, which enabled the republicans to communicate with whomever they wished, anywhere in the world. He used Sinn Féiners in the railway system and among the seamen to move letters

---

55. See, e.g., "Statement of Michael J. Lynch" (Military Archives of Ireland (MAI), Bureau of Military History (BMH) WS 511), 57–58.

and packages, with only small amounts captured by the British.[56] This element sought to cause confusion among the British by obscuring the IRA's plans and intentions. The IRA kept information on a need-to-know basis and the British complained about insufficient intelligence sources. The IRA, controversially, shot many civilians whom it accused of spying for the enemy.[57]

Another supporting capability is counterintelligence. Collins, in addition to his many other responsibilities, was also IRA director of intelligence. In this capacity, he established the "Squad," a group of assassins that specifically targeted British military and police intelligence assets. While the Squad killed many individual intelligence agents, particularly in the Dublin Metropolitan Police, one of its most famous operations was the Bloody Sunday killings of November 21, 1920, when the rebels killed a dozen and a half army officers working in intelligence throughout Dublin.[58] Collins's counterintelligence actions, while not perfect, blinded the British.[59] Within this element was public affairs, which, for the republicans, fell under two people. The first was an Englishman, Robert Erskine Childers, who was an ardent Irish nationalist. As Dáil director of publicity, he produced the *Irish Bulletin*, which provided the "official" republican, Sinn Féin, and Dáil views of events. The other man was IRA chief of propaganda, Piaras Béaslaí, who was chiefly responsible for publishing the IRA's biweekly (later weekly) journal *An t-Óglác* (*The Volunteer*),[60] which published some fifty issues from 1918 to 1922. *An t-Óglác* provided IRA units throughout Ireland with information they could not otherwise get.

The Irish War of Independence ended with an international truce (July 11–December 6, 1921); formal negotiations, started in October and lasted until both sides signed the Anglo-Irish Treaty in December. The Dáil narrowly ratified the treaty in January 1922. Those against the treaty, however, fought a civil war against the provisional government from June 1922 until the following spring. Ireland proclaimed the republic in 1949.

The Irish experience clearly predates Mao Zedong's purported originality as regards the concept of protracted popular struggle. Further, there is evidence that it was the IRA method that influenced and inspired other movements. Robert Briscoe, for

---

56. Collins to Mid Clare Brigade, September 8, 1919, Collins Papers, MAI A/0362/xxii; Collins to O'Daly, February 2, 1921, and O'Daly to Collins, February 3, 1921, Mulcahy Papers, University College, Dublin, Archives, P7/A/4.

57. Peter Hart, *British Intelligence in Ireland, 1920–21: The Final Reports* (Cork: Cork University Press, 2002); Gerard Murphy, *The Year of Disappearances: Political Killings in Cork, 1921–22* (Dublin: Gill and Macmillan, 2010).

58. Richard Abbott, *Police Casualties in Ireland, 1919–1922* (Dublin: Mercier Press, 2000).

59. T. Ryle Dwyer, *The Squad and the Intelligence Operations of Michael Collins* (Cork: Mercier, 2005).

60. Óglaigh na hÉireann (Defense Forces Ireland), *An tÓglach Magazine*, Military Archives, accessed September 27, 2019, http://www.militaryarchives.ie/en/collections/online-collections/an-toglach-magazine-1918-1933.

example, was a Jewish-Irish republican who assisted in IRA arms smuggling. He met with Vladimir (Ze'ev) Jabotinsky, founder of the pro-Zionist Irgun, in 1933 in London to provide information on IRA practices for the coming fight in Palestine. The Irish fought a popular insurgency almost a generation before Mao's two May 1938 speeches regarding a protracted "people's protracted war," and Jabotinsky received information from Briscoe five years before these speeches.

For his part, Brinton published his ideas in the spring of 1938, and Mao's works were largely unavailable in English until Samuel Griffith translated one short book in 1940, while the main writings on the people's war were unavailable in English until the later 1940s.[61] Renowned historian Ian Beckett has noted that revolutionaries as far-ranging as Burma, India, Zionists in British Palestine, and Cyprus, as well as the British Special Operations Executive in World War II, studied the IRA.[62] Journalist-historian Tim Pat Coogan has even claimed that Mao himself studied Michael Collins's ideas from the Irish Revolution.[63]

The consequence of this analysis is that the theory of "generational war" falls apart. Fourth-generation warfare developed in full *before* the third generation of maneuver warfare. Moreover, because Brinton found, through historical case studies, similar patterns stretching back to well before the twentieth century, 4GW could even precede the 2GW (massed firepower). Thus, the entire theory is suspect. Although these theories are really myths, there is no doubt that the methods first employed by the IRA would later go on to inspire a rash of similar, but communist, movements, possibly including Mao's.

Conclusion

As should be more than evident by this point, asymmetric war by any name is nothing new. While asymmetrical effects are real, its use as a political act and threat in the modern sense translated directly at the dawn of modern politics in the late eighteenth

---

61. Mao Zedong, "Problems of Strategy in Guerrilla War Against Japan" and "On Protracted War," in *Selected Military Writings of Mao Tse-Tung* (Beijing: Foreign Language Press, 1968), 153–86 and 187–268; *Mao Tse-tung on Guerrilla Warfare*, trans. S. Griffith, Fleet Marine Corps Reference Publication (FMFRP) 12–18 (Washington, DC: US Marine Corps, 1989, repr. from 1940).

62. I. F. W. Beckett, *Modern Insurgencies and Counter-Insurgencies: Guerillas and Their Opponents since 1750* (New York: Routledge, 2001), 17–18; Michael Silvestri, "'The Sinn Fein of India': Irish Nationalism and the Policing of Revolutionary Terrorism in Bengal," *Journal of British Studies* 39, no. 4 (2000): 454–86; Robert Briscoe, *For the Life of Me* (Boston: Little, Brown, 1958), 264; Bernard Weinraub, "An Irish Legend's Life and Mysterious Death," *New York Times*, October 9, 1996, 13; Paul Majendie, "Michael Collins: Irish Hero or Terrorist?" *Los Angeles Times*, November 11, 1990.

63. Tim Pat Coogan, *Path to Freedom: Articles and Speeches by Michael Collins* (New York: Roberts Rinehart, 1996), viii; Tadhg O'Sullivan, "French View of the Big Fellow," *The Irish Times*, April 25, 1997; Pierre Joannon, *Michael Collins: Une Biographie* (Paris: Tableronde, 1978).

century. The use of protracted popular war is of at least early twentieth-century origin, if not older; after all, Sun Tzu wrote about it more than two millennia ago.[64] The Irish fought their revolution and passed on their knowledge to multiple revolutionary groups and, perhaps, Mao, among others. Thus, the use of these multifaceted, multidomain conflicts is far from new. To suggest otherwise in the face of the evidence surpasses credulity and merely perpetuates this myth born of historical ignorance. Moreover, the theorists of 4GW and nontrinitarian warfare are simply wrong because Mao was obviously not the genitor but only one of several who recognized the truths of multifaceted, multi-domain insurgency.

While it is impossible here to survey how every asymmetric theory found purchase, examples in the Western Hemisphere illustrate the diversity of intellectual transmission. Fidel Castro fought the Cuban Revolution (1953–59) against Fulgencio Batista's regime in the inaccessible rural regions of western Cuba against ill-trained and demoralized security forces. One of Castro's compadres, the intellectually arrogant Argentinian Ernesto "Che" Guevara, believed what he saw in Cuba would work anywhere and forced several disparate concepts together. He took Bakunin's belief in the validity of rural insurrection, combined with Mao's concept of revolutionary education, and the Pisacanian-Bakunian-Nechayevian propaganda of the deed to develop a theory known as "Foco" or *foquismo*, which indicates the focus, or focal point, of the revolution. *Foquismo* held that Mao's first stage of rural revolution, politicization through education of the masses, was unnecessary. One did not have to wait until the time was ripe for revolutionary action: one could create the conditions with revolutionary violence.[65] The problem for Guevara was that his theory was as overconfident as it was deadly. The concept worked neither for him (he was captured and shot in 1967) nor his imitators. Revolutionaries in Argentina (Montaneros), Uruguay (MLN-T: Movimiento de Liberación Nacional-Tupamaros), and Brazil (ALN: Ação Libertadora Nacional) used what amounted to *foquismo* in an urban environment into the 1970s, but all failed. Around the same time, inspired by these movements and Carlos Marighella's strategy of "urban guerrilla warfare," "classic" political terrorism arose to foment revolution in successive decades and around the world.[66]

Regardless, since the end of the 1940s, people have looked primarily at Mao as the prototypical guerrilla theorist. Everything guerrilla seems to be described or judged in terms of Mao. Indeed, with the perpetuation of Maoist hagiography, other schools of thought on guerrilla warfare have been overlooked. The era after the 9/11 attacks is even frequently referred to as "post-Mao."

---

64. E.g., Sun Tzu, *The Art of War*, ed. and trans. S. Griffith (Cambridge: Cambridge University Press, 1963), 96–97: "Therefore, against those skilled in attack, an enemy does not know where to defend; against the experts in defence, the enemy does not know where to attack."

65. Ernesto "Che" Guevara, *Guerrilla Warfare* (Lincoln: University of Nebraska Press, 1985); Régis Debray, *Revolution in the Revolution?* (Harmondsworth, UK: Penguin, 1967).

66. Carlos Marighella, *Minimanual of the Urban Guerrilla* (Brasilia, 1969).

Mao Zedong.

This Maoism seemed nearly universal in academia, government, and the military, especially with regard to counterinsurgency. General David Petraeus wrote the US military's counterinsurgency (COIN) manual (FM 3-24) for his return to Iraq as commander in 2007, and he fell for Mao in FM 3-24. Mao's name is mentioned eighteen times in the text, more than any other theorist. Interestingly, the 2014 version removed almost all overt references to Mao, but the influence remains, especially regarding the connection of Mao as the father of protracted popular war. The Maoist concept of the three-phased insurgency became, and remains, US military doctrine.[67]

Nonetheless, the Irish Revolution could be the archetypal protracted popular war that Hammes and van Creveld described. Each of the elements they described was borne out in Ireland. It is largely through ignorance that the Irish revolutionary period is understudied, which is regrettable since the more modern asymmetric wars retain most of the same essential elements. Indeed, the People's Republic of China's concepts of comprehensive national power and "unrestricted warfare" and the Russian Gerasimov doctrine are examples of updated versions of the same ideas, even though not necessarily connected by direct linkages.[68]

In short, then, two things have happened: Mao's proximate influence has been mythologized, and a myth of new asymmetrical warfare has come along for the ride. Such things matter a great deal. During these types of conflicts, leaders look to history to help make decisions. While the general social sciences are of value due to their presumed predictive qualities, in addition to their explanatory capabilities, few expect historians to predict the future. This situation also provides a warning about history

---

67. Field Manual (FM) 3-24/Marine Corps Warfighting Paper 3-33.5: *Insurgencies and Countering Insurgencies* (Washington, DC: Department of the Army, 2014), 4–8.

68. Qiao Liang and Wang Xiangsui, *Unrestricted Warfare* (Beijing: PLA Literature and Arts Publishing House, 1999); Valery Gerasimov, "The Value of Science Is in the Foresight: New Challenges Demand Rethinking the Forms and Methods of Carrying Out Combat Operations," *Military-Industrial Kurier* (February 27, 2013), in *Military Review*, January–February 2016, 23–29.

by nonspecialists. Hammes, for example, misidentified the character of the Irish War of Independence, saying that its purpose was to defeat British military power. His ignorance of the conflict could be excused if his mistakes were not so critical.[69]

The problem with the spurious misuse and ignorance of history that led to this myth, of the supposedly new innovation of asymmetric war, is that misunderstanding the problem hampers finding a solution. Although dynamite did not produce the revolutionary climate that the nineteenth-century anarchists sought, neither did the rifle. What these weapons allowed was smaller groups of insurgents to start a conflict and fight a protracted defensive war that would hopefully gain in popularity over time. Consequently, the combination of high explosives and modern firearms provided the technological elements of the modern situation, while protracted war and revolutionary theory gave the conceptual elements. Each practitioner sought to use this classic strategy of exhaustion as a base upon which he built his own expression of it.[70]

The book of Ecclesiastes (1:9) says that there is "nothing is new under the sun," which seems to hold for revolutionary conflicts too. Guerrilla warfare is supposed to be the method of the weak against the strong, a method of resistance against tyranny. Resistance groups, however, have frequently degraded into mere criminality, preying on the people they claim to represent. The incompetence and indiscipline, plus half-baked complaints of "oppression" used to justify barbarism and banditry, betray the harsh truth about most revolutionaries: all too often they represent none but themselves and are hardly distinguishable by their actions from those they claim to fight. Their promises about the rights of the people have a disturbing, common tendency to disappear on the rare occasions when they win. In these instances, they remain as oppressive as those they overthrew, or worse. What rapidly becomes clear is that political-doctrinal writings combined with modern technologies cannot make up for a lack of overwhelming public support. The doctrine became the way, the weapons became the means, but, thanks to a lack of support, few insurgent groups have achieved their ends. The politicos, analysts, and pundits are right: there was, indeed, a change in small wars, but they were off by at least two hundred years. Everything else was merely an evolution in revolutionary affairs.

69. T. X. Hammes, "Insurgency: Modern Warfare Evolves into a Fourth Generation," *Strategic Forum* 214 (January 2005): 3. China's comprehensive national power and "unrestricted warfare" refer to the use of all elements of a nation's power—diplomatic, informational, economic, and military—to achieve the government's goals in the international arena. The so-called Gerasimov doctrine is essentially the same concept; the use of all "weapons" against one's enemies.
70. Debray, *Revolution in the Revolution*, 67; Ian F. Beckett, *Modern Insurgencies and Counter-Insurgencies: Guerrillas and Their Opponents since 1750* (New York: Routledge: 2004), 151.

7. TECHNOLOGICAL DETERMINISM: EXPLAINING SUCCESS AND FAILURE IN WAR

Rob Johnson

> "It's a miracle, Sir."
> "If it is, Colour Sergeant, it's a four-five caliber, short-chamber, Boxer-primed miracle."
> "And a bayonet, Sir—with some guts behind it."
> —*Colour Sergeant Bourne and Lieutenant Chard in the movie* Zulu

In the movie *Zulu*, a British officer reflects on how his small detachment had defeated, miraculously, a much larger force. His conclusion was that rifle technology had determined the outcome. His subordinate was quick to qualify the judgment, attributing success to human factors—the soldiers and their courage. This fictional conversation goes to the heart of a prevailing idea about war: that outcomes are dependent on superior technology. Yet, arguably, the role of technology is exaggerated as the single most important factor. The paradox of the fictional conversation in *Zulu* is that both characters favor their preferred interpretation of success and mythologize either the modern rifle or the bayonet.

Determinism is a way of trying to ascertain causation, but as an explanation for change, its singularity leaves it open to the charge that it fails to address context, the diverse reasons for change, or alternative explanations.[1] As a way of thinking, it appears too mechanistic and limited.

The notion of determinism can be traced back to Democritus (460–370 BCE), who, dissatisfied with the idea that humankind was at the whim of capricious gods, looked instead for physical laws that controlled the motion of atoms.[2] He concluded that everything, including our minds, consists merely of atoms in a void. All the events in the world could now be connected in an eternal deterministic causal chain with a single possible future, even one that would periodically repeat itself in a cosmic "great cycle." Later, Epicurus (341–270 BCE), troubled by the tyranny that this determinism imposed, especially the loss of human free will or the moral

---

1. *Does Technology Drive History? The Dilemma of Technological Determinism*, ed. M. R. Smith and L. Marx (Cambridge, MA: MIT Press, 1994).

2. Gregory Vlastos, "Ethics and Physics in Democritus," *Philosophical Review* 54–55 (1945–1946): 578–92 and 53–64.

responsibility it implied, modified the theory of Democritus with "chance." This opened the possibility of breaking the causal chain and reasserting human responsibility over iron determinism.

There are compelling reasons for technologies to be considered as the dominant explanation for change in human history and we refer to the Stone, Bronze, and Iron Ages in recognition of their importance. But can we refer to technological determinism? The subject has been examined most critically by social scientists, who reject determinism in favor of action-and-reaction or challenge-and-response drivers, but there is still an inherent assumption in much of the scholarship that historical change is characterized by continuous social improvement and that modernization is therefore inherently progressive. It is also striking that governments and political analysts still tend to look for trends, even though they are astonishingly unreliable in terms of their accuracy or predictive capacity. Trends appear plausible in retrospect but there are disagreements among theorists about gradients, sheer events, and sample sizes, which make trend analyses subjective.[3] The implication for the study of war in history is that trends are not a reliable model for understanding change, even though we can define eras by the prevailing technology, such as gunpowder or industrial systems. While some trends move at a sufficiently slow pace to offer some degree of reliability, there may be concurrent changes of different velocity, and the varied nature of technological change is perhaps the least predictable of all.

At the turn of the current millennium, Manuel De Landa addressed, through a materialist philosophy of history and the science of dynamics, the fundamentals of change.[4] He argued that there is no single path of change, but rather endless fractures, branches, and new combinations through time. He rejected technological determinism to argue that there are no path-dependent changes, but changes in relative importance and "accumulations" of effects. Rejecting any single explanatory driver of change, he concluded the source of all physical forms, including technologies, were just the result of accumulated changes across a very wide range of factors, from the environment to "accidental" events. Nevertheless, there is often a strong desire to employ a single, dominant factor to explain global and historical phenomena, such as economics, ideologies, or technology and these have all the hallmarks of determinism.

There is a close relationship between determinism and "inevitability," not least in questions such as the causes of war. Despite their apparent inflexibility, there is still some latitude for chance and alternatives in causal mechanisms that concern time, processes, and events. If one were to examine the period between 1894 and

---

3. Perci Diaconis, "Theories of Data Analysis: From Magical Thinking through Classical Statistics," in *Exploring Data Tables, Trends, and Shapes*, ed. D. C. Hoaglin et al. (Hoboken, NJ: Wiley, 1985), 4–36.

4. As in, history produced from material conditions, as opposed to ideas. See Manuel De Landa, *A Thousand Years of Nonlinear History* (New York: Zone, 1997), 259–61 and 265.

the last weeks of European diplomacy before the outbreak of the First World War, a major continental conflict might have appeared unlikely in 1900 or even in 1913. But assessed in terms of mobilization by various powers and diplomatic exchanges in July 1914, a war appeared, at that late point, to be inevitable. Furthermore, in looking for the *origins* of that war, one could imply a long-term causation and that might make it seem that the war had been inevitable, and it is just a question of discerning the factors that accumulated. The origins approach would favor determinism, while an examination of the *causes* of the war would suggest a more short-term, perhaps diverse set of decisions, reactions, and events that produced the conflict. This issue has divided historians, particularly in the 1960s when the German scholar Fritz Fischer posited—much to the shock of many of his colleagues—that Germany had been pursuing a predetermined program of aggression and expansion from about 1897.[5] The context of this interpretation was significant because few German academics in the 1960s could accept that Germany in the 1890s had been following a plan of domination similar to that of Hitler, since the implication was that Germany was a nation condemned to expansionist wars, and that Hitler had not been some aberration in their history after all.[6] They preferred the more accommodating interpretations of the interwar years, when statesmen, like British prime minister David Lloyd George, had suggested the Europeans had collectively slithered into war, almost by accident.[7] That was the antithesis of determinism.

Faith in the idea of determinism has not dissipated. There is considerable debate about the extent to which one's genetic construction, and therefore "nature," determines a person's susceptibility to disease or longevity, and perhaps even other traits, such as personality. At a collective level, it was once believed that racial types determined forms of behavior, such as willingness to take risks, acumen for problem-solving, and suitability to govern. Faith in science is strong and with it the belief that scientific advances, especially in technology, will provide technical solutions to global problems. It is predicated on the idea that all problems *can* be solved through some appropriate engineering. Economic conditions are treated in similar ways. Markets are notoriously unstable, but faith in the idea of inevitable economic improvement and wealth generation is remarkable and conspicuous. Economic setbacks are invariably received in shock, whereas global history suggests that the ebb and flow of economic performance, not constant improvement, is normative.

Economic and technological explanations for the outbreak of the First World War were mythologized by communist historians in the twentieth century. They argued that war and revolution were "inevitable" because of capitalist competition and

---

5. The English translations are *Germany and the Origins of the First World War* (London: Chatto and Windus, 1967), and *The War of Illusions* (London: Chatto and Windus, 1975).

6. Georg G. Iggers, *The German Conception of History: The National Tradition of Historical Thought from Herder to the Present* (Middletown, CT: Wesleyan University Press, 1968).

7. David Lloyd George, *War Memoirs*, vol. 1 (London: Nicolson and Watson, 1933), 32.

massive investments in armaments. Yet the communist interpretation was exposed as fallacious by the events of the late twentieth century and the collapse not of the capitalist system, but of the communist Soviet Union.

Technology in History

Technology is often seen as the strongest determining factor of historical change at the macro level, despite evident setbacks through time.[8] The material culture of antiquity is the basis of the argument for technological determinism, and the examples most cited are the shifts from stone to bronze weapons, then iron, which had parallels in the development of the iron-bladed plow. The improved cutting power and durability of iron weapons and tools has been used as the marker for a significant change in civilizations. But even if one were to accept the preponderance of iron as a dominant mechanism for change, we would still need to account for all the other elements that played their part in the historical shift in Afro-Eurasia and, at the same time, ask why some human communities either did not go through the same development or retained traditional systems, perhaps because their alternatives were more suited to their climate, resources, and social structure despite their adoption of iron technology. Archaeologists also point out that technologies can sometimes be abandoned when the systems that had sustained them collapse.[9]

Just as there are several driving forces that create change, technology is itself actually a category of explanations, in the plural, not in the singular.[10] The capabilities of weapons, their ease of manufacture, their appropriateness to the tasks required, and their utilization in tactics, command, and training all play their part in how and where they are adopted. Moreover, weapons technologies can be fetishized, even when their utility is questionable.[11] After 1943, Hitler's Third Reich was faced with large-scale offensives on multiple fronts but, ideologically, there was considerable faith in the idea that German military prowess, biological supremacy, and technological skill would ensure victory. The regime authorized accelerated research and development in a series of exquisitely engineered *Wunderwaffen* (wonder weapons) that ranged from remote armored vehicles and jet-propelled aircraft to the Fieseler

---

8. W. H. McNeill, "Men, Machines and War," in *Men, Machines and War*, ed. R. Haycock (Waterloo, ON: Laurier University Press, 1988); chap. 11–15 in Martin van Creveld, *Technology and War: From 2000 B.C. to the Present* (Oxford: Oxford University Press, 1991).

9. Eric H. Cline, *1177 BC: The Year Civilization Collapsed* (Princeton, NJ: Princeton University Press, 2014).

10. Jeremy Black, "Determinisms and Other Issues," *Journal of Military History* 68, no. 4 (2004): 1219.

11. Matthew Ford, *Weapon of Choice: Small Arms and the Culture of Military Innovation* (London: Hurst, 2017): 1–2.

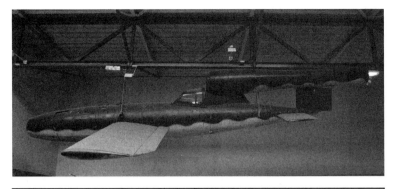

A Fieseler Fi 103R manned V-1 missile captured by British soldiers in 1945. The German *Luftwaffe* tested many sorts of "wonder weapons" in the later stages of World War II.

Fi 103R "Reichenberg" manned variant of the V-1 missile, and ballistic rockets like the V-2.[12] Yet within months, in spite of the weapons' advanced nature and potential, Nazi Germany was defeated.

Despite the failure of Nazi wonder weapons to turn the tide of war, there is still a tendency to emphasize technologies as an explanation for change. Regardless of the proclivity to regard technology as the primary driver of change, war has always been and remains an activity driven by humans, as Thucydides, the historian of the Peloponnesian War, so eloquently reminded us. In his lifetime, he strongly advocated technological developments, especially the necessity for a strong Athenian navy, but he acknowledged that, in war, the human dimension will always assert itself.[13] For Thucydides and many of the classic military historians of antiquity and early modernity, war was the result of fear and miscalculation, a desire to protect honor or to serve one's interests. It was also, in some extreme circumstances, simply a question of survival. In other cases, it could be the desire to end the uncertainty of a threat, a policy driven by the domestic pressure to act, the response to a perceived injustice, or the reaction to some incursion.[14] Less honorably, it could be the manifestation of what historian Jeremy Black calls a bellicose culture, or the fulfillment of some ambition or opportunism.[15]

Global history further indicates that some wars are the result of error, through misinterpretation or prejudice. In terms of internal wars, where populations revolt

12. Adam Tooze, *The Wages of Destruction: The Making and Breaking of the Nazi Economy* (London: Penguin, 2007), 517.

13. Thucydides, *Histories*, 1.14.3, 2.75–76, and 7.36.2–3.

14. Ned Lebow, *Why Nations Fight* (Cambridge: Cambridge University Press, 2010); Jeremy Black, *Why Wars Happen* (London: Reaktion, 1998), 16, 17, and 22; Geoffrey Blainey, *The Causes of War* (London: Macmillan, 1973).

15. Black, *Why Wars Happen*, 16–17.

against their own rulers, there is a correlation between worsening conditions (be they political, economic, or social) and violence. For example, when food prices increase and cross a particular threshold, the likelihood of violence is much greater, particularly if expectations of improvement have been raised.[16] Theoretically, this gives us measurable indicators of the point at which humans are likely to resort to armed conflict, but it still is far from automatic or determined. Critically, it indicates that the outcome of a war will be related to its human causes, and the means by which it is fought, the technology, is only an enabler to these objectives.

When confronted with a significant change in war, often through some unexpected setback or victory, there is a reexamination of causation and invariably a search for the dominant factor that determined its outcome. Take, for example, the detailed study of the Battle of Gettysburg: Could one prioritize the lethality of the modern rifle and its Minié ammunition, or General Lee's decision-making? Or would we emphasize the resistance of tactical commanders like Joshua Chamberlain at Little Round Top, or perhaps a range of other factors? Critically, the battle has been seen as the "turning point" of the Civil War, after which material, strategic, and operational advantages lay in federal hands, suggesting accumulations of factors rather than a single technological cause. Similarly, if one were to assess the reasons for setback and success in the storming of Omaha Beach at Normandy in 1944, would one attribute it more to the determination of US troops, to the fixed nature of German defense, or to Allied firepower? What degree of importance would we attach to the Normandy landings, compared with Soviet efforts or other strategic elements in the Second World War, such as the scale of American industrial and military capacity to account for the outcome of the conflict?

Technology, in the form of weapons or the means of mobility, has frequently been invoked as a determining factor, even though technologies are really just the products of their historical period. In other words, even when certain technologies appear to be dominant on the battlefield, they may only have that dominance because of a host of other factors, such as the way those technologies are used or the effectiveness of the organizations to which they belong.

What we need to do is broaden our understanding of how technology fits within war itself. War has been defined as organized violence with a purpose, but, essentially, it is a lethal activity that, in many cultures, creates a sacralized response over time: it is therefore an activity that transcends a brief fight or skirmish fought with certain technologies. War changes with every encounter, and so even if a particular technology is effective in an initial battle, it may not, under later circumstances, prove quite so decisive.

---

16. The United Nations' FAO food price index correlates with "food riots" in several African countries around 2008 and the so-called Arab Spring conflicts in 2011. See Paul Collier and Anke Hoffler, "Greed and Grievance in Civil War," May 2000, accessed February 2021, https://papers.ssrn.com/sol3/papers.cfm?abstract_id=630727.

In its fundamental elements, as Carl von Clausewitz posited, war consists of reason and passion, but also chance, together forming a "remarkable" trinity in constant tension and therefore prone to unexpected outcomes.[17] For Clausewitz, the actions and violence of war were the product of the interaction of three forces: (1) irrational emotions and actions ("primordial violence, hatred, and enmity"); (2) nonrational forces ("the play of chance and probability" and the "genius" or "insight" of the commander) that produce friction; and (3) purely rational forces (war's direction through policy and reason). This idea of *forces* makes a more appropriate mechanism for understanding the way in which new technologies and techniques have developed. War, Clausewitz reminded us, is "not an isolated act," but "a series of blows," a "duel," and a struggle.[18] The desire by its participants to seek out advantages and to win creates a dynamic of adaptation, escalation, and maneuver, and it is this that drives technological development in the instruments and practice of war. He did not identify technology in his calculations of war's nature, as his was a search for the true essence of all war, throughout history, not a specific era.[19]

The escalatory logic of war, which Clausewitz had identified, demands constant reassessment of horizons, milestones, cost-benefit analyses, and options. While war consists of the efficient deployment of the appropriate tools, such as the technology of weapons and transportation, it also demands a suitable "rational calculus" (Clausewitz's phrase), meaning bringing into alignment objectives, methods, and the means to achieve them. Clausewitz insisted that superior "means"—the technology—would not be enough. War consists of paradoxes, dynamics, and surprises, so these reinforce the adaptive and iterative nature of war. The common denominator in this variability is the human, and therefore the operator of the technology, rather than the technology itself.

The impression often given is that the changing character of war is technologically driven. To some extent our thinking has been influenced by the military revolution debate that began in the 1950s.[20] One argument was that the organization and progress of modern states was a direct consequence of the development of gunpowder weapons, which produced mass armies around 1650. A development based on this theory was that siege and fortress technologies, and their sheer expense, demanded the professionalization of both bureaucracy and armies.[21] This development also extended to navies of the period, which were even more technologically dependent

17. Carl von Clausewitz, *On War*, ed. and trans. M. Howard and P. Paret (Princeton, NJ: Princeton University Press, 1989), I.1.28 and II.2.

18. Clausewitz, *On War*, I.1.2 and 8.

19. Andreas Herberg-Rothe, "Clausewitz's 'Wonderous Trinity' as a Coordinate System of War and Violent Conflict," *International Journal of Conflict and Violence* 3, no. 2 (2009): 204–19.

20. Michael Roberts, *The Military Revolution, 1560–1660: Inaugural Lecture Delivered before the Queen's University Belfast* (Belfast: Marjory Boyd, 1956).

21. Parker, *The Military Revolution*, chap. 1.

from the sixteenth century onward. Critics argued that an infantry revolution had occurred as early as the fourteenth century, while others posited that the greatest shift in military change occurred in the seventeenth century, or even, the eighteenth century.[22] Other observers then noted that, over a period of four hundred years, what had occurred was surely a military evolution or a "punctuated evolution" (of spurts of change).[23] Nevertheless, the guiding idea was still that a technology, in this case gunpowder weapons, had determined a transformation in military affairs and in the very states that supported these militaries.

Arguably the greatest acceleration of the "military revolution" using technology as the sole standard occurred in the nineteenth century, with developments in rifling, steam (and then oil-fired) propulsion, the internal combustion engine, developments in chemicals and explosives, and rudimentary automation in the machine gun and recoilless artillery. The twentieth century was marked by another step change in technological advance with aviation, missiles, and nuclear weapons.[24] After 1945, it was thought that major industrial war was too costly to be an instrument of policy, and statesman looked to limited wars to achieve national objectives. This was, in fact, contrary to the ideas of Clausewitz and represented a significant change, some would say, in the very nature of war. That judgment would not satisfy many historians and military theorists who see, even in the cases of nuclear confrontation, the same elements that have always existed. It certainly appeared that possession of nuclear weapons determined constraints, but nuclear-armed powers continued to engage in wars: for example, the Soviet invasion of Afghanistan in 1979 and the American war in Vietnam.

In more recent times, another significant change was identified at the end of the First Gulf War in 1991, which was a conflict that seemed to be the culmination of conventional, combined air-land maneuver, and "high-tech" warfare. It was characterized by overmatching coalition firepower and air supremacy. There were significant developments in computing capacity, such as Blue Force Tracker, which plotted geographically all Allied units in real time; embryonic advances in robotics, more substantial developments in remotely piloted air systems (RPAS), and a range of smart mines, torpedoes, and missiles.[25] The proportion of smart, guided, precision weapons

---

22. Rogers, "England's Fourteenth-Century RMA," 15–34.

23. Rogers, "Military Revolutions of the Hundred Years' War," 76–77; see also *Medieval Military Revolution*, and Chapter 4 in this volume, by John France.

24. Various claims have been made for other technologies, such as Roger Edwards, *Panzer: A Revolution in Warfare, 1939–45* (London: Arms and Armour, 1989). Tim Benbow argues there have been twenty-seven military revolutions; see *The Magic Bullet? Understanding the Revolution in Military Affairs* (London: Brassey's, 2004), 18. Andrew Krepinevich identifies ten; see *Cavalry to Computer: The Pattern of Military Revolutions* (New York: National Affairs, 1994).

25. Bernard I. Cohen, "The Computer: A Case Study of Support by Government, Especially the Military, of a New Science and Technology," in *Science, Technology and the Military*, ed. E. Mendelsohn et al. (Dordrecht, Neth.: Kluwer, 1988), 119–54.

Operation Crossroads: the underwater detonation of a twenty-one kiloton nuclear weapon at Bikini Atoll in 1946. The proliferation of nuclear weapons in the 1950s and 1960s nonetheless occurred alongside an assortment of conventional, limited, and proxy wars.

used in the conflict grew steadily thereafter, as did their costs. On the other hand, this was also an era when "low-tech" solutions had a greater presence on the battlefield. They included cheap drones (to conduct tactical surveillance or drop grenades), improvised explosive devices (IEDs), fast pickup trucks mounted with heavy machine guns ("technicals") and armored vehicle-borne IEDs in the form of fuel tankers, used in conjunction with armor, swarms of men with assault rifles, and spearheaded by suicide bombers.

Determinist Failings

New technology often attracts the most attention in war. Some see, in technology, trends that offer new opportunities, while others are more alarmed by its threatened disruption. Technology is, of course, integral as a weapon or enabler in war but there is often a trade-off in its value and use. Take, for example, the Bronze Age warrior of Homeric Greece. He was lightly armed with helmet, shield, spear or sword, breastplate, and greaves (leg protectors). The weight of his technology was deliberately limited to enhance his mobility. This principle endured for centuries. The combination of mobility and weapon systems demanded tactics, namely a method for using warriors and their weapons most effectively, and changes in those tactics have occurred as new weapon systems have emerged or fresh trade-offs have been required.

Technological explanations for change have also had their critics because contextual aspects, including the culture that legitimates certain technologies, are omitted or misinterpreted. So, for example, the European partition of Africa in the nineteenth century was reduced to a formula of supremacy in weapons technology. The author and wit Hilaire Belloc quipped in his infamous couplet that "whatever happens we have got / the Maxim gun, and they have not."[26] Certain colonial campaigns were cited to reinforce the idea, such as the French conquest of Samori Touré and the Fulani Empire, the British defeat of Cetshweyo and Lobengula in southern Africa, or the Battle of Omdurman in 1898, in which a Sudanese *Mahdiyya* army of fifty thousand was routed by breech-loading artillery, magazine-fed rifles, and machine guns.[27]

The so-called technology gap was, however, a selective analysis of history. Such a gap between African and European forces only really appeared in the second half of that century, and, for the preceding decades, Europeans were not always successful because of diseases, vast distances, limitations in available manpower, and greater parity in weapons technology. Indeed, colonial conflicts often featured large numbers of locally recruited levies armed with similar technologies to those used by the forces being attacked by the Europeans. Moreover, the destruction of Custer's Seventh Cavalry at Little Big Horn in 1876, the disastrous fate of General Hicks's Egyptian brigade (armed with modern Remington rifles and Krupp artillery) in Darfur in 1884, and the Italians at Adowa in 1896 (equipped with similar modern weaponry) indicated that, even at the end of the century, superiority in weapons technology offered no guarantees of success.

In the case of South Asia in the eighteenth century, there was no attempt to show the British had a technological superiority to account for their colonial success. This was because South Asian armies who opposed them possessed not only parity in weapons but they often enjoyed numerical superiority in artillery. Instead, the British conquest of India was attributed to military success based on better training, discipline, and drill. These were regarded as the products of the military revolution in Europe, leading to exclusively military explanations for the British takeover. Critics noted that this explanation failed to account for a more powerful macroeconomic explanation, namely the displacement of indigenous economies by a global expansion

---

26. Hilaire Belloc, *The Modern Traveller* (London: Edward Arnold, 1898).

27. Bruce Vandervort, *Wars of Imperial Conquest in Africa, 1830–1914* (London: UCL Press, 1998), 175–77; Richard J. Reid, *Warfare in African History* (New York: Cambridge University Press, 2012), 99–101.

ZULU SOLDIERS AND KRAAL

Zulu warriors. The British possession of the Martini-Henry rifle did not prevent their defeat by the Zulu at the Battle of Isandlwana in 1879.

of a seaborne empire.[28] Randolf Cooper condemned the "racist diatribe" that had perpetuated the military supremacy myth and its "technological determination."[29] Nevertheless, the Indian subcontinent was not simply "bought out" and rendered an economic client without a great deal of military activity. Military fiscalism had a part to play as a mutually reinforcing process (as this was a system whereby military personnel, armaments, and administration could be paid for by the relentless acquisition of taxable territory).[30] In addition, military forces, including Indian personnel under British officers, acted boldly against a number of significant threats from the 1740s to the 1890s. Some two-thirds of the British Army in India were made up of Asian personnel. The case of South Asia reveals that military technology is only part of a socioeconomic and cultural system that can explain changes and outcomes.

28. A form of economic determinism was advocated by Alvin and Heidi Toffler in *War and Anti-War: Survival and the Dawn of the Twenty-First Century* (Boston: Little, Brown, 1993), 19.

29. R. G. S. Cooper, *The Anglo-Maratha Campaigns and the Contest for India: The Struggle for Control of the South Asian Military Economy* (Cambridge: Cambridge University Press, 2003), 310–11.

30. Deborah Avant, "From Mercenary to Citizen Armies: Explaining Change in the Practice of War," *International Organization* 54, no. 1 (2000): 41–72; for the origins of military fiscalism, see John Brewer, *The Sinews of Power: War, Money, and the English State, 1688–1783* (London: Unwin Hyman, 1989).

Innovations appear in technology but may not reach an optimum military effectiveness for some time because institutions, cultures, and socioeconomic systems have to be built around them.[31] The stirrup is a classic example. It appeared initially in Eurasia, offering greater accuracy and rate of fire by mounted archers using the steppe bow. The ability to hold the rider in the saddle while making thrusts with a weapon was refined over time until, with a modified saddle, it was possible to make use of a longer lance, armor protection for the rider and horse, and specific tactics appropriate to the weight and energy of a mounted soldier. This technological combination reinforced an emergent sociopolitical system that ensured sufficient funds were available to sustain this military unit.[32] At Hattin in 1187, however, adversaries learned to circumvent the strength of knights and their supporting armored infantry, using their own missile harassment tactics and the advantages afforded by the environment to defeat them.[33] Similar technologies that require contextual systems of support and sustainment to become effective would include the tank, the surveillance aircraft, and the aircraft carrier.[34] For example, Tonio Andrade has indicated how the West's development of math and ballistics gave it significant advantages over China from the 1840s: although the Chinese had developed gunpowder, they lacked the scientific infrastructure to fully exploit its development.[35]

Clearly technology is not an absolute and independent element in history but part of an integrated whole.[36] It is often not the technology itself but the human response to it that drives change. There is experimentation, adaptation, and varying perceptions that will affect what is adopted and utilized. During the stalemate on the Western Front in the First World War, for example, a number of technological and organizational options for change were examined. Although, rather simplistically, the Allied victory in 1918 is sometimes attributed to certain technological advances, such as the tank, it is clear that tactical and doctrinal improvements were as important, and the outcome of the war was the result of a complex interaction of factors, from the relative deterioration of the German, Austro-Hungarian, Bulgarian, and Ottoman

---

31. Knox and Murray, "Thinking about Revolutions in Warfare," 4, 9–10, and 11–12.

32. A controversy erupted over the extent to which the stirrup was the technology that determined the rise of "feudalism"; see Alex Roland, "Once More into the Stirrups: Lynn White Jr., 'Medieval Technology and Social Change,'" in *Technology and Culture* 44, no. 3 (July 2003): 574–85. On feudalism as a purported "system," see Chapter 3 in this volume, by Richard Abels.

33. See John France, *Great Battles: Hattin* (Oxford: Oxford University Press, 2017), 95–101; Steven Runciman, *A History of the Crusades: The Kingdom of Jerusalem and the Frankish East*, 3 vols. (Cambridge: Cambridge University Press, 1968), II:457–59; Eva Rodhe Lundqvist, *Saladin and the Crusaders: Selected Annals from Masalik al-absar fi mamalik al-ansar*, vol. 5 (Lund, Swed.: Studia Orientalia Lundensia, 1992).

34. Williamson Murray and MacGregor Knox, "Conclusion: The Future Behind Us," in *Dynamics of Military Revolution*, 181 and 186–87.

35. Andrade, *Gunpowder Age*.

36. Black, "Determinisms and Other Issues," 1220.

economies to the erroneous strategies adopted by the Central powers from the beginning of the war, or the surge of US resources from 1917. Indeed, despite the technological innovations of that conflict, while having an impact at the tactical level in the *way* the war was fought, it is far harder to claim that they determined the outcome.[37]

Influential advocates after the First World War posited that technology would provide the solution to costly stalemate in the future, but their reflections were driven, understandably, by their recent experience of immobile trench warfare.[38] Moreover, technological failures are all too often overlooked, as are the misuses and limits of promising systems. The German use of poison gas and early nerve agents in 1915–18, for example, was a strategic error since it depended on prevailing winds and atmospheric conditions, which often favored their enemies. Germany also chose not to deploy the weapon against civilian populations of cities, even though the strategic effect of such attacks would have been considerable.

Judgments about the importance of technology in determining an outcome are made after an event and are done so selectively.[39] The technologies that underperform are frequently overlooked, although the failures of obsolete systems are frequently cited.[40] The American "ball" tank and Russian Tsar tank were mobility failures, but these powers succeeded against Germany in the Second World War. While the Germans deployed advanced technologies, they lost the war. Germany made some use of the Messerschmitt 262 as a jet fighter but failed to affect the outcome of the war, while the Focke-Wulf Triebflügel was a Nazi rocket-propelled helicopter that failed in trials, demonstrating that, for all of Germany's advanced research, it too suffered technological setbacks.

There are other examples where a seemingly advanced technology or technological errors made little impact on the actual outcomes of a military campaign. In 1689, the British Army found its innovative plug bayonet reduced firepower and was deficient in hand-to-hand combat, but it nevertheless succeeded in the campaign in Scotland.[41] Early breech-loading iron guns of the Venetian fleet were often a greater threat to their crews than their enemies, yet their navy was one of the most successful in the early

---

37. Dennis Showalter, "Mass Warfare and the Impact of Technology," in *Great War, Total War: Combat and Mobilization on the Western Front, 1914–1918*, ed. R. Chickering and S. Förster (Cambridge: Cambridge University Press, 2000), 73–93.

38. J. F. C. Fuller, *Armament and History: The Influence of Armament on History from the Dawn of the Classical Age to the End of the Second World War* (repr., Boston: Da Capo, 1998); *Military Innovation in the Interwar Period*, ed. W. R. Murray and A. R. Millett (Cambridge: Cambridge University Press, 1996): 6.

39. Eliot Cohen, "Stephen Biddle on Military Power," *Journal of Strategic Studies* 28, no. 3 (June 2005): 413–24.

40. Ofer Fridman, "Revolutions in Military Affairs That Did Not Occur: A Framework for Analysis," *Comparative Strategy* 35, no. 5 (2016): 388–406.

41. Hugh MacKay, *Memoirs of the War Carried on in Scotland and Ireland (1689–91)* (Edinburgh, 1693), 52.

modern period.[42] In the siege of Venice in 1849, the Austrian army failed in its experimental use of balloon bombing, but captured the city some months later.[43] And, in a final example, the Prussian Dreyse needle gun, while inferior to the French Army's Chassepot rifle, was sufficient, when combined with bold maneuvers, to ensure German victory over France in 1871.[44] Technological determinism has therefore been applied selectively to explain success, but rarely to account for defeat or even a victory despite a failed or flawed technology.

Revolutions in Military Affairs (RMA)

The idea of military revolution, as a paradigm shift, appeared in Soviet thinking in the Second World War, but the concept is usually associated with technological developments in the United States during the Cold War.[45] In its definition, it is the synchronization of doctrine, strategy, operations, tactics, and technologies to produce a dramatic breakthrough in war fighting. In the last decade of the twentieth century, it came to be associated with the blending of information technology, telecommunications, and satellite technology, which enabled a faster, global, networked response to any threat. It was usually connected with the expeditionary projection of power by the United States in the early 2000s.

The revolution in military affairs (RMA) is so closely linked to new technologies that one critic has referred to the "machinization" of thinking and practice in the American military.[46] It offered the opportunity for low casualties, domination of the electromagnetic bandwidth, supremacy in the skies, and absolute operational success on land and at sea. Long-range and precise missiles reinforced the United States' ability to strike anywhere in the world. It has been, therefore, an assertion of American military prowess over all potential and actual enemies. The Iraqis in 2003, for example, were expected to be in "shock and awe" at the firepower and rapidity of American operations, such that their capitulation would occur in a very short period of four weeks. It was claimed that a combination of speed and maneuver, enabling the actions of special forces, the delivery of precision firepower, and the comprehensive

---

42. John Francis Guilmartin, "The Earliest Shipboard Gunpowder Ordnance: An Analysis of Its Technical Parameters and Tactical Capabilities," *Journal of Military History* 71, no. 3 (2007): 649–69.

43. Lee Kennett, *A History of Strategic Bombing* (New York: Charles Scribner's Sons, 1982), 6.

44. Wawro, *Franco-Prussian War*; David Gates, *Warfare in the Nineteenth Century* (New York: Palgrave, 2001), 76.

45. Matthew Mowthorpe, "The Revolution in Military Affairs (RMA): The United States, Russian, and Chinese Views," *Journal of Social, Political, and Economic Studies* 30 (Summer 2005): 137–53; Fanourious Pantelogianis, "RMA: The Russian Way," *Cyberwar, Netwar, and the Revolution in Military Affairs*, ed. E. Halpin et al. (London: Palgrave Macmillan, 2006), 158.

46. Jeremy Black, *War and the New Disorder in the 21st Century* (New York: Continuum, 2004), 140.

use of psychological operations represented a "profound" shift in war fighting.[47] But, while technology aided the conventional defeat of Iraq, it did not prevent a prolonged insurgency.

The RMA was also a manifestation of American confidence and anxiety. When the Soviets believed that the United States was acquiring an advantage through a "military-technical revolution" in the 1970s, the Americans had eagerly sought to embrace and develop the idea. RMA is an aspiration to achieve a decisive and rapid success in the operational dimension but, equally, a search for the conventional victory to avoid protracted warfare and its associated strategic defeat, which is an anxiety derived from the Vietnam War. The RMA is therefore much more than an operational technique, for it suggests some extensive change in organization, doctrine, tactics, intellectual approach, and even social and political acceptance, all of which are connected to, or wrought by, some technological development. The inclusiveness and opacity of the term is, however, also the weakness of the concept because it could be an attempt to explain all elements of modern war, without being precise about what, specifically, is the nature of the breakthrough.[48]

The RMA was nevertheless an attractive proposition. The information age, which emerged in the 1980s with the connectivity of computing and satellite communications, offered an opportunity for further technological breakthroughs in military affairs. Some likened the advent of "net-centric warfare" as the equivalent to the shock of the French revolutionary and Napoleonic approach to operations in the 1790s.[49] Bill Owens, vice chairman of the Joint Chiefs of Staff, suggested the new RMA could "lift the fog of war," while the digitized battlespace, part of a "system of systems," would reduce friction, provide total situational awareness, and reduce the time in the decision-making cycle.[50] In fact, war is far less certain than these judgments would presume.

Where we might advance ideas of technological effects on war with more confidence would be in terms of communications, propulsion, and precision. From the early modern period, when the printing press began to speed up communication in the West, and then offer its democratization, mass communications have had an increasing influence on the conduct of war. Political groups and states recognized

---

47. Max Boot, "The New American Way of War," *Foreign Affairs* 82, no. 4 (July–August 2003): 1.

48. Jeremy Black, "The Revolution in Military Affairs: The Historian's Perspective," *RUSI Journal* 154, no. 2 (2009): 89 and 98.

49. Arthur Cebrowski and John Garstka, "Network-centric Warfare: Its Origins and Future," *US Naval Institute Proceedings* 124, no. 1 (January 1998): 1. The analogy to the French revolutionary and Napoleonic period was meant to suggest a complete transformation of war, with sudden and unexpected victories through unorthodox tactics.

50. William Owens, *Lifting the Fog of War* (New York: Farrar, Strauss and Giroux, 2000), 15; David Kirkpatrick, "Revolutions in Military Technology, and Their Consequences," *RUSI Journal* 146, no. 4 (2001); David F. Ronfeldt and John Arquilla, *In Athena's Camp: Preparing for Conflict in the Information Age* (Santa Monica, CA: RAND, 1997).

Two M1A1 Abrams tanks and a Bradley Fighting Vehicle crossing the desert during Operation Desert Storm in 1991. The successful merging of land, sea, air, and electronic warfare prompted theorists to discuss a new sort of "net-centric" warfare.

the potential it offered and the threat it posed, orchestrating information campaigns alongside their military efforts. The guerrilla commander T. E. Lawrence ("of Arabia") once remarked that the printing press would become the greatest weapon in the arsenal of the modern commander, for insurgency was, in essence, "a war of communications."[51] Radio, telephony, and then the internet have expanded the possibilities for military operations. Radios fitted to turrets of vehicles, to aircraft cockpits and to shipping and guidance systems have enabled greater dispersal and survivability, coordination, and synchronization. Nevertheless, communications have also enabled irregular warfare to a significant extent.

Man-made propulsion has transformed warfare. From a dependence on animal transportation, the development of the steam engine, motor, propeller, jets, and rocketry has enabled a global reach for military units and the positioning of satellites for worldwide surveillance, communications, and targeting. This, too, has enhanced the gradual development of precision, from the rifling of firearms and artillery in the eighteenth century to GPS and "smart" ordnance in the twentieth and twenty-first centuries. It is now possible to locate, select, and destroy individual targets with

51. T. E. Lawrence, "The Science of Guerrilla Warfare," *Encyclopaedia Britannica*, 14th ed. (1929): 951.

pinpoint accuracy, a far cry from the wasteful and costly expenditures of ammunition, personnel, and combat power of the past. In the Allied bombing of Germany in the Second World War, while 1,415,745 tons of bombs were dropped, there are estimates that as few as 1 in 10 of this ordnance hit its intended targets. As a result, the standard method was to carpet an area with waves of bombing in order to destroy a specific target, but the loss in aircraft (over 33,000) and their crews (over 160,000) was heavy.[52]

The development of computing power enhanced by wireless communications has enabled remote and robotic weapon systems, and produced advances in intelligence, surveillance, and reconnaissance (ISR). Robots and automated systems are developing rapidly, giving rise to optimism in the US military that such systems will provide a "third offset," or strategic advantage. Technology is the heart of the system, combining robotic autonomy, miniaturization, the analytical potential of processing "big data," and new forms of manufacturing.[53]

In conflicts in the early twenty-first century in Syria, Iraq, Libya, or sub-Saharan Africa, despite the novelty of new and emerging technologies, each of the elements of the nature of war was present, including friction and technological failures. In Syria and Iraq, for example, the allegiance and the cohesion of the people were important, the political purpose of governance was still extant, and the conflicts were sacralized by the religiously inspired belligerents perhaps even more sincerely than those of the 1990s. Nevertheless, technologies did have an important role in the conflict against Daesh (ISIS) astride the Syrian-Iraqi border in the 2010s. Rebels in Syria were overmatched by precise and overwhelming firepower, and all sides made use of new technological innovations, from accurate guided munitions to tablet-enabled calibration of mortar fire. Yet, on the other hand, resistance to the Syrian regime was neither driven by the issue of new technology alone nor was its outcome determined solely by technology. Few would deny that human motivation was still the most significant single aspect driving the conflict, so we cannot say it was entirely "technologically determined."

In the 1860s, in his study of combat, Ardant du Picq wrote, "Man is the fundamental instrument in battle. . . . Nothing can be prescribed . . . without knowledge of his state of mind, his morale, at the instant of combat."[54] He believed that technological advances cannot change the human condition and therefore humanity's response to combat. Human "friction" always intervenes in conflict. Things go wrong, individuals and weapons fail, and attrition imposes itself, in one form or another, on all operations.

---

52. Overy, *The Bombing War*. See also Chapter 5 in this volume, by John Curatola.

53. Secretary of Defense Chuck Hegel, "Reagan National Defense Forum Keynote," November 15, 2014, accessed February 2019, https://www.dod.defense.gov/News/Speeches/Speech-View/Article/606635/.

54. Ardant du Picq, *Battle Studies: Ancient and Modern Battle*, in *Roots of Strategy 2*, ed. S. Brooks (Mechanicsburg, PA: Stackpole, 1987), 65.

It is for this reason that linear models of war (in which military professionals assert that conflict follows specific phases of initial entry, full combat, stabilization, and then a restoration of peace) are misleading and reinforce the impression of determinism. Such neat arrangements fail to account for the reality of war, not least its dynamic and escalatory nature. An alternative to this linearity is to regard war as consisting of three parts that reflect the distribution and contestation of power: latent power, dynamic conflict events, and then technological or organizational adaptation to those events. Note that there is not necessarily a "conclusion," since so many conflicts do not end in a linear fashion but transform and continue, either as a new lethal episode or a less intense or violent power-political dynamic, as occurred after the Western military interventions in Afghanistan, Iraq, and Libya in the early 2000s.

Examining historical examples allows us to assess more honestly the relative importance of technological advantages and developments. The results indicate that while technologies can make a significant tactical and operational impact, their ability to effect a strategic change is far less certain or common. It is for this reason that the detonation of the atomic bombs in 1945 was so exceptional—it ushered in a strategic change more far-reaching than even the gunpowder or aviation revolutions. A more robust historical framework encourages us to seek other ways of assessing change in war that are not linear or couched solely in terms of new technology.

Technology may be new and apparently influential, but it sometimes lacks the accompanying infrastructure or exploitation of its potential, and so it is no more likely to determine the outcome of a conflict than other factors. For example, the French deployed the innovative mitrailleuse machine gun in their war of 1870–71 against Prussia and the German states—an apparently revolutionary weapon—but their reluctance to use it at the front line (treating it like artillery) reduced its effectiveness and France lost the war. A single technology is therefore far less likely to produce a revolution but, despite this, many analysts still favor systemic change as having the capacity to determine outcomes.

There are alternative assessments of change that are not deterministic. One of these is to evaluate the industrial form of warfare, which defined the twentieth century, with the legacies and consequences that it produced. Industrialization itself placed an emphasis on the routinization of production and of mass. It also privileged technology over technique.[55] One consequence of that was the undue emphasis placed on exquisite, highly engineered solutions or the dependence on the ballistic missiles of the Cold War and space race. The industrial era also placed great store in the scientific solution and ruthless rationalism. The challenge of this triumph of the rational-logical is that industrialized forces tended to ignore or underestimate the human-emotional aspects of conflict, causing surprise. By way of historical example, this manifested in the approach to risk-taking taken by the Imperial Japanese forces and the astonishment

---

55. Azar Gat, *Fascist and Liberal Visions of War: Fuller, Liddell Hart, Douhet, and Other Modernists* (Oxford: Oxford University Press, 1998).

of the British garrison of Singapore in 1942, which believed an offensive against it would be illogical. They were surprised by an amphibious and landward assault by inferior numbers of well-trained and disciplined Japanese troops. The fall of Singapore exposed the fallacy of deterministic faith in technology in another symbolic way. The vast British naval guns, which protected both land and seaward approaches, were rendered irrelevant by the Japanese maneuver. On the other hand, the British had underestimated the quality of Japanese aircraft, and their ships had been sunk by the technological superiority of their enemies.

The industrial era had also been characterized by a greater emphasis on bureaucracy, which can produce slow processes and an overdependence on quantification. Industrial approaches favor systemization—which stifles the innovators, or those with initiative, on whom adaptation, experimentation, and change depend. This in turn means that professionalization, which is the hallmark of the industrial era, is also its undoing, in that conformity is prized over disruptive thinking. It implies that determinism may be related to rigid thinking and an antithesis to change.

Among the changes that have occurred in modern, industrial war, we observe in particular a sustained high-intensity war having a definitive end being replaced by unending, constant conflict of episodic intensity. In the late nineteenth and early twentieth centuries' wars, major powers enjoyed technological supremacy over others but, at times since, there has been a degree of technological parity, at least at the tactical level. Technology also mattered less to the insurgent forces of the post-1945 period. The French were defeated in Indo-China and Algeria, despite their technological superiority, by adversaries making use of protracted guerrilla warfare, local superiority of numbers and artillery (e.g., at Dien Bien Phu in 1954), and attrition.

The technological disparity was even greater in the American intervention in Vietnam. The United States possessed more advanced aircraft, helicopters, communications, and vehicles, but the North Vietnamese and their insurgent cadres in the south were supplied with advanced mines, technically more robust small arms, and sophisticated surface-to-air missiles. The American temptation was to make greater use of firepower, particularly to counter the frustration of not being able to get to grips with an elusive adversary. In the defense of locations like Khe Sanh, technological superiority achieved significant tactical victories, but the military advantages afforded by technology or firepower were not enough to achieve a decisive outcome, and the weakness of the American strategy was a dependence on the unstable and unpopular South Vietnam government. Critics noted that the United States could not bomb its way to victory and contrasted the successful British counterinsurgency methods in Malaya from 1948 to 1955, which did not depend on technology, but on gaining the trust of the majority of Malays, promising a political solution to a competent Malaysian government, and isolating the insurgents in irrelevant backwaters of the country in a low-intensity, painstaking campaign.[56]

---

56. John Nagl, *Learning to Eat Soup with a Knife: Counterinsurgency Lessons from Malaya to Vietnam* (Chicago: University of Chicago Press, 2005), 190.

Conclusion

Technological-determinist interpretations of war are common. It is easy to refer to new developments in weapons as marking turning points in the conduct of war.[57] All too often, however, as noted above, technological failures are overlooked.[58] Moreover, less technologically advantaged peoples defending their lands, insurgents and guerrillas, have, at times, challenged and beaten apparently technologically superior military forces in the past. Determinism is largely a myth, and technology as the sole determining factor in wars' outcomes has been mythologized.

Dependence on certain technologies or systems can lead to failure. For example, in operations in the 1990s, airpower, while influential, did not fulfill the expectations of its advocates as a conflict-winning weapon system without ground contingents. Technologies confer certain advantages, and may even be essential to selected outcomes, but they do not, on their own, constitute a solution in every case. Their combination with other systems (such as communications), personnel (specialists), techniques (such as tactics), and situations (e.g., in the common objective of a coalition or part of a grand strategy) is more likely to produce success.

The solution to so many of these apparently technical challenges is to return to the centrality of the human in war. The human is the motivational force and the point of vulnerability in conflict. Despite the advocates of a decisive result in war, brought about by breaking an adversary, physically and morally, through some new weaponry or technologically enabled system, such phenomena are rare in practice and often very costly.

We may therefore conclude that the unifying element of all the approaches, frameworks, and options in the history of war is the human. It is not that the human stands in a dichotomous relationship with technology, but rather that the human is most effective as a belligerent when fused with technology.[59] In other words, when we can see the human as just another form of technology (in this case, "bio-tech") it becomes easier to conceive of a harmonious and efficient application of human-technological systems. The humans' use of tools and technology dates back to their earliest origins, and while they are unpredictable and unique as individuals, their collective behavior is often far easier to map and forecast. To defeat humans, one needs to attack their central operating system, namely the mind. The routes to do this, to compel the target to make a choice that is compliant, can be to induce hesitation or paralysis through fear or confusion; to deter by appealing to its risk calculus; to demoralize by depriving

---

57. E. C. Sloan, *The Revolution in Military Affairs* (Montreal: McGill University Press, 2002); William Owens, "The Emerging US System of Systems," *US Naval Institute Proceedings*, May 1995, 36–39; W. H. Manthorpe Jr., "The Emerging Joint System-of-Systems: A Systems Engineering Challenge and Opportunity for APL," *Johns Hopkins APL Technical Digest* 17, no. 3 (1996): 305–10.

58. Sydney J. Freedberg Jr., "Artificial Stupidity: Learning to Trust Artificial Intelligence (Sometimes)," *Breaking Defense*, July 5, 2017.

59. Keegan, *History of Warfare*, 366–85.

it of information, fuel, health, or life; or to create options that influence its choices and make it predictable.

History indicates that war is a combination of three forms of technology: human, physical, and cognitive. They can be tackled together or individually to produce significant results. Nevertheless, it is the dynamic nature of war, and the variable characteristics of the human in conflict, that have defied the myths of determinist explanations and brutally exposed the fallacies of mythologized interpretations of the past.

EPILOGUE: TO BRAVELY GO . . .

> Myths are not lies. Nor are they detached stories. They are imaginative patterns . . . that suggest particular ways of interpreting the world. They shape its meaning.
>
> —*Mary Midgley*[1]

Hans von Wees has written that myths derive from two groups: modern scholars and the historical sources they utilize.[2] But one need not be an academic to mythologize the past, and unfamiliarity with the nuances and subtexts of sources from any historical period can lead both professional and amateur historians, as well as politicians, journalists, and even seasoned military professionals, down misleading paths. One could argue, in fact, that scholars who publish exclusively in less-accessible academic journals effectively cede their ability to counter it. And there have been consequences.

Consider, for example, an extremely well-known movie featuring warfare: *Braveheart* (1995), starring Mel Gibson in a gripping story of a Scottish orphan who wages a nationalistic war of revenge against King Edward I "Longshanks" of England. The film was a commercial and critical success, winning Best Picture and four other Oscars in 1996 (and being nominated in five other categories) and dozens of awards and nominations in other industry competitions.[3]

Among medieval scholars, however, *Braveheart* is one of the most frequently derided films for its historical inaccuracies. The most blatant of these is probably the depiction of the Battle of Stirling Bridge (September 11, 1297), which was, indeed, a triumph by Gibson's real-life character, William Wallace, and the Scots over an English force on the River Forth. As the name implies, there was a bridge involved—one that is completely absent in the film. Gibson's volunteer comrades (who had actually been conscripted) looked fearsome with their faces painted in blue (a forgotten custom by the thirteenth century) and clothed in short kilts (not invented until the seventeenth century).[4] And so on and so forth.[5]

---

1. Mary Midgley, *The Myths We Live By* (London: Routledge, 2011), 1.

2. Hans von Wees, *Greek Warfare: Myths and Realities* (London: Gerald Duckworth, 2004), 1.

3. "*Braveheart* (1995)," Awards, Internet Movie Database, accessed September 22, 2019, https://www.imdb.com/title/tt0112573/awards.

4. "*Braveheart*: Full of Mistakes Which Make Scotland Look Better," *Politics.Co.UK*, August 26, 2014.

5. For a candid ripping, see Michael Livingston, "Medieval Matters: The Many Sins of *Braveheart*," Tor.com, accessed September 22, 2019, https://www.tor.com/2018/11/29/medieval-matters-the-many-sins-of-braveheart/.

Yet most consequential has been *Braveheart*'s mythologizing of William Wallace's cause. The movie's principal theme is one of Scottish nationalism. Oppressed Highlanders rebel against the cruel English, who rape their women, steal their lands, and deny their rights. Wallace fights and dies for freedom; taking his inspirational place is then another historical figure, Robert I "the Bruce," who, in the movie's epilogue, leads the Scots over the English at the 1314 Battle of Bannockburn.

It would be difficult to find a film with more of a political impact on national politics. *Braveheart* was a driving force for devolution, the 1997 referendum in which voters elected to transfer some powers from the government of the United Kingdom to Scotland. The following year, the House of Commons passed the Scotland Act, which formalized the transfer and reestablished the Scottish Parliament (defunct since 1707).[6] Two decades later, further powers have devolved to the north. How does *Braveheart* fit in? The 1997 vote was held on the 700th anniversary of William Wallace's victory at Stirling Bridge. The devolution effort was spearheaded by the Scottish National Party, which made frequent use of *Braveheart* themes and distributed leaflets featuring a picture of Mel Gibson in character; so too did the Scottish press lean on such imagery.[7] These efforts played on the overall notion pushed by the movie: that Scotland needed to unite to escape the clutches of political power emanating from London. *Braveheart* would be evoked again in September 2014, when Scotland voted on a referendum for independence from Great Britain that nonetheless failed.[8]

From whence comes *Braveheart*'s nationalistic overtones? Its screenwriter, Randall Wallace, has readily admitted his preference for the legendary account called "The Wallace," a Middle English poem written in the 1470s by a man named Blind Harry—over a century and a half after Wallace's execution in 1305. Blind Harry's *Wallace* is a Scottish liberator, fighting a nationalistic war against an essentially colonizing English monarchy.[9] The poem's historical problems have long been known, as has its bias and agenda. As one critic wrote in 1974:

> Blind Harry's *Wallace* is a conscious blending of folk-myth and Chaucerian literary conventions. "Blind Harry's" intention in this blending is to

---

6. "Devolution," UK Government: Delivering for Scotland, accessed September 22, 2019, https://www.deliveringforscotland.gov.uk/scotland-in-the-uk/devolution/#.

7. Mure Dickie, "'Braveheart' Screening Stokes Scottish Debate," *Financial Times*, June 23, 2014; and Steve Blandford, *Film, Drama and the Breakup of Britain* (Bristol: Intellect, 2007), 68; quoting Sally J. Morgan, "The Ghost in the Luggage: Wallace and *Braveheart*: Post-colonial 'Pioneer' Identities," *Cultural Studies* 2, no. 3 (1999): 375–92, at 376–77.

8. Robert Brent Toplin, "Could a Movie Help Lead to the Departure of Scotland from the UK?" History News Network, accessed September 23, 2019, https://historynewsnetwork.org/article/159433.

9. The oldest edition of "The Wallace" is from 1488; for the text and commentary, see *The Wallace: Selections*, ed. A. McKim (Kalamazoo, MI: Medieval Institute Publications, 2003).

make the "actis and deidis of the illustere and vailyand campioun, Schir William Wallace" seem more the doings of a "gracious god of Scotland" than those of a Scottish marauder who in actuality struck only one blow against the English, for which he was shortly hanged.[10]

Nonetheless, Randall Wallace justified his privileging of the legend on the basis that "the actual facts of [William] Wallace's life as established by historians are miniscule."[11]

But while William Wallace's biography is indeed incomplete, historians have nonetheless unearthed significant context for his life and rebellion.[12] Many sources predate Blind Harry's poem, and their details call into question his overly fantastic rendering. As Michael Prestwich has noted, "While patriotism and personal ambition must have played a major part in inspiring the [Wallace's] rising" of 1297, the proximate causes involved Edward I's demands for Scottish money, possessions, and men to serve on his overseas military campaigns.[13] In short, what we might today call "nationalism" was only one factor of Wallace's militancy and probably not the primary one.[14]

Regardless, in the 1990s, the film was understood as a stirring reminder of Scotland's distinctive nationhood and real enough history of enduring English ills. A military event (the Battle of Stirling Bridge) was transmitted popularly through a partial rendering, then visually dramatized for a massive, worldwide audience, and, finally, appropriated for political purposes. In short, the story became mythologized and a medieval clash of arms unpredictably affected the affairs of the modern world! This fits the mold of Mary Midgley's "imaginative patterns" quoted above. The *Braveheart* story is not a lie per se or even fully erroneous: it is, rather, a particular rendering of past texts and contexts that excludes certain details while centering others.

One person's myth is another's reality, and convenient devices can defy diminishment. Wallace-as-Scottish-nationalist is likely here to stay. Likewise, the mythologized concepts and constructs in this volume carry significant cultural and social meaning, and some have even served useful (and often profitable) political and strategic

---

10. John Balaban, "Blind Harry and 'The Wallace,'" *Chaucer Review* 8, no. 3 (1974): 241–51, at 250.

11. As quoted in Constantine Santas et al., *The Encyclopedia of Epic Films* (Lanham, MD: Rowman and Littlefield, 2014), 104.

12. See the website of the Society of William Wallace, e.g., "English Accounts of Wallace," accessed September 23, 2019, http://www.thesocietyofwilliamwallace.com/wallaceenglish.htm.

13. Michael Prestwich, *Edward I* (Berkeley: University of California Press, 1988), 476–77.

14. On whether "nationalism" existed at the turn of the fourteenth century, see Dauvit Broun, *Scottish Independence and the Idea of Britain: From the Picts to Alexander III* (Edinburgh: Edinburgh University Press, 2007), 280–82.

purposes. They demonstrate the very real application of the past in the present. But when a particular *belief* about the past overshadows its *realities*, everyone ought to take notice. For in the halls of bookstores, universities, industries, and government walk people of influence all too ready to make weighty decisions on the basis of good stories and neat, tidy, and convenient explanations.

John D. Hosler

SUGGESTED READING

Military history is as old as recorded history itself. Listing all of the recommended books for the times and places discussed in these essays would be tedious and overly long, but we have attempted to meet the spirit of coverage and offer titles below that have been formative in the field of military history. Traditionally, as in other historical fields, military history publications in the English language are dominated by a focus on "the West," centering the warfare of Europe and North America, often to the exclusion of other regions. Due to this volume's themes, there remains a noticeable Western bent in the recommended readings. It is our hope, however, that the included global and/or non-Western titles below will serve to illustrate the breadth of the field as a whole.

General Surveys of Military History

Black, Jeremy. *War and the World: Military Power and the Fate of Continents, 1450–2000.* New Haven, CT: Yale University Press, 2000.

Lee, Wayne E. *Waging War: Conflict, Culture and Innovation in World History.* New York: Oxford University Press, 2016.

The Makers of Modern Strategy: From Machiavelli to the Nuclear Age. Edited by Peter Paret. Princeton, NJ: Princeton University Press, 1986.

Morillo, Stephen, Jeremy Black, and Paul Lococo. *War in World History: Society, Technology, and War from Ancient Times to the Present.* 2 vols. New York: McGraw-Hill, 2008.

The Routledge History of Global War and Society. Edited by Matthew S. Muehlbauer and David J. Ulbrich. New York: Routledge, 2018.

The West Point History of Warfare. Edited by Clifford J. Rogers and Ty Seidule. New York: Rowan Technology, 2014–2020.

Religion and War

Blin, Arnaud. *War and Religion: Europe and the Mediterranean from the First through the Twenty-First Centuries.* Berkeley: University of California Press, 2019.

Buc, Philippe. *Holy War, Martyrdom, and Terror: Christianity, Violence, and the West.* Philadelphia: University of Pennsylvania Press, 2015.

Graziano, Manlio. *Holy Wars and Holy Alliance: The Return of Religion to the Global Political Stage.* New York: Columbia University Press, 2017.

New, David S. *Holy War: The Rise of Militant Christian, Jewish and Islamic Fundamentalism.* Jefferson, NC: McFarland, 2002.

Religion and the American Civil War. Edited by Randall M. Miller, Harry S. Stout, and Charles Reagan Wilson. New York: Oxford University Press, 1998.

War and Religion: An Encyclopedia of Faith and Conflict. Edited by Jeffrey M. Shaw and Timothy J. Demy. 3 volumes. Santa Barbara, CA: ABC-CLIO, 2017.

Western Way of War

The Cambridge History of Warfare. Edited by Geoffrey Parker. Cambridge: Cambridge University Press, 2009.

Hanson, Victor Davis. *Carnage and Culture: Landmark Battles in the Rise of Western Power.* New York, Anchor Books, 2007.

———. *The Western Way of War: Infantry Battle in Classical Greece.* Berkeley: University of California Press, 1989.

Lynn, John A. *Battle: A History of Combat and Culture from Ancient Greece to Modern America.* Cambridge, MA: Westview, 2003.

Nolan, Cathal J. *The Allure of Battle: A History of How Wars Have Been Won or Lost.* Oxford: Oxford University Press, 2017.

Sharman, Jason C. *Empires of the Weak: The Real Story of European Expansion and the Creation of the New World Order.* Princeton, NJ: Princeton University Press, 2019.

Feudalism and Medieval War

Bachrach, Bernard S., and David S. Bachrach. *Warfare in Medieval Europe, c. 400–c.1453.* New York: Routledge, 2016.

Contamine, Philippe. *War in the Middle Ages.* Translated by Michael Jones. Oxford: Basil Blackwell, 1984.

France, John. *Victory in the East: A Military History of the First Crusade.* Cambridge: Cambridge University Press, 1996.

Haldon, John. *Warfare, State and Society in the Byzantine World, 565–1204.* New York: Routledge, 1999.

Nicholson, Helen. *Medieval Warfare: Theory and Practice of War in Europe, 300–1500.* London: Palgrave Macmillan, 2004.

Rogers, Clifford J. *Soldiers' Lives through History: The Middle Ages.* Westport, CT: Greenwood Press, 2007.

Military Revolutions

Gray, Colin S. *Strategy for Chaos: Revolutions in Military Affairs and the Evidence of History.* London: Frank Cass, 2002.

Jacob, Frank, and Gilmar Visoni-Alonzo. *The Military Revolution: A Revision.* London: Palgrave Pivot, 2016.

Lorge, Peter. *The Asian Military Revolution: From Gunpowder to the Bomb.* Cambridge: Cambridge University Press, 2008.

Parker, Geoffrey. *The Military Revolution: Military Innovation and the Rise of the West, 1500–1800.* 2nd ed. Cambridge: Cambridge University Press, 1996.

Reassessing the Revolution in Military Affairs: Transformation, Evolution and Lessons Learnt. Edited by Jeffrey Collins and Andrew Futter. Initiatives in Strategic Studies. London: Palgrave Macmillan, 2015.

Shimko, Keith L. *The Iraq Wars and America's Military Revolution.* Cambridge: Cambridge University Press, 2010.

Strategic Air Power

Black, Jeremy. *Air Power: A Global History.* Lanham, MD: Rowman and Littlefield, 2016.

Boyne, Walter J. *The Influence of Air Power Upon History.* Barnsley, UK: Pen and Sword, 2005.

Budiansky, Stephen. *Air Power: From Kitty Hawk to Gulf War II: A History of the People, Ideas and Machines That Transformed War in the Century of Flight.* New York: Penguin, 2005.

Higham, Robin. *100 Years of Air Power and Aviation.* College Station: Texas A&M University Press, 2003.

The Routledge Handbook of Air Power. Edited by John Andreas Olsen. New York: Routledge, 2018.

Van Creveld, Martin. *The Age of Airpower.* New York: Public Affairs, 2012.

Asymmetrical Warfare and Terrorism

Arreguín-Toft, Ivan. *How the Weak Win Wars: A Theory of Asymmetric Conflict.* Cambridge Studies in International Relations. New York: Cambridge University Press, 2005.

The Bear Went Over the Mountain: Soviet Combat Tactics in Afghanistan. Edited by Lester W. Grau. London: Frank Cass, 1998.

Boot, Max. *The Savage Wars of Peace: Small Wars and the Rise of American Power.* New York: Basic Books, 2014.

Hybrid Warfare: Fighting Complex Opponents from the Ancient World to the Present. Edited by Williamson Murray and Peter R. Mansoor. New York: Cambridge University Press, 2012.

Lynn, John A. *Another Kind of War: The Nature and History of Terrorism.* New Haven, CT: Yale University Press, 2019.

Paul, T. V. *Asymmetric Conflicts: War Initiation by Weaker Powers.* Cambridge Studies in International Relations. Cambridge: Cambridge University Press, 1994.

Technology and War

Biddle, Stephen. *Military Power: Explaining Victory and Defeat in Modern Battle.* Princeton, NJ: Princeton University Press, 2004.

Black, Jeremy. *War and Technology.* Bloomington: Indiana University Press, 2013.

Boot, Max. *War Made New: Technology, Warfare, and the Course of History, 1500 to Today.* New York: Gotham Books, 2006.

Gray, Colin S. *Weapons Don't Make War: Policy, Strategy, and Military Technology.* Lawrence: University of Kansas Press, 1993.

Roland, Alex. *War and Technology: A Very Short Introduction.* Oxford: Oxford University Press, 2016.

Van Creveld, Martin. *Technology and War: From 2000 B.C. to the Present.* New York: Free Press, 1991.

Contributor Biographies

Andrew Holt (PhD, University of Florida) is Professor of History at Florida State College at Jacksonville. He is co-author (with Alfred J. Andrea) of *Sanctified Violence: Holy War in World History* (Hackett, 2021); editor of *The World of the Crusades: A Daily Life Encyclopedia*, 2 vols. (Greenwood, 2019); and co-editor of *Great Events in Religion: An Encyclopedia of Pivotal Events in Religious History* (ABC-CLIO, 2016), *Seven Myths of the Crusades* (Hackett, 2015), and *Fighting Words: Competing Voices from the Crusades* (Greenwood, 2008).

Everett L. Wheeler (PhD, Duke University) is Scholar in Residence at Duke University. His research focuses on ancient military history, military theorists (ancient and modern), the Roman army, and the Eastern frontier of the Roman Empire, especially eastern Anatolia and Transcaucasia. His publications include *Stratagem and the Vocabulary of Military Trickery* (1988), a translation of *Polyaenus Strategika* and related texts (1994), and *The Armies of Classical Greece* (2007).

Richard P. Abels (PhD, Columbia University) is Professor Emeritus and former Chair of the History Department at the United States Naval Academy, where he taught for thirty-five years. He is the recipient of the Naval Academy's civilian excellence awards in teaching, research, and service and the author of three books: *Æthelred the Unready: The Failed King* (Penguin, 2018), *Alfred the Great: War, Kingship and Culture in Anglo-Saxon England* (Routledge, 1998), and *Lordship and Military Obligation in Anglo-Saxon England* (University of California Press, 1988).

John France is Professor Emeritus in the History Department at Swansea University. He is a medievalist and his main interests lie in crusading and military history in the earlier part of the Middle Ages. Among his notable books are *Victory in the East: A Military History of the First Crusade* (Cambridge University Press, 1994), *Western Warfare in the Age of the Crusades 1000–1300* (UCL Press, 1999), and *Perilous Glory: The Rise of Western Military Power* (Yale University Press, 2011).

John Curatola (PhD, University of Kansas) is Professor of History at the US Army School of Advanced Military Studies. A retired Marine Lieutenant Colonel, his published works focus on World War II, airpower, and the Cold War and include *Bigger Bombs for a Brighter Tomorrow* (McFarland, 2015) and the forthcoming *Autumn of Our Discontent: Fall 1949 and the Genesis of NSC-68*.

William Kautt is Professor of Military History at the Command and General Staff College. His research interests include political violence, urban and guerrilla warfare, terrorism, countermobility operations, arms smuggling, and intelligence. He is author of *The Anglo-Irish War, 1916–1921: A People's War* (Praeger, 1999), *Ambushes and Armour: The Irish Rebellion, 1919–1921* (Irish Academic, 2010), *Ground Truths: British Army Operations in the Irish War of Independence* (Irish Academic, 2014), and *Arming the Irish Revolution: Gunrunning and Arms Smuggling, 1911–1922* (University Press of Kansas, 2021).

Rob Johnson is the Director of the Changing Character of War (CCW) research center at Oxford University. His primary research interests are in the history of war and strategy with a particular focus on the wider Middle East, but he is also concerned with how we conceive of future conflict environments. He is the author of *Lawrence of Arabia on War: The Campaign in the Desert 1916–18* (Osprey, 2020), and co-editor of *The Conduct of War* (Routledge, 2020) and *Military Strategy for the 21st Century* (C. Hurst, 2020).

John D. Hosler (PhD, University of Delaware) is Professor of Military History at the Command and General Staff College. He is the author or editor of several books, including *The Siege of Acre, 1189–1191* (Yale University Press), which was named a 2018 Book of the Year by the *Times Literary Supplement* and *The Financial Times*.